INTERFAITH DIALOGUE

INTERFAITH DIALOGUE

A Catholic View

MICHAEL L. FITZGERALD
and
JOHN BORELLI

SPCK

ORBIS BOOKS
Maryknoll, New York 10545

First published in Great Britain in 2006

Society for Promoting Christian Knowledge
36 Causton Street
London SW1P 4ST

British Library Cataloguing-in-Publication Data
A catalogue record for this book is available from the British Library

ISBN-13: 978–0–281–05383–4
ISBN-10: 0–281–05383–9

First published in the United States of America in 2006

Orbis Books, Maryknoll, NY 10545

Founded in 1970, Orbis Books endeavors to publish works that enlighten
the mind, nourish the spirit, and challenge the conscience. The publishing
arm of the Maryknoll Fathers and Brothers, Orbis seeks to explore the
global dimensions of the Christian faith and mission, to invite dialogue
with diverse cultures and religious traditions, and to serve the cause of
reconciliation and peace. The books published reflect the views of their
authors and do not represent the official position of the Maryknoll
Society. To learn more about Maryknoll and Orbis Books, please visit our
website at www.maryknoll.org.

Library of Congress Cataloging-in-Publication Data
Fitzgerald, Michael L.
    Interfaith dialogue: a Catholic view / Michael L. Fitzgerald and John
Borelli.
        p. cm.
    ISBN-13: 978–1–57075–652–8 (pbk.)
    1. Catholic Church—Relations. 2. Christianity and other religions.
    3. Catholic Church—Doctrines. I. Borelli, John. II. Title.
BX1787.F58 2006
261.2—dc22

                                                    2005033400

Scripture quotations are taken from The Jerusalem Bible, published and
copyright © 1966, 1967 and 1968 by Darton, Longman & Todd Ltd and
Doubleday, a division of Random House, Inc., and used by permission.

1 3 5 7 9 10 8 6 4 2

Typeset by Graphicraft Ltd, Hong Kong
Printed in Great Britain by Ashford Colour Press

Contents

Contents

Foreword

Interfaith relations is very much an issue of our times. It is an area whose importance has become more widely recognized in recent years as relationships between different faiths have become a matter of great social and political concern. But interfaith relations have been a concern and an area of engagement by the Catholic Church for 40 years: ever since the publication in 1965 of the Second Vatican Council's Declaration on the Relation of the Church to Non-Christian Religions (*Nostra Aetate*) on 28 October 1965. That document, together with the references to other religions that form part of the Dogmatic Constitution on the Church (*Lumen Gentium*), constitute the doctrinal basis for the Catholic Church's commitment to interfaith relations. We should add to this another conciliar text that was vital for enabling and shaping the Catholic Church's outreach to other faiths, namely, the Declaration on Religious Liberty.

The Pontifical Council for Interreligious Dialogue (formerly the Secretariat for Non-Christians) is the office within the Roman Curia that is responsible for implementing the provisions of *Nostra Aetate*. Archbishop Michael Fitzgerald was Secretary of this office from 1987 until 2002 and succeeded Cardinal Arinze as President in October 2002. He is an Arabic scholar by training and there can be no doubt that he is uniquely well qualified to write a book entitled *Interfaith Dialogue: A Catholic View*. What Archbishop Michael offers is an authoritative voice in an area that is crucially important but also sensitive and delicate. Some chapters have been contributed by Dr John Borelli, special assistant for interreligious affairs to the President of Georgetown University, Washington DC, who worked for many years for the US Conference of Catholic Bishops. This collection of talks and articles will be an invaluable reference book for people who work in this area, and will be very instructive for Catholics generally and for those who wish to know the Catholic Church's view of interfaith relations.

Interfaith relations are part of the life of the Catholic Church. It is not something marginal but integral to the Church's outreach to the world. The Pontifical Council has adopted the phrase 'Dialogue and Proclamation' to indicate the two distinct but related ways in which the Church takes forward its mission. Moreover, interfaith work requires people who combine a deep fidelity to the faith of the Catholic Church with a genuine openness to people of other religions. These qualities are most luminously evident in the person of Pope John Paul II. During his pontificate he was a tireless teacher of the Catholic Faith while presiding over some of the boldest initiatives in interfaith relations. The Day of Prayer for Peace at Assisi in 1986 was a watershed in relations between the Catholic Church and other faiths. Members of other faiths responded enthusiastically to the Pope's invitation to 'come together to pray'. At the time, Archbishop Runcie of Canterbury said that only one Church and only one religious leader could have convened such a day. The exercise was repeated in 1999, on the eve of the Great Jubilee of the Year 2000, and again in 2002. The leadership of the Pope in this area has provided both the context and the confidence that the Pontifical Council for Interreligious Dialogue has needed in order to do its work. Archbishop Michael, like his predecessor, Cardinal Arinze, has been both resourceful and effective in taking forward the whole enterprise.

This collection of Archbishop Michael's writings, together with the contribution of John Borelli, cover a range of quite fundamental topics which will address the questions and concerns people have about the relationship of the Catholic Church to people of other faiths. Part I addresses the whole issue of religious pluralism. This raises profound philosophical and theological questions to which the Church has had to respond. Part II of the book deals with Christian–Muslim relations. This is Archbishop Michael's particular area of specialization and is an area that has taken on a particular urgency in the light of 9/11 and its aftermath. Part III broadens the horizon to consider religions other than Islam, and also deals with some wider issues that are central to the agenda of interfaith work in the future.

It should be noted that these essays do not touch on Catholic–Jewish relations. Because of the quite special nature of the relationship between the Church and Judaism, there is a separate office in the Vatican that deals with Catholic–Jewish relations. It is called the Commission for Religious Relations with the Jews. This, too, is an area where the Pope has broken new ground and it is important to bear that in mind while reading this book.

This is a timely and very useful compendium of writings, which I know will be warmly welcomed throughout the Church.

Kevin McDonald
Archbishop of Southwark,
Chairman of the Committee for Other Faiths,
Catholic Bishops' Conference of England and Wales

Acknowledgements

To the late Pope John Paul II, for his profound teaching on inter-religious relations and the wonderful example he gave in this field.

To Cardinal Francis Arinze, my predecessor as President of the Pontifical Council for Interreligious Dialogue, for his leadership during the 15 years I worked under him.

To my colleagues in the council for their constant collaboration.

To Mrs Ruth McCurry of SPCK for her encouragement, constructive criticism and prodding without which this book would never have seen the light of day.

To Dr Penelope Johnstone for her valuable help in preparing the texts for publication.

To Dr John Borelli for his willingness to contribute to this project.

To many friends, both Christians and people of other religions, who, perhaps unknowingly to them, have shaped the contents of these chapters.

Abbreviations

AA	*Apostolicam Actuositatem* (Decree on the Apostolate of Lay People)
Can.	Canon
CCC	*Catechism of the Catholic Church*
CD	*Christus Dominus* (Decree concerning the Pastoral Office of Bishops in the Church)
DH	*Dignitatis Humanae* (Declaration on Religious Freedom)
DJ	*Dominus Jesus* (Of the Unicity and Salvific Universality of Jesus Christ and the Church)
DM	*Dialogue and Mission* (1984)
DP	*Dialogue and Proclamation* (1991)
EN	*Evangelii Nuntiandi* (On Evangelization in the Modern World)
GS	*Gaudium et Spes* (Pastoral Constitution on the Church in the Modern World)
LG	*Lumen Gentium* (Dogmatic Constitution on the Church)
MAA	Mir Ahmed Ali, *The Holy Qur'an. With English Translation of the Arabic Text and Commentary according to the Version of the Holy Ahlul-Bait*, Karachi, Muhammad Khaleel Shirazi, 1964
NA	*Nostra Aetate* (Declaration on the Relation of the Church to Non-Christian Religions)
NMI	*Novo Millennio Ineunte*
PCID	Pontifical Council for Interreligious Dialogue
PNE	*Directory for the Application of the Principles and Norms of Ecumenism*
RH	*Redemptor Hominis*
RM	*Redemptoris Missio* (On the permanent validity of the Church's missionary mandate)
UR	*Unitatis Redintegratio* (Decree on Ecumenism)
UUS	*Ut Unum Sint* (On commitment to Ecumenism)
YA	Yusuf Ali, *The Holy Qur'an. Text, Translation and Commentary*, Beirut, Dar al Arabia, 1968.

My personal journey in mission

MICHAEL L. FITZGERALD

The very fact that we have come to Assisi from various quarters of the world is in itself a sign of this common path which humanity is called to tread. Either we learn to walk together in peace and harmony, or we drift apart and ruin ourselves and others. We hope that the pilgrimage to Assisi has taught us anew to be aware of the common origin and common destiny of humankind. Let us see in it an anticipation of what God would like the developing history of humanity to be: a fraternal journey in which we accompany one another toward the transcendent goal which he sets for us.

These words were spoken by Pope John Paul II at the conclusion of the Day of Prayer for Peace which was held in Assisi on 27 October 1986. I and my fellow Missionaries of Africa had seen some of the events on television. We watched for about five minutes and then went into the Chapter room to do serious work. We were not aware that we were letting history go by, and little did I realize that this Assisi event was marking a watershed in my own life. How I got to this point, and what happened afterwards, forms the content of this introductory chapter.

I was born in Walsall, a town in the West Midlands of England, into a Catholic family, but my parents, both doctors, had many non-Catholic friends, and they sent me to non-Catholic schools because they thought the education there would be better. To the best of my knowledge there were no pupils of other religions in these schools. The few of us who were Catholics were to some extent set apart: we did not attend religion classes, but were given maths problems to solve; nor did we attend morning assembly, since this included prayers, and so we were made to act as policemen, taking down the names of those who arrived late. Yet, despite this, I can say that we were always treated with respect.

My parents had arranged for a teacher at the Catholic parish school, Miss Quigley, to come once a week to teach me the catechism. It was perhaps from her that I first heard about the missionary work of the Church in Africa, and read books such as *Wopsy: The Adventures of a Guardian Angel*, which told exciting tales about life in Africa. I do know that, from very early on, I wished to be a priest, and indeed a missionary. Some boys from the parish had gone to join the Missionaries of Africa (White Fathers) and, at the age of 12, I insisted on leaving the local grammar school and going to junior seminary, first in Scotland and then in the south of England.

Looking back, the education we received at that time was not really very good from the academic point of view, apart from Latin and French. Nevertheless, coming as we did from a variety of backgrounds, we learnt to accept one another, to work and play together, and this could be considered as a preparation for the necessary cultural adaptation which missionary life would later demand.

The thoughts of all of us during these years at junior seminary, of both boys and teachers, were focused on 'black Africa' and the conversion of the Africans. There was hardly any mention of Islam, and indeed most felt that the apostolate among the Muslims was a waste of time. In those pre-Vatican II days dialogue, as a dimension of the Church's evangelizing mission, was not part of the common vision.

It was only during my study of philosophy in senior seminary that one of the staff members, who had done his studies in Tunisia, regaled us with stories of contacts with the Arabs. This started my interest in an aspect of the work of the White Fathers that had been there ever since the Society was founded in Algeria. I volunteered to go to Algiers for my novitiate, and was somewhat disappointed to be sent to Holland instead. However, to my delight, in the following year I was chosen to go for theological studies in Carthage, Tunisia. It was there that I started learning Arabic and acquired some rudimentary knowledge of Islam. We used little booklets prepared by George Letellier, a French White Father who was director of the Manouba, a training centre for missionaries where they were taught Arabic thoroughly as a key to understanding Islam. We also had visits from our senior confrères working in Tunisia, such as André Demeerseman, who had a deep knowledge of Tunisian culture. We students admired his example of inculturation (the term was not yet used at that time), but we were sometimes exasperated by his prudence regarding the explicit preaching of the Christian gospel. We were thus made more aware of the White Father tradition in North Africa, initiated by the founder, Cardinal Lavigerie, and later developed into a missionary theory by Henri Marchal. This tradition advocated a persevering presence of missionaries and efforts to affect society, bringing to it gospel values, rather than working for individual conversions.

At the end of the period in the senior seminary I volunteered to work among Muslims, with Nigeria as the first choice and Tunisia as the second. But after ordination to the priesthood I was sent to Rome for further studies in theology. It was the exciting time of the Second Vatican Council. It was of course too early for the lectures at the university to reflect the new thinking coming out of the council, particularly with regard to the attitude of the Catholic Church towards other religions. Yet there was the opportunity to attend special lectures given by experts. These included Karl Rahner, who would later develop his theory of anonymous Christians, which though it has lost favour was certainly influential, and Yves Congar, whose work in ecumenism helped to shape his vision of the Church. We knew too that our superior general, together with the superiors general of other missionary congregations, was actively engaged in preparing a text expressing the missionary vision of the Church which would be respectful of different cultures and even of different religions. The documents of the council, *Lumen Gentium* on the nature of the Church, *Gaudium et Spes* on the role of the Church in the modern world, *Ad Gentes* on the Church's missionary task, *Dignitatis Humanae* on religious liberty, and *Nostra Aetate* on the relations of the Church to other religions, were to form the basis of my later theological work.

My mind was turned towards teaching theology in seminaries for the African clergy or for our own missionary candidates. To my surprise, just as I was finishing my doctorate, I was asked to accept an appointment on the staff of the Pontifical Institute of Arabic Studies (known as IPEA from its title in French), which had recently had to transfer from the Manouba, Tunis, to Rome. 'Think about this carefully,' said Fr Volker, the superior general, 'because this will determine the rest of your life.' I was hardly likely to object, however, since this was in line with what I had asked for at ordination. Of course there was a need to prepare for this task. This took me to the School of Oriental and African Studies (SOAS), London University, for a three-year undergraduate degree. The lecturers, whether Christians or Muslims, did not appear to object or even be surprised that a missionary priest should be studying Arabic. There were friendly contacts with the mosque in Regent's Park where from time to time, though perhaps not enough, I asked the help of the Imam. I remember one day the Imam visited SOAS for a discussion in the common room, and he turned to me and said, 'Father Michael, please explain the Trinity in five minutes.' This was perhaps a flattering request but not one that I responded to, as I knew already that the deep truths of our religions cannot be shared in such a superficial way.

There was contact too with the Selly Oak Colleges in Birmingham where Dr John B. Taylor was lecturer in Islamics, paving the way for the future Centre for the Study of Islam and Christian–Muslim relations. I was invited to a seminar at Selly Oak on *Preparatio Evangelica*, a term the Second Vatican Council had taken up from Eusebius of Caesarea, an early Father of the Church. The council stated that whatever was good or true in non-Christian cultures could be considered as a preparation for the gospel. This was my first exposure to theological reflection on dialogue. Professor R. C. Zaehner of Oxford was one of the participants. I would later make much use of his books *At Sundry Times* and *Mysticism Sacred and Profane*.

After London, I returned to Rome, to the IPEA, to start teaching and to continue the study of the Qur'an and Qur'an commentary. I followed the classes of Robert Caspar, a sound scholar who nevertheless showed great sympathy for Islam. I would follow his line when I had to take over teaching his courses. This, however, was to come later since almost immediately I was alerted to a vacancy in the Department of Religious Studies at the University of Makerere, Kampala, Uganda. I was encouraged to apply for the post, and to my surprise was accepted. Arriving at Makerere I found that there was already a Muslim lecturer in the department, but he had thought it useful to have a Christian colleague sharing the teaching of Islamics, since the students were of both religions. I wondered what he would let me do, whether he would reserve the more religious topics for himself and leave me with the history of Islam. In fact, he let me do whatever I liked and made no attempt to control my teaching. This openness and trust were immensely encouraging. It impressed me then, and has always remained with me as an example of interreligious relations. Yet it led to the strange situation of a Catholic priest teaching Islam to Muslim students.

The majority of these students were Ismailis, followers of the Aga Khan, who knew little about Sunni Islam, which I had studied, and therefore realized that they could learn something from me; while I, in turn, learnt a good deal from them. In addition, I never hid the fact that I was a priest, and my respectful attitude to their religion helped to create a climate of mutual acceptance. Relations with the students were very cordial. One young woman said afterwards that she would have preferred to have had a Muslim lecturer, but none of the students contested my position. It is worth insisting on this, since it is important. Some years later, during a Christian–Muslim meeting in Arusha, Tanzania, some Muslim participants from West Africa proposed that no non-Muslim should be allowed to teach Islamics. This was scotched by the Muslim co-chair, Badru Kateregga, at that time Ambassador of Uganda to Saudi Arabia, who declared: 'I had a Christian as a lecturer on Islam at Makerere [he was referring to me]. He it was who encouraged me to specialize in Islamics so that I eventually became a lecturer in this subject in Nairobi. And now I have trained a Christian lady to take my place.' It seems to me that this mutual confidence and this cooperation in scholarship is an essential ingredient in Christian–Muslim relations.

After two most enjoyable years in Uganda I was brought back to Rome to resume teaching at the IPEA, which has now become the Pontifical Institute for Arabic and Islamic Studies (PISAI, following its Italian title). One year later I was appointed Director, at a time when the Institute was expanding its programmes to include English-speaking students in order to address the needs of Christian–Muslim relations in Africa and Asia. One of the early students in this section was Bishop Benvenido (Benny) Tudtud from the Philippines. He had asked for, and been granted, a sabbatical year to study Islam in order to be able to understand the numerous Muslims in his diocese. On his return to the Philippines he initiated a dialogical approach which was to have a tremendous impact both in the Philippines and beyond.

We were lucky, at the PISAI, to be able to invite as guest lecturers such well-known figures as George Anawati, an Egyptian Dominican specialist on Islam; Louis Gardet, a French Thomist who had worked with Anawati and whose writings provided a sound theological approach to Islam; and Roger Arnaldez, a professor at the Sorbonne. There were also Muslims: Mohammed Arkoun and Ali Merad, both Algerians, who were professors in French universities; Abdelmajid Méziane, who later became the Minister for Religious Affairs in Algeria; and Abdelmajid Charfi, who as Minister for Education in Tunisia helped to bring in a reform of religious education in the country. Their presence was the occasion for a public lecture that would bring the various aspects of Christian–Muslim relations to a wider audience. With the same end in view we started the publication of *Encounter, Documents for Christian–Muslim Understanding*, a periodical providing every month an article on some aspect of Islam and Christian–Muslim relations. A further innovation of these years was the launching of a specialist journal, *Islamochristiana*, giving both historical and contemporary material concerning dialogue and interaction between the two religions.

There is a tradition that the Director of the PISAI is chosen as a consultor of the Pontifical Council for Interreligious Dialogue (PCID). So my connection with the PCID goes back to 1972. It was through the Secretariat for Non-Christians, as it was then known, that I was introduced to formal Christian–Muslim dialogue. The first meeting I attended was the consultation organized by the World Council of Churches in Broumana, Lebanon, in 1972. At the time it did not seem to me to be a very satisfactory meeting. Too many topics were addressed, and so nothing was studied in depth. A number of the participants, both Christian and Muslim, appeared to form a group, almost a clique, around the figure of Professor Wilfred Cantwell Smith. On the Muslim side there was a sensation of censorship being applied, thus preventing open discussion. Yet the WCC followed up Broumana with regional meetings, one of which was held in Hong Kong. On a journey to the Philippines I had the privilege of attending a gathering in Manila where the Filipino participants in the Hong Kong meeting were relating their experience. I was struck by the words of a leading Muslim from Mindanao, Senator Tamano. He spoke about the benefit of meeting with people from other countries and getting to know about Christian–Muslim relations in other areas. This led him, he said, to realize that such relations need not be marked by conflict. This helped to convince me that international gatherings can indeed serve to promote Christian–Muslim understanding.

Another international gathering was held in Tripoli, Libya, in 1976, organized by the Arabic Socialist Union of Libya and the Vatican Secretariat for Non-Christians. This had been intended as a private meeting between two international delegations, but the Libyan government, with extreme generosity, sent out invitations far and wide, so that the discussions took place before an audience of some 500 people. The final communiqué, prepared rather hastily, included two clauses that the Vatican side had to reject. This gave a bad reputation to the Tripoli meeting, and made many suspicious of Christian–Muslim dialogue. The positive aspects tended to be completely overlooked.

During these same years, I was involved in meetings with delegations to the Vatican from Saudi Arabia, Iran and Indonesia, and took part in a difficult meeting, at Chambésy-Geneva, on the concept of mission as understood by Christianity and Islam. I can still hear the voice of Bishop Kenneth Cragg pleading for a less partisan approach. The ecumenical dimension of work in Christian–Muslim relations, and in interreligious dialogue in general, has become a strong feature of my own convictions. Yet ecumenical cooperation is not always easy, as is borne out by another experience. Early in 1978 I was invited to attend an inter-Christian exchange on relations with Muslims in Europe, organized by the Conference of European Churches at Salzburg. What remains in my mind about this meeting is that the group discussing the theological underpinning for Christian–Muslim relations could not come to any agreement, not even to disagree. The final report from the consultation carried an eloquently blank page for the section entitled 'Theology'.

That same year I handed over the direction of the PISAI to one of my colleagues, and left Rome for the Sudan where I had been appointed. The next two years were spent doing parish work in the town and district of New Halfa, in northern Sudan, not far from the Ethiopian border. Our task was to minister to the Christian population, mainly southerners who had come to the northern region looking for work. But at the same time we were cooperating with local Muslims who helped us run a centre for adult education. This was a practical experience of two aspects of the Church's mission, which I would see defined later as proclamation and dialogue. It was not always easy making this double commitment understood. The Christians tended to resent the attention given to Muslims and the fact that the Church premises were open to them. On the other hand some of our Muslim friends felt that we were wasting our time with 'these blacks', an attitude which only served to convince us that we were right to give this form of Christian witness. We insisted with the Christians that the Church cannot be a 'club', but must be at the service of the whole population. In turn we struggled with the Christians in order that they gain more respect. We came to appreciate the line taken by Archbishop, now Cardinal, Gabriel Zubeir Wako, the first Sudanese Archbishop of Khartoum: his fearless defence of the Christian community, his tireless work on behalf of human rights and his constant advocacy of non-violent methods.

The Sudanese interlude over, I returned to Rome expecting to take up teaching again in the PISAI. Instead I found myself elected to the General Council of the Missionaries of Africa, and so the next six years were spent in administration and animation. This entailed a fair amount of travelling in Europe and in Africa, and even in Brazil, visiting communities and individuals, encouraging them in their missionary life and work. The team I belonged to, the General Council, did try to stimulate an interest in dialogue with Muslims, but without a great deal of success.

It was during the General Chapter of 1986, which brought to a close this period of my life, that the Assisi event took place. Again I was prepared to return to PISAI but instead I was appointed to work in the Vatican as the Secretary of the Secretariat for Non-Christians. This entailed an enlargement of scale and a widening of horizons. Up to this point I had been concerned with Christian–Muslim relations. Now my field of work extended to all religions, with one exception: Judaism. In the Vatican, responsibility for Catholic–Jewish relations is carried by a special commission that comes under the Pontifical Council for Promoting Christian Unity. Yet the range of religions or religious groups is extremely wide – from the Ahmadiyya to the Zoroastrians. Ideally I should have asked for some time for study in order to prepare for this new task, but in fact I had to start straight away, picking up bits of knowledge as I went along.

I was now the immediate collaborator of Cardinal Arinze, the President of the Secretariat, from whom I have learnt much, in particular the deep respect that is due to the local churches. Our office was at the direct service of Pope John Paul II. I was soon to realize how much his example and teachings influenced the Catholic approach to people of other religions. Many Christians who had followed the events of the Day of Prayer for Peace at Assisi, on television or through the press, felt reassured by it that meeting with people of different religions is not against one's own faith.

One of my first tasks as Secretary was to help to organize the 1987 Plenary Assembly of the Secretariat, which brought together some 30 bishops from many different parts of the world. The agenda included the discussion of the first draft of a document which was to become *Dialogue and Proclamation*, eventually published in 1991. The preliminary work on this document, which became a joint venture of the PCID and the Congregation for the Evangelization of Peoples, brought me into contact with Jacques Dupuis, one of the leading Catholic theologians on religious pluralism. I realized how delicate this topic is, and how much room there is for misunderstanding. I will come back to this in more detail later in the book.

Yet theological reflection was not confined to official documents. To foster dialogue within the Church, Cardinal Arinze took the initiative of arranging two theological consultations, one in India on 'Jesus Christ Lord and Saviour and the encounter with religions' and the second in Abidjan, Côte d'Ivoire, on 'The Gospel of Jesus Christ and the encounter with traditional religions'. The proceedings of these consultations were published in the journal of our office. In 1988 the Secretariat was renamed the Pontifical Council for Interreligious Dialogue, and the journal's name was changed from the *Bulletin* to *Pro Dialogo*. This journal reproduces whatever the Pope writes or says about interreligious relations, such as his discourses in the Vatican and speeches during his pastoral visits around the world. It contains articles, book reviews, and news of dialogue events and meetings.

Not all the Secretary's time is spent sitting behind a desk. There are many visitors to receive, there are meetings to attend, talks to be given, in Rome, in Europe and further afield. In 1990 I was given the opportunity of joining a party of monks and nuns from Europe who were taking part in an exchange programme with Buddhist monastics in Japan. The experience of living in a Buddhist monastery, even if only for a couple of weeks, did certainly help me to get some understanding of Buddhism from within. The importance of silent meditation, the attention to the present moment inculcated through the menial work tasks allocated to the monks in training, the humility required to go out begging in the streets – appreciation for these features of Buddhism grew through sharing in them. The programme included visits to prominent Buddhist monasteries including Mount Hiei, near Kyoto. The abbot of the monastery, the Venerable Etai Yamada, had attended the 1986 Prayer in Assisi, and had been so impressed that he decided to organize a similar event in his monastery the following year. This has continued every year since then. I was to meet Etai Yamada again in 1992 and, through an interpreter, was able to have a conversation with him. He reminded me in some ways of John Paul II, with his strong convictions, his deep spirituality and his great attention to young people.

At the end of 1991 I received an unexpected call to see Cardinal Sodano, the Secretary of State. I was wondering what it was all about, but the Cardinal said to me 'The Holy Father wants to make you a bishop. Come back tomorrow at the same time with your answer.' What could I say? I accepted, and was ordained bishop by Pope John Paul II in St Peter's Basilica on 6 January 1992. This did not entail a move from Rome, as I was given a titular diocese, Nepte, which is the modern Nefta in Tunisia. I have been twice to this rather pretty oasis, but nobody there knows I am the bishop. Nor did the fact of being a bishop in any way change the nature of the work I was doing, though it has facilitated relations at different levels.

As a bishop, however, I am on occasions asked to administer confirmation and also to confer ordination. One such invitation was to Birmingham, to a very multicultural parish, and during my stay I was taken to the Sikhs' large purpose-built *gurdwara* in Handsworth. The visit took place on a Saturday morning. Perhaps because of this, the building was crowded with people, all doing different things. There was a wedding party in one hall; in another room there were people reciting the Scriptures, while others seemed to be receiving instruction; in the *langar*, the communal kitchen, women were chanting prayers as they made *chapatis*. It was most impressive. Later, a delegation from this gurdwara came to visit us in Rome, and we engaged in formal exchange on the role of Scripture in our respective religions. Other Sikhs have taken part in multireligious meetings that we have organized, for instance a consultation on marriage and the family in the modern world and a reflection on the role of religions in society. I had always felt that greater attention should be given to the Sikhs, and so it was with joy that we welcomed religious leaders from the Golden Temple in Amritsar when they came for another Day of Prayer for Peace in Assisi in January 2002. In December of 2003 I was able to return this visit.

One of the features of the work in the PCID is its ecumenical dimension. Our office, almost from its first years, had established a strong working relationship with the corresponding office in the World Council of Churches. Staff members from Geneva were invited to attend the PCID's plenary assemblies and, as Secretary, I represented our office at the meeting of the Advisory Committee of the WCC's office on interreligious relations and dialogue. There was a feeling of complete acceptance, of not being treated as a mere observer but as a full participant. Though not always fully agreeing with all the opinions expressed, I have come to appreciate and respect the thinking and writing of Stanley Samartha, Wesley Ariarajah and Hans Ucko. These good relations have developed into common projects, such as joint reflections on interreligious marriage, consultations on interreligious prayer and a programme highlighting the contribution of Africa to the religious heritage of the world.

Though the brief of the PCID does not extend to relations with Jews, I was also appointed as a consultor of the Vatican's Commission for Religious Relations with the Jews. This has taken me to meetings with Jews in Rome, New York, Jerusalem and, most recently, Buenos Aires. There has also been an involvement in trilateral dialogue among Jews, Christians and Muslims, organized on an ecumenical basis. Such a dialogue is by no means simple, and the current political situation presents added difficulties, yet such efforts are always needed.

The PCID has a group of consultors (advisors) who live in a number of different countries. They are appointed for a five-year term, and the custom is to meet with them in their respective continents at least once during their mandate. In September 2002, after earlier meetings in Dar es Salaam and in Damascus, we were gathered in Korea with our Asian consultors and secretaries of interreligious commissions from different countries. Cardinal Arinze was presiding. My two Asian colleagues and myself formed the rest of the team. It was at this time that the Cardinal was told of his impending appointment to head another office of the Roman Curia and I was told that I would be taking over as President of the PCID. After the Korean engagements, the Cardinal returned to Rome and I stayed on to preside over an already planned Catholic–Buddhist dialogue, which was to take place in Tokyo.

So a new phase in my life opened, one that is still ongoing. I am able to build on the good work of my predecessors, particularly Cardinal Arinze with whom I had been working closely for 15 years.

I was asked one day if I had an episcopal coat of arms. I said no, but it set me thinking, and with the help of a heraldic expert I devised one: a palm tree to represent Nepte, my titular diocese; a star evoking the Feast of the Epiphany, which was the day on which I was ordained bishop; and a Celtic cross in a verdant field to recall my Irish descent. For a motto I chose *Fructum dabit*, 'It will give fruit'. These words come from Psalm 1, 'he is like a tree that is planted by running water, yielding its fruit in due season'. This, for me, is a good expression of what dialogue means. One cannot expect immediate results. There is a need to prepare the ground, to build up confidence, to establish friendship, so that relationships can grow stronger. One has to be patient and persevere in hope. Fruit will certainly come in due time.

Forty years ago:
Vatican II, dialogue and lay leadership

JOHN BORELLI

Preparations

As a way to encourage bishops to take a positive view towards inter-religious relations during the Second Vatican Council, Pope Paul VI established the Secretariat for Non-Christians (now known as the Pontifical Council for Interreligious Dialogue) on 19 May 1964. This was between the second and third sessions. Three days earlier, 16 May, the council's Coordinating Commission agreed that a proposed chapter on relations with Jews for the original schema on ecumenism would become a separate document and would include relations with other religious groups and with Muslims in particular.[1] Probably few in the Catholic Church took notice of these developments although most were aware of monumental shifts in Church policies and teachings taking place over the course of the council's four sessions. Of all the important changes, renewing the Catholic community and shaping it into the Church we are today, it was the creation of an office for interreligious dialogue in 1964 and the passage of a declaration in October 1965 connecting interreligious dialogue with the council's vision of the Church as a communion and dialogue of salvation that would have the greatest impact on my future.

In May 1964, I was preparing for high school graduation and the conclusion of the first four years of an anticipated 12-year pro-gramme in seminary education. Minor seminary covered the first six years and thus two years of college. In September 1964, I was to return to St Francis de Sales Preparatory Seminary, in Oklahoma City, for two more years of study and preparation and then a decision about the next six years of major seminary. High school graduation was still an important passage, even in the seminary. We wore caps and gowns and received hearty congratulations from family, friends, faculty and fellow students. In 1964, I sensed that I was at the beginning not only of a long period of preparation but also of a set of major changes in the life of the Catholic Church. I was preparing to be a priest for the Diocese of Oklahoma City and Tulsa, and to their credit, the seminary faculty hosted speakers who kept us informed of the liturgical renewal and other changes in doctrine and practice that would impact significantly on our lives. We had watched the opening of the council in 1962, and Bishop Victor J. Reed returned each year to Oklahoma with much to tell us about the future. As much as an adolescent could, I had committed myself to a life of service to a Church that was adjusting to the times.

Far from population centres where our numbers were high, Catholics in Oklahoma were barely 2 per cent of the population in 1964. A few older Catholics remembered the first missions to Indian Territory prior to statehood in 1907, and my parents were born six years after the first bishop was appointed (1905). We nurtured a pioneer religious identity and bonded together in parishes, schools, and other diocesan projects and enterprises. In the post-Second World War years, Oklahoma had a proportionally large number of young priests who seemed eager to experiment with the suggestions of the 'new theology' already old hat in Europe. The pastor of Christ the King parish in Oklahoma City implemented a 'dialogue mass' for the daily 8.30 morning liturgy, and all grammar school students were expected to attend. The 'dialogue mass' format was an interim step drawing the faithful into attentive participation in the liturgy. Benedictine sisters with a love for liturgical prayer and singing and an assistant pastor with an excitement for liturgical studies assisted the pastor. When I entered first grade in September 1952, I walked into this little world. By eighth grade, in 1960, the assistant was pastor and had pulled the altar away from the wall, as a prop for Lenten renewal in the parish. Presiders faced the assembly. When I suggested to the Principal of the school that I wait to instruct the new crop of altar boys until after Lent, Sister told me with marked determination that 'we are never going to put the altar back.' Our first pastor, Charles A. Buswell, was a bishop in Colorado and would be among the council fathers, and in Oklahoma and elsewhere, we were designing new churches for the liturgical changes yet to be made official. I had already grown accustomed to the full and active participation of the laity in the liturgy as the source of Christian life.[2]

The reform of the liturgy was the first major step taken by the Second Vatican Council in the renewal of the Catholic Church and probably had the widest impact on the lives of Catholics. As an eighth grader at age 13, I was reading aloud at mass and felt comfortable in the sanctuary. A quarter of the proposals sent to Rome in the preparatory phase of the council pertained to the liturgy, and Vatican II would be the first universal council in the history of the Western Church to compose a document on liturgical questions for a single rite.[3]

Thus, the promotion of interreligious conversation and understanding would be only one item on a list of monumental steps for this Council. Like the rest, it did not come without preparation and effort to connect the new course with past efforts. For centuries, missionaries, diplomats and other travellers reported, often with a profound appreciation, what they had learned about other religious traditions. There were also examples of efforts by some Catholic leaders to promote peaceful relations especially with Muslims. Through the centuries, few scholars had the tools for proper research into other religious traditions although the Council of Vienne in 1312 had called for the establishment of schools of Arabic, Greek, Hebrew and Syriac at given major European universities.[4] In 1965, the Second Vatican Council reiterated this fundamental need for scholarly study of other religions and for communities of Christians and for missionaries and other pastoral workers to be accurately informed. Vatican II did more than reiterate; it took the bolder step in recognizing positive values in other religions and calling for genuine dialogue not just on those things which unite us but on our differences as well.[5] This happened in the final session in 1965.

During the following two years, 1966–8, I completed my last two years of college at St Louis University. Taken in isolation from these times and changes, the circumstances that led me from minor seminary in Oklahoma City to an urban Catholic and Jesuit university with a highly reputable department of philosophy would seem remarkable; but those were times on the cusp of change. Several of us, given the chance to state our preferences for major seminary, asked for the opportunity to finish college on a university campus rather than in a seminary. There I majored in philosophy, loved the courses, continued to study literature and history, and carried a third minor in theology. During the fall term of my senior year, Fr Karl Rahner, one of the leading theologians of Vatican II, was on campus giving a series of talks. My Jesuit scholastic friends handed out passes to each session, every seat filled to capacity.

I never once gave up the thought of eventually studying theology, but my experiences and surroundings challenged me to consider other ways of doing it. Seminaries generally offered ministerial degrees, but I now hungered for academic studies. I figured that the Church needed smarter, more professionally trained leaders, but I also observed that there were three 'lay' theologians, one woman and two men, in St Louis University's Department of Theology. I took courses from two of them, and I could see myself in their shoes. As 1967 unfolded, I decided to suspend formal preparations for the priesthood. I did not ask for a leave; rather, I wanted to be free to explore possibilities in the highly charged environment of Church life after the council. I never again asked to be a candidate for the priesthood or even pondered the possibility, for the council's call for lay leadership was too strong. As one author has put it recently, 'nothing could ever be the same again for the fortunes of laypeople in the Church after the Second Vatican Council.'[6]

Acting upon decisions

In September 1968, I started graduate studies in the Department of Theology, Fordham University, a Jesuit university in New York City. My intention was to focus on 'historical theology', a theological orientation that took account of the development of doctrine, which had aided many in the Church to embrace the changes of the council. John XXIII had asked bishops to read the signs of the times, and this implied the importance of historical factors in understanding Church doctrines and practices. At Fordham, two of my four instructors that first semester were Protestants. Vatican II's commitment to ecumenism was also being implemented. In addition to biblical, systematic and historical studies in the theology programme, there was a section entitled 'History of Religions'. I had chosen Fordham because I wanted to focus on theological anthropology with an eye for historical development of Christian understanding of human nature oriented towards God. Thomas Berry, the Passionist priest who headed History of Religions and with a background in Chinese studies, told me I could do the same thing by studying other religions and focusing on the interface between Christian theology and the thought systems of other religions. I told him I would think about it.

By dropping my seminarian status, I also gave up a divinity school deferment from military draft during the height of the Vietnam War. My local draft board in Oklahoma City allowed me to complete my first semester before ordering me to present myself for military draft. In February 1969, I reported for the required two years of military service and, after eight weeks of basic training, was pooled with other college graduates to spend thirty weeks studying Vietnamese and another eight weeks in military intelligence training. I spent most of 1970 in Vietnam as a language-trained interrogator, where many of my counterparts in the South Vietnamese army were Buddhists. A Jesuit professor at St Louis University continued to advise me, as he had served as my tutor for graduate studies during my senior year, and pointed out the Buddhist sites in and around Da Nang and Hue where I was stationed. I visited them with Vietnamese friends and read extensively about Buddhism, Hinduism and Chinese religions.

I returned to Fordham in January 1971, completed the requirements for a Master's degree in theology, switched to a focus on history of religions for doctoral studies and defended a dissertation on a Hindu theologian in February 1976. Fr Berry's sympathetic vision for the insights of other religions flowing from an appreciation of genuine religious experiences seemed exactly what the Catholic Church needed to implement Vatican II's call for interreligious dialogue. I had studied Sanskrit and Chinese to access the religious traditions of India and China and had incorporated a dialogical approach as a significant element in my use of the history of religions method within a theological context. I sensed that my future involved developing and implementing the insights and recommendations of the council's Declaration on the Relation of the Church to Non-Christian Religions (*Nostra Aetate*) and that my contribution as a layperson would be as a scholar and university professor. My work brought me into contact and friendship with Hindu, Buddhist and other scholars. I would work collegially with them testing my interpretations of Hindu, Buddhist and other traditions with their understanding of the traditions, and my life would involve intellectual exchanges reaching deeper insights into these traditions and improving theological understanding and relations among peoples of different faith traditions. I would encourage students to develop a positive appreciation of other religions to enrich their lives and for the sake of peace. In 1986, I addressed a serious deficiency in my education when I was accepted as a National Endowment for the Humanities fellow at New York University for a five-month term to study Islam.

While I was teaching in New York in the late 1970s, the chairman of the ecumenical commission for the Archdiocese of New York, Msgr James Rigney, Rector of St Patrick Cathedral, invited me to become a member of the commission. Someone said that the commission desired an infusion of creativity and energy from new members. I agreed to assist with ecumenical relations but stated my real interest was interreligious dialogue. Fifteen years after the Second Vatican Council, there were no interreligious dialogues involving the Archdiocese of New York beyond dialogues with Jewish leaders. There were of course several ecumenical dialogues. In 1981, Msgr Rigney asked me to represent the archdiocese at an ecumenical leadership institute co-sponsored by the Bishops' Committee for Ecumenical and Interreligious Affairs and a national network of Catholic diocesan ecumenical officers. I attended and met several key figures, particularly the ecumenical officer for the Archdiocese of Los Angeles. He knew first hand that dioceses needed help immediately for interreligious relations. Together, he and I formed a support committee serving the network of diocesan officers drawing upon the expertise of Catholic scholars of religions and diocesan staff who were already gaining experience with interreligious contacts. This was the Faiths in the World Committee for the National Association of Diocesan Ecumenical Officers. It met annually from 1982 and organized programmes for diocesan staff who attended the annual National Workshop on Christian Unity. With few exceptions, the same person, usually a priest, is responsible for ecumenical and interreligious relations for a diocese. From this time forward, I did not miss an annual meeting of the Faiths in the World Committee nor failed to attend the annual workshop on Christian unity from 1984 until 2003–4. What was significant for me was that I was engaged in the work of restoring Christian unity and in promoting interreligious relations at the same time. I had moved with the flow of events from before the Second Vatican Council, through my formal education, and to teaching from an ecumenical and interreligious perspective and serving a network of Catholic dioceses.

In those early days, I was blessed with another good teacher, John F. Long, SJ, who had returned to New York after a decade and a half serving on the staff of the Secretariat for Christian Unity. He guided me in understanding Vatican II's vision of the Church and especially the implications for ecumenical relations. In 1982, I held a part-time position as a staff writer and researcher for the archdiocesan commission while holding down a full-time teaching position at the College of Mount St Vincent. In 1985, with a few others, I founded the Catholic–Muslim Dialogue of New York. In 1986, I was asked to assist with the US chapter of the World Conference of Religions for Peace by serving as secretary-general on a part-time basis. I added this to my teaching and diocesan support work. Every day of my life seemed to involve service to interreligious relations.

By 1987, the national episcopal conference had funded a proposal to expand the staff of its national secretariat, and I left academic life to embark on a 16-year career as Associate Director of the Secretariat for Ecumenical and Interreligious Affairs at the US Conference of Catholic Bishops. I was the first on that staff to take up interreligious activity in any formal way. Besides numerous consultations with Catholics and other Christians and special events and projects with Muslim, Buddhist, Hindu and multireligious and interreligious groups, I assisted in the inauguration of three ongoing Catholic–Muslim dialogues, which met annually in the Mid-Atlantic, Mid-western and West Coast regions of the USA, and an ongoing dialogue with Buddhists and one with Hindus. I also continued to do interreligious work hand-in-hand with ecumenical work, staffing Byzantine Orthodox relations for eight years and Anglican–Catholic relations for the next eight years.

John F. Hotchkin, the Chicago priest and genius for ecumenical relations, who was director of the office until his death in 2001, wanted me to do both. He knew first hand that bishops and other Church leaders in the USA had come to recognize the importance of ecumenical relations and relations with Jews, but he was also aware that many still needed to be convinced of the necessity of interreligious relations, especially of Christian–Muslim relations. In those times before September 11, 2001, the best course for promoting interreligious relations seemed to be to link these efforts with ecumenism through the vision of the Church as a communion of the baptized in relationship with one another and the whole of humanity. In addition, by continuing to engage in ecumenical relations, I gained so much that I might otherwise not have noticed, especially the progress among various Christians towards full communion. Furthermore, other Churches needed to develop interreligious relations too, and all Christians share the same profound implications of interreligious relations as they address their differences with one another and seek to overcome any lack of unity.

As a layperson, I was usually in a minority, and sometimes a minority of one, among Catholic participants in these projects. Bishops were generally grateful for my assistance, often going out of their way to express gratitude. They appreciated expertise, usually offered by scholars and experienced practitioners, and consulted with respect and usually in a collegial manner. Scholars and representatives of religious groups were eager to offer time and talent to promoting ecumenism and interreligious understanding. Working as a layperson, I could encourage others, like myself, with the knowledge that their views would be heard and all their efforts could make a difference in achieving the goals we were setting for these dialogues and other ecumenical and interreligious projects.

In 1990, the Vatican Secretary of State appointed me a consultor to the Pontifical Council for Interreligious Dialogue, and I have remained a consultor long enough to celebrate its fortieth anniversary in 2004. This office has worked steadfastly in interreligious relations from 1964 to 2004, and my personal journey from 'dialogue mass' in Oklahoma to exchanging views on interreligious relations with bishops from around the world has been as remarkable as it has been enjoyable and fulfilling.

The Pontifical Council has been generous in offering me opportunities for international experience and encouraging me to comment on interreligious events and policies. The President and members of the staff have become friends and have acted with equanimity in our interactions. Forty years after the Second Vatican Council, Church leaders did not expect a layperson to have held the responsibilities that I had while working for a national conference of bishops. If you check the *Annuario Pontificio,* you will not find very many names of laypersons. In the 2004 edition, the names of four nuns, one laywoman, and three laymen appear among the consultors of the PCID.

Forty years after Vatican II, my status as a layperson stands out in stark contrast to what remains the norm especially on visits to Rome. These visits for meetings have often included an audience with Pope John Paul II. Vigilant at the stairs and doorways of the papal palace, Swiss Guards and other officials have singled me out as if I did not belong with this group. Once, in 1995, in such a line, a priest on the staff smiled and suggested that the Church needs more laymen like me. I am sure he intended this as a positive comment about my contributions to interreligious work and an expression of openness towards the future, but I was amused at how the thought had occurred to him in this particular situation and how I had the same thought 30 years earlier. Is ordination still a hidden requirement for all positions of leadership in the Catholic Church?

As I compose these reflections in the year 2004, I have returned to academic life serving as Special Assistant to the President of Georgetown University in Washington, DC. This is the oldest Catholic university in the USA, founded in the year of the republic (1789) by the first bishop of the USA, John Carroll. Although Church officials suppressed the Jesuit order between 1773 and 1814, the men who created Georgetown University and John Carroll himself were Jesuits, and the university is the oldest of 28 universities and colleges in the USA founded by the Society of Jesus. In 1995, at their 34th General Congregation, the Jesuits committed themselves and their institutions to promote interreligious dialogue: 'To be religious today is to be interreligious in the sense that a positive relationship with believers of other faiths is a requirement in a world of religious plur-alism.'[7] The President of Georgetown University, Dr John DeGioia, the first layman to serve as president of a Jesuit university, asked me to consider assisting him in exploring how this university can do more to promote interreligious understanding.

My initial conversations with Dr DeGioia leading to his invitation and my acceptance were a completely unanticipated set of events, but these circumstances were not unlike those at other major crossroads in my life. Decisions taken often involved little conscious choice on my part, but circumstances led to possibilities and to further and even unimaginable avenues. With a faith nurtured by family and by countless others who conveyed joy and enthusiasm for partaking in the life of the Church, I habitually looked for a 'calling' or vocation in my situations. My parents chose to move to Christ the King Parish for reasons other than the fact that Msgr Buswell had implemented a dialogue mass for the daily school liturgy; yet, the formation in liturgical prayer and song had an enormous impact on the rest of our lives. My parents were probably reluctant, like all parents, to recommend that I attend minor seminary, but Bishop McGuinness, who knew them well enough as friends to ask my father for his skills and expertise for diocesan projects, had urged them to encourage me to be a priest when he held me as a toddler. Had I not gone to St Francis Seminary, I most likely would not have paid as much attention to the Second Vatican Council and almost certainly would not have gone to St Louis University. Completion of my undergraduate education there prepared me to make a decision to attend Fordham for graduate studies. Like most draftees, I would happily have preferred to pursue other priorities and to forfeit the opportunity to become a first-hand participant in the intensely emotional and complicated war in Vietnam that continues to divide Americans to this day. This interruption in graduate studies with the almost accidental chance to study Vietnamese, and be attuned to the language and culture of the Vietnamese people, resulted in my first interreligious experiences. Connections at Fordham recommended me to a full-time position in New York City, when teaching jobs were scarce, but at a college with a unique history with the Archdiocese of New York. By teaching at the College of Mount St Vincent, I was noticed for membership on the ecumenical commission even though my interests and expertise were in the history of religions, Asian religions and interreligious dialogue, not in ecumenism. Had I not been asked by Msgr Rigney to attend that first ecumenical leadership institute, I might never have met the ecumenical officer from Los Angeles, Msgr Vadakin. Together, we launched the Faiths in the World Committee, which preceded the opening in interreligious relations on the bishops' staff by five years. Had I been selected, instead of someone else and a priest, to be the executive director of the secretariat in 2002, since I was appointed the interim director after Fr Hotchkin's death, I would not be at Georgetown University today.

When I was young, Catholics usually referred to vocations to the priesthood or religious life. Even Vatican's II Dogmatic Constitution on the Church (*Lumen Gentium*) uses the term with a double-edged meaning favouring ordination and consecrated life: 'The family is, so to speak, the domestic church. In it parents should, by their word and example, be the first preachers of the faith to their children; they should encourage them in the vocation which is proper to each of them, fostering with special care vocation to a sacred state' (LG 11). Having a vocation is true for everyone who believes that God is involved in their lives, speaking to them and making known greater possibilities for building the kingdom. Vatican II's Decree on the Apostolate of Lay People (*Apostolicam Actuositatem*) contains a chapter on 'The Vocation of the Laity to the Apostolate'. Much of my life has been spent discerning what specifically belongs to the vocation of the laity in the life of the Church. Taking my ecumenical and interreligious interests and work to the environment Georgetown University provides seemed the right step to take at the time. This journey does not seem to be on its final leg.

Many decisions involve some regrets. I regretted giving up the many good aspects of my service at the episcopal conference, especially the opportunities to nurture ecumenical and interreligious friendships and to work collegially, ecumenically and interreligiously, with so many dedicated persons serving the restoration of Christian unity and the promotion of interreligious understanding. I remain in contact with many I had come to know over these years although our official work together has ceased. In addition, looking back, I would have expected by this time not to be an exception in Church circles implementing the commitment of the Catholic Church to ecumenical and interreligious relations. Committed as we are to the goals and ideals of the Second Vatican Council, lay leaders find ways to adjust and continue to make their contributions to the life of the Church, but I regret that I was not able to promote lay leadership within the structure better than I did.

Finally, I would be remiss if I did not mention that a sacramental partnership and bond of friendship long ago create the foundation for any contribution I have been able to make along the way. I met Marianne at St Louis University in January 1967, appropriately, I suppose, during the greeting of peace at one of the masses on campus. We were engaged in December 1969 and were married in January 1971 less than 30 days after my return from Vietnam. During our first years together, we were both graduate students, then took turns supporting one another, and then held full-time teaching positions while raising our three children: Stephen, Claire and Eleanor joined us in 1974, 1978 and 1980 respectively. I completed my doctorate in 1976, and Marianne finished hers in 1981 in psychiatric mental health nursing. In 2002, she met all the requirements to be a certified nurse practitioner. If I boast of not having missed a committee meeting or workshop for 20 years, or if I was able to participate in events and dialogues, it was because she encouraged me to keep going and was willing to manage the household by herself on those occasions. Having defended her dissertation and preparing to return to full-time teaching in the fall and with our children turning one, three, and seven that summer or in a few weeks thereafter, she permitted me to attend the ten-day institute in Minnesota that led eventually to a full-time position in service to the Church. I once counted 100 travel days in a calendar year while working for the conference of bishops. Her generosity, hard work, support and shared enthusiasm for the lay vocation in the Church, assistance with discernment and companionship for 35 years of marriage are essential aspects of my personal journey through interreligious relations, which I have been privileged to follow.

Part I

DIALOGUE IN GENERAL

1

The Catholic Church and interreligious dialogue

'Interreligious dialogue is a part of the Church's evangelising mission' (RM 55). This clear statement, found in John Paul II's missionary encyclical *Redemptoris Missio* (1990), recognizes the important role of interreligious dialogue in the Church's life. This was not a new idea, since it already appears in the documents of the Second Vatican Council. Recent popes have developed the bare outlines of these documents, and Paul VI's journeys, and John Paul II's visits, talks and teachings, emphasized the importance of relations with people from other religious traditions.

In interreligious relations, formal meetings and learned discussions certainly have their place, but these relations involve much more than theological discussion. Theology arises from experience, and I wish to situate the whole question of interreligious dialogue within the context of everyday life. I shall first look briefly at the goal of dialogue and the forms it might take. A document of 1991, *Dialogue and Proclamation* (DP), building on an earlier document of 1984, gave the following definition:

> In the context of religious plurality, dialogue means 'all positive and constructive interreligious relations with individuals and communities of other faiths which are directed at mutual understanding and enrichment', in obedience to truth and respect for freedom.   (DP 9)

From this it can be seen that interreligious dialogue is a response to religious plurality, a phenomenon which is increasing as communications become easier and more rapid. In recent years both the awareness of diversity and the need and desire for dialogue have grown. Moreover, the term chosen to define dialogue is 'relations', showing that dialogue does not only mean verbal exchange but includes many kinds of human interaction.

Such relations, which to qualify as dialogue must be positive and constructive, can exist between individual believers at an informal level, or between representatives of communities. It should be noted that dialogue takes place between people, not between systems.

The goal of dialogue is first 'mutual understanding', to try to understand others as they want to be understood. Each person has to be open, ready to listen, to put aside prejudice and to learn from the other. At the same time, each must have the freedom to express their own conviction.

A further goal is 'mutual enrichment'. Relations with people of other religions must never degenerate into rivalry or polemics – trying to score points. Where the relationship is positive, it will lead to admiration for what is good in the other religion, and encourage us to deepen our knowledge not only of that religion but of our own as well.

Forms of dialogue

The 1984 document, *Dialogue and Mission* (DM), was perhaps the first to present four forms of dialogue. These were briefly and conveniently summarized in DP:

> The *dialogue of life*, where people strive to live in an open and neighbourly spirit, sharing their joys and sorrows, their human problems and preoccupations.
>
> The *dialogue of action*, in which Christians and others collaborate for the integral development and liberation of people.
>
> The *dialogue of theological exchange*, where specialists seek to deepen their understanding of their respective religious heritage, and to appreciate each other's spiritual values.
>
> The *dialogue of religious experience*, where persons rooted in their own religious traditions share their spiritual riches, for instance with regard to prayer and contemplation, faith and ways of searching for God or the Absolute. (DP 42)

This typology is not exhaustive, nor are the definitions perfect. In particular, instead of the *dialogue of theological exchange* I would prefer the *dialogue of discourse*, or *of formal exchange*, since the subject may not necessarily be confined to theological issues. However, this division into four forms has proved its worth pedagogically, and I shall follow it, as we look at ways in which true dialogue can be encouraged and practised.

Dialogue of life

From the description above it can be seen that the dialogue of life is not something passive, not mere coexistence; it requires openness, a desire to enter into relations with others. Its aim is to establish good neighbourly relations, to ensure that people live in peace and harmony.

How can this be done? Perhaps the first thing is to stimulate an active interest in the other, especially people of a different religion. Acquiring knowledge about others, through reading or direct contact, helps to overcome prejudices and encourage understanding. Paying visits to one another's homes is a normal way of increasing neighbourliness. 'Sharing joys and sorrows' could include presenting congratulations at a marriage or birth, offering condolences at a bereavement, or giving a helping hand. Life itself provides occasions for meeting.

Sometimes these visits may be organized. Westminster Interfaith, an initiative of the Catholic Archdiocese of Westminster, London, every year holds a walk ('Pilgrimage of Peace') through the streets of London, a different area each time. The walkers, or pilgrims, go from one place of worship to another, from the Baptist chapel to the Buddhist temple, from the synagogue to the Sikh gurdwara, from the Anglican or Catholic church to the Hindu temple. In each place the local community is able to receive the group on its own terms, offering an opportunity for rest and refreshment, but also a chance to learn something about the host community. The walkers too, as they go along, are drawn to share their own stories, as pilgrims do. This annual walk thus helps people of different religious traditions to grow in unity, while at the same time they give a united witness to the wider public.

Another organized form of the dialogue of life is the *Duyog Ramadan* programme in the Southern Philippines. This is a programme to help Christians accompany (the meaning of the word *duyog*) Muslims during the fasting month of Ramadan. By appropriate sermons and talks, and special programmes on the radio,

Christians are made aware of how Muslims observe Ramadan and why. In this way greater understanding can be built up, and possible tensions overcome.

Acknowledging the feasts of people of other religions is a way of showing recognition and esteem for them. Since 1967 our Pontifical Council for Interreligious Dialogue (PCID) has sent a message of greetings to Muslims for 'Id al-Fitr, the feast concluding the month of Ramadan. In recent years our council has also been sending a message to Buddhists for Vesakh, and to Hindus for Diwali. These messages are well received, and are certainly a way of building up good relations.

A very obvious example of the dialogue of life is seen in inter-religious marriages. While the Church does not encourage these, since the difference of religion can bring added strain, these marriages should be upheld and helped to work. In France and in England, and in other places, there are already groups of couples of mixed faith, who meet for sharing, reflection and support.

Dialogue of action

After having mentioned the four forms of dialogue, DP goes on to say:

> The importance of dialogue for integral development, social justice and human liberation needs to be stressed. Local churches are called upon, as witnesses to Christ, to commit themselves in this respect in an unselfish and impartial manner. There is need to stand up for human rights, proclaim the demands of justice, and denounce injustice not only when their own members are victimised, but independently of the religious allegiance of the victims. (DP 44)

The document here addresses Christians, in particular Catholics, and local churches, but they are not the only ones working for greater respect for human rights. In Pakistan for instance, where Christians constitute a very small minority of the population, it is encouraging to see that Christians and Muslims have been protesting together against certain measures, such as the proposal to include religion on identity cards, or the blasphemy law. It is not of course only religious bodies that 'stand up for human rights', but also neutral bodies, which can often be more effective.

The passage from DP continues: 'There is need also to join together in trying to solve the great problems facing society and the world, as well as in education for justice and peace' (DP 44).

Religious bodies need to collaborate more in humanitarian aid, for instance to help refugees, in assistance after natural disasters, reconstruction after war, reconciliation. One example is a joint project of the Italian Episcopal Conference and the Chinese Red Cross, in financing a training school for nurses in mainland China. This project is facilitated by the Schweizer Temple in Japan, a Buddhist institution, and a neighbouring Christian house of prayer.

This need for collaboration seems to me to have been the inspiration behind an organization such as the World Conference of Religions for Peace (WCRP). The founders – a Unitarian, a Jew and a Buddhist – felt that all religions were faced with the same problems, and that they would benefit by trying to tackle them together rather than separately. The first world conference was held in Kyoto in 1970, and the decision was taken to establish a permanent organization. A Catholic bishop, Archbishop Angelo Fernandes of New Delhi, gave enthusiastic support, and was chosen as the first president. One of the distinctive features of WCRP is that it brings into play the respective religious motivations for commitment to justice and peace. Recently the movement has become more action oriented. It contributed to setting up an interreligious council in Sarajevo, and has set up a similar council in Sierra Leone, which has become engaged in the rehabilitation of child soldiers.

There can be networking too, with many religions joining in on equal terms, as with local interfaith councils – generally concerned more with local social problems than with religion as such. One such example is the Inter Faith Network for the UK, which brings together institutions and persons from all the faiths and provides a forum for making representation to the government.

Work for justice and peace is an integral part of the Church's mission, it forms part of its *diakonia,* and has to be carried out at all levels. The services of education, medical work and social action are not confined to the Church's members but are offered to all. Similarly, members of the Church, either as individuals or as recognized religious bodies, may work within already existing structures, state or private. And there are other initiatives, in the countries of the Maghreb for instance, where Christians are involved alongside

Muslims in private associations. A great deal of confidence is needed to be able to work harmoniously together, and this kind of action can truly be considered a form of dialogue.

Dialogue of discourse

Perhaps the most familiar 'type' of dialogue, formal exchange, can take many different forms. The dialogue can be bilateral, Christian–Jewish, Christian–Muslim; or trilateral, Jews, Christians and Muslims together; or multilateral, with people of many different religious traditions taking part. Each has its own special advantages.

Meetings will also differ in the number of participants, ranging from large congresses to groups that can meet in people's homes. Some are unique experiences, while others may be occasional or regular meetings. Again, the topics addressed may be theological or social issues. The way of organizing the meetings can differ: the choice of participants may be through inviting individuals or by institutions selecting their own representatives.

This dialogue of discourse, first with Muslims, has included meetings between our council and the Al Albait (Jordan) on religious education, rights of children, women in society, religion and nationalism, use of the earth's resources, human dignity. With the World Islamic Call Society (WICS), which has its headquarters in Tripoli, Libya, we have discussed mission and da'wa, tolerance, religion and the media, and the role and formation of priests and imams. With Buddhists, we have held meetings on convergence and divergence, the human condition and the need for liberation, ultimate reality and the experience of Nirvana, Buddha and Christ, personal detachment and social commitment. Another meeting, in Bangalore, was on word and silence. With Hindus, meetings have been held in New Delhi on working for harmony in the contemporary world, in Madurai on issues in Hindu–Christian dialogue, in Pune on Hindu and Christian cosmology and anthropology, in Parma and Rome on artisans of peace.

If the dialogue of discourse is to succeed, certain conditions need to be fulfilled: preparation should be carried out jointly, it should be serious preparation while still leaving room for spontaneous discussion. Care must be taken to avoid polemics, but also not to restrict the exchanges to a purely academic approach. There will be a certain amount of repetition, especially when new people are brought into the dialogues. Very often meetings wish to end up with a common statement, and it is best not to try to say too much, so that there can at least be some common ground. Continuity is good. It is obvious that confidence grows when people meet at frequent intervals.

Dialogue of religious experience

To some extent this can be a specific form of the dialogue of discourse, when the topics for discussion are selected from the realm of spirituality. One example is the Christian–Muslim seminar on holiness held at the Pontifical Institute of Arabic and Islamic Studies in 1985, with papers on the concept of holiness, the teaching on the paths to holiness and concrete examples of holy people, in the two religions.

A similar discussion of spiritual teaching occurred in the encounters of the Ribat al-Salam, a group that used to meet at the Trappist monastery of Tibhérine, in Algeria, until the assassination of the seven monks. Besides providing an opportunity for sharing, these encounters were particular in that they included a considerable time given over to prayer.

The dialogue of religious experience is being developed among monastics, and an international secretariat has been set up to stimulate and coordinate this Monastic Interreligious Dialogue (MID). While the American group started by welcoming in particular monks and nuns from the Tibetan tradition, in Europe more contact has been made with the Zen tradition of Japan. The experience includes periods of two to three weeks in a monastery of the other tradition, developing a dialogue without words. This has flourished mainly between Buddhists and Christians, since they share the tradition of monasticism.

It should not be thought that dialogue of religious experience is confined to monastics. Interreligious prayer can be considered a form of this particular dialogue, and is a growing phenomenon. The World Day of Prayer for Peace, held in Assisi in October 1986, has encouraged many people to come together to pray. People may feel a need to pray together at times of crisis or disaster. There can be more private occasions too. Different sensibilities have to be respected, and it is not generally possible to find forms of prayer that can be shared.

Yet, provided the participants are attentive and listen with respect to another tradition's prayers, this can be a true form of dialogue.

In this regard, certain conditions should be underlined. First integrity, that there should be no compromise of one's own religious convictions. Second respect, not embarrassing people by inviting them to say words or perform gestures with which they are not comfortable. Finally humility, acknowledging the limitations of human symbols and accepting the signs of God's presence.

It may be useful here to quote a passage from DM:

> This type of dialogue can be a (source of) mutual enrichment and fruitful cooperation for promoting and preserving the highest values and spiritual ideals. It leads naturally to each partner communicating to the other the reasons for his own faith. The sometimes profound differences between the faiths do not prevent this dialogue. Those differences, rather, must be referred back in humility and confidence to God who 'is greater than our heart' (1 John 3:20).   (DM 35)

Dispositions for dialogue

To conclude, it may be good to say something about the dispositions needed for dialogue. There is a need for a balanced attitude. It is true that the Holy Spirit is at work both in the hearts of individuals and in the religious traditions to which they belong. This does not mean that everything in these traditions is good; however, they cannot be dismissed simply as evil or without value. There is need for openness and receptivity as well as discernment.

A further disposition required is a strong religious conviction. Without this there would be a danger of indifference to religious values, a temptation not to take others' religious convictions seriously. Or if one's own beliefs are not strong enough, a challenge might lead to a defensive or even aggressive attitude. We need a respectful and receptive approach to the convictions and values of the other.

Connected with this is an openness to the truth. The conviction that the fullness of truth is to be found in Jesus Christ does not rule out such openness. Provided the Christian realizes that truth is something by which we are to be grasped rather than for us to grasp, the meeting with others can help towards a deeper understanding of the truth. Dialogue can thus become a true learning process.

For this to be realized a contemplative spirit is needed. Through contemplation one is able to discover and admire what God is doing through the Holy Spirit, in the world, in the whole of humanity. Prayer in which a dialogue with God is developed provides a solid foundation for dialogue with others.

Finally there are patience and perseverance. One cannot look for quick results. There are obstacles: ignorance, prejudice, suspicion, self-sufficiency as well as sociopolitical factors, which may make genuine encounter difficult. Many things have to be explained again and again, and this can cause weariness. Nor should failures or disappointments lead to discouragement. The fruits will come in their own good time; yet it may be true here as elsewhere, that one will reap where another has sown. It is God who gives the increase.

One final quotation:

> It must be remembered that the Church's commitment to dialogue is not dependent on success in achieving mutual understanding and enrichment; rather it flows from God's initiative in entering into dialogue with humankind and from the example of Jesus Christ whose life, death and resurrection gave to that dialogue its ultimate expression.   (DP 53)

2

Theological considerations on pluralism

Introduction

Contemporary discussion about the plurality of religions and inter-religious relations has taken a more practical turn. The question that is being asked is whether religions, or civilizations marked by religions, must necessarily be in conflict. Are the different religions and the cultures that they help to shape like so many celestial bodies on paths that will inevitably collide? If the answer to such a question is yes – with obvious negative results – then how can we ensure damage limitation? If no definite answer can be given, then further questions arise: how can a possible clash of religiously influenced cultures be avoided? What would be the role of interreligious dialogue as a preventive measure?

We start from the contemporary context, not so much for its own sake but rather to show that there is a need for theological reflection. Quick or superficial answers are inadvisable; I shall not try here to evaluate all the different theological positions regarding religious pluralism, but to present some reflections based on traditional Catholic teaching.

Religious pluralism

Not a new phenomenon

In its introductory paragraph the Declaration *Nostra Aetate* of the Second Vatican Council states:

> Men look to their different religions for an answer to the unsolved riddles of human existence. The problems that weigh heavily on the hearts of men are the same today as in the past. What is man? What is the meaning and purpose of life? (NA 1)

Answers to such questions have been asked of all the religions. If we look first at the Scriptures, we see that the Jewish people, chosen by God to bear witness to monotheism, had to accomplish their mission in a religiously pluralistic environment: Judaism could not ignore the religious reality with which it was surrounded.

Christianity also soon became aware of religious pluralism. There was the growing consciousness, painful perhaps, of the early community that it was distinct from Judaism, with the theologically founded but very practical consequence that observance of the full Jewish law was not required of Christians. Then came the encounter with polytheism, as symbolized by the shock sustained by Paul in Athens. The Christian Church was soon confronted also by emperor worship, and was seen to be in rivalry with Eastern cults such as Mithraism. As Christianity spread from the Mediterranean area to other parts of the world it met with other religious expressions. Later it found itself also face to face with a new religion, Islam.

Islam did not set out to be a new religion. Indeed according to its own self-perception it is the original religion, indeed *the* religion that God willed for humankind. Yet Islam was born in a religiously plural environment, where Jews and Christians did not accept its message and remained as distinct communities. Other groups too were recognized as having a legitimate status: Sabaeans (Mandaeans) and Majus or Magians (Zoroastrians). In its later expansion Islam had to come to terms with other religions, for instance Hinduism, with its temples and rites so foreign to the Islamic spirit. Long before the rise of Islam, Hinduism itself experienced religious differentiation. Hinduism is not in fact a unified religion, but this term was used to cover a multiplicity of different traditions. Yet there grew up some traditions that proved to be completely distinct, such as Jainism and Buddhism.

Later history has brought the formation of new religious groups, or new religions, such as Sikhism in India, the Baha'i religion in Iran and Tenrikyo in Japan, to give just a few examples from former centuries. The religious map of the world has always been subject to change.

Pluralism today

If even regarding the past it would be incorrect to see the world divided into religious 'blocs' – Christianity, Islam, Buddhism, Hinduism, with only the Jews, because of their dispersal, scattered to various regions – this would reflect even less the present reality. With the increased mobility of the modern world, the religions are brought into contact more than ever.

John Paul II, in his first encyclical *Redemptor Hominis,* stated that the Second Vatican Council had presented to the Church 'a view of the terrestrial globe as a map of various religions'. In a later encyclical, *Redemptoris Missio,* he added another aspect:

> Our times are both momentous and fascinating. While on the one hand people seem to be pursuing material prosperity and to be sinking ever deeper into consumerism and materialism, on the other hand we are witnessing a desperate search for meaning, the need for an inner life, and a desire to learn new forms and methods of meditation and prayers. Not only in cultures with strong religious elements, but also in secularized societies, the spiritual dimension of life is being sought after as an antidote to dehumanization. (RM 38)

This search for meaning has given rise to a new type of pluralism. Margins are moving, and some people are looking to more than one tradition. Others, while professing to belong to one tradition (usually Christian), follow practices of another: all of which can present new theological and pastoral problems.

Theological reflection on religious pluralism

If theology is *fides quaerens intellectum* (faith seeking understanding), this faith has to try to come to grips with the reality of religious pluralism, and attempt to make some sense of it. The light of revelation is thrown on this reality, revelation that has come down to us in various ways, but finally in the Son, concretized in the Scriptures and received through tradition. Theological reflection will attempt to produce a satisfying synthesis. It is important to note that theology, since it starts from faith, is always particularized. There will be a Buddhist explanation of reality (avoiding the term theology, since Buddhists do not usually speak of God), an Islamic theology, a Christian (perhaps even a Catholic) theology. To try to develop a 'world theology' which would be acceptable to all would be an impossible task.

This does not mean that the underlying universality should be overlooked by particular theologies. One of my predecessors, Piero

Rossano, used to emphasize the need to pay attention to *homo religiosus*. If similar phenomena are found in different religious traditions, is this not because the human being is naturally inclined to offer cultic expression to belief in the Transcendent? Theological reflection should be aware of both the similarities and the differences, the latter coming from particular frameworks of reference.

For Christians the particular framework is provided by the fullness of revelation given in Jesus Christ. For Catholic theology this remains central.

Jesus Christ, the way

A fundamental teaching of the Christian faith, one that has been restated forcefully by the Second Vatican Council and to which Pope John Paul II constantly returned, is the universal dimension of the incarnation. The council document *Gaudium et Spes* states that 'by his incarnation, he, the son of God, has in a certain way united himself with each man' (GS 22). The whole of humanity has been affected, from the beginning of time to its end, extending to all geographical areas. So the Son of Man identifies himself with the person in need: 'I tell you solemnly in so far as you did this to one of the least of these brothers of mine, you did it to me' (Matt. 25.40). No time limit is indicated for this identification. It would appear to hold good for the period before the incarnation as much as after it. As the divine Word takes flesh and comes into time, so the divinity that is beyond time or outside of time allows its influence to be felt throughout the whole of time.

To this must be added the fact that the incarnate Word opens up the way of salvation for all. As *Gaudium et Spes* says also:

> for since Christ died for all, and since all are in fact called to one and the same destiny, which is divine, we must hold that the Holy Spirit offers to all the possibility of being made partakers, in a way known to God, in the paschal mystery. (GS 22)

The paschal mystery, the death and resurrection of Jesus, is indicated as the way to salvation, and a way open to all. The whole teaching of Paul is to be borne in mind. It is through death to self, implying death to sin, that the human person comes to true life in Jesus Christ. This personal re-enactment of the paschal mystery is operated through baptism, the foundation of the Christian life. The continuous living of this mystery which baptism demands is sustained particularly by the Eucharist through which the paschal mystery is made present.

Now we should remember too the traditional teaching of the Church that salvation is not confined only to those who have received the sacrament of baptism. There is the possibility of the *baptism of blood*. There is also the possibility of the *baptism of desire*. As the *Catechism of the Catholic Church* puts it, 'Every man who is ignorant of the Gospel of Christ and of his Church, but seeks the truth and does the will of God in accordance with his understanding of it, can be saved' (CCC 1260). The *Catechism* adds: 'It may be supposed that such persons would have *desired Baptism explicitly,* if they had known its necessity' (CCC 1260).

This teaching does of course raise problems. How is ignorance of the gospel and of the Church to be understood? In today's pluralistic world it might be imagined that everyone has the opportunity of coming into contact with the Church and hearing the gospel. In point of fact, though, and some of the members of my own missionary society can bear witness to this, there are people who have never in their lives met with a Christian. Moreover, the mere encounter with a Christian does not necessarily provide an opportunity to know and understand the gospel message and to appreciate the importance of the Church. A Muslim, who will know something of Jesus from the Qur'an, may not feel impelled to seek further knowledge from the Christian Scriptures. This should not be categorized immediately as *culpable* ignorance. The *Catechism,* when treating of the stages of revelation, speaks of the covenant with Noah, which 'remains in force during the times of the Gentiles, until the universal proclamation of the Gospel' (CCC 58). It does not make explicit when this universal proclamation will have been completed.

It has been suggested that different religions aim to bring people to distinct goals, not just as intermediate ends, but for their final destination. This would seem difficult to accept. Surely from the Christian point of view, and this is the one adopted in Christian theology, there can be only one salvation, as is expressed in the glossary appended to the second English edition of the *Catechism:* 'The forgiveness of sins and restoration of friendship with God, which can be done by God alone'. It is the idea of friendship with God that is to be noted. In fact the Scriptures go further and speak about sharing in divine life as the ultimate reward for human beings who live in friendship with God.

It is Jesus who is the way to this divine life. How then can other religions play any role? According to our Christian faith, Jesus is certainly the way, and the way he has followed himself leads through the narrow gate of death to resurrection to new life. The human person is invited to enter, with the assistance of divine grace, into this way of dying and rising.

The different religions can help in this process, for they contain elements that are true and holy. They enshrine precepts and doctrines that 'often reflect a ray of that truth which enlightens all men' (NA 2). They may inculcate a manner of life and conduct that is to be highly regarded. As Paul VI said in *Evangelii Nuntiandi*, the religions possess 'a splendid patrimony of religious writings' and they 'have taught generations of men how to pray' (EN 53). Such are the elements that can help to dispose the followers of the different religions to enter into the paschal mystery. It may be through turning the mind away from self and towards God in prayer; through the practice of right thinking and right speaking; through the service of one's fellow human beings. In such ways the religions provide the possibility for developing a life of friendship with God, though they themselves would not necessarily express what they are doing in these terms. It must be remembered nevertheless that the gift of God's grace is always necessary, and it is this grace that introduces a person into the saving mystery of Christ.

This does not mean that all religions are perfect, and that it does not matter to which religion one belongs. Vatican II teaches us to recognize elements of truth and holiness in the religions. It never puts them on a par with the One, Holy, Catholic and Apostolic Church. The religions can provide help along the way of salvation, but they are not independent ways of salvation. As the document *Dialogue and Proclamation* says:

> Concretely, it will be in the sincere practice of what is Good in their own religious traditions and by following the dictates of their conscience that the members of other religions respond positively to God's invitation and receive salvation in Jesus Christ, even while they do not recognize him as their Saviour. (DP 29)

So, it states further: 'the mystery of salvation reaches out to them, in a way known to God, through the invisible action of the Holy Spirit' (DP 29).

The role of the Spirit

Can anything more be said about this 'invisible action' of the Holy Spirit? First let us look at the Christian presentation of the message.

The Spirit is present both in the one who proclaims the good news of salvation in Jesus Christ and in the one who responds to this proclamation. To the one the Holy Spirit will suggest the words necessary for the right presentation of the message. To the other the Spirit will give the necessary predisposition to be open and receptive to the good news (cf. DP 64). In other words, the presentation of the gospel message is not carried out in a vacuum.

Moreover, those receiving the message may well have been influenced by authentic values in their own religious traditions. This brings us to what could be called the collective dimension of the Spirit's action, which is most important for interreligious dialogue. One of the goals of interreligious dialogue is to 'acknowledge, preserve and encourage the spiritual and moral good found among non-Christians, as well as their social and cultural values' (NA 2). The presence of these values is attributed to the work of the Spirit who, as Vatican II teaches, was 'at work in the world before Christ was glorified' (*Ad Gentes* 4). Perhaps this is why Paul, while exhorting the Philippians to let their tolerance be evident to everyone, including presumably those around them who did not share their faith, could exhort them to fill their minds with 'everything that is true, everything that is noble, everything that is good and pure, everything that we love and honour, and everything that can be thought virtuous or worthy of praise' (Phil. 4.8).

Such goodness can exist not only in individuals but also 'in the rites and customs of people' (LG 17).

In a powerful passage in his Letter to the Romans, Paul speaks again of the work of the Spirit. He says first of all that 'the Spirit himself and our spirit bear united witness that we are children of God' (Rom. 8.16). He then speaks of creation's eager expectation for the mystery of divine sonship to be fully revealed. This is put in a striking way: 'From the beginning till now the entire creation, as we know, has been groaning in one great act of giving birth' (Rom. 8.22). Can it not be said that the Spirit is present in this groaning, as in the united witness? It may be difficult at times to distinguish what is purely human and what is of the Spirit, precisely because the Spirit unites himself to the human spirit.

This action of the Spirit is not to be separated from that of the Word made flesh. Rather it is the Spirit that gives effect to that potentially salvific contact with the whole of humanity established by the Word precisely in becoming incarnate and entering into humanity. This is true for those who lived before the historical event of the incarnation as it is for those who have come into existence after this event. The declaration *Dominus Jesus* concludes its section on the Holy Spirit with the following clear statement:

> In conclusion, the action of the Spirit is not outside or parallel to the action of Christ. There is only one salvific economy of the one and triune God, realized in the mystery of the incarnation, death and resurrection of the Son of God, actualized with the cooperation of the Holy Spirit and extended in its salvific value to all humanity and to the entire universe. (DJ 12)

Ambiguity and weakness

To attribute what is good and noble in religious traditions to the action of the Spirit does not imply blanket approval of these traditions. Reflecting on the Day of Prayer for Peace, held in Assisi in October 1986, John Paul II spoke of unity and diversity. The order of unity, in creation and redemption, he presented as of divine origin, whereas divergences, even in the religious field, would go back to a 'human fact'. He was referring to differences 'in which are revealed the limitation, the evolution and the falls of the human spirit which is undermined by the spirit of evil in history' (*Discourse to the Roman Curia*, 22 December 1986, n. 5).

It must be admitted, of course, that such an observation applies also to Christianity, since the Christian faith is lived out by people who are weak and sinful. This is stated clearly in the Decree on Ecumenism of Vatican II (*Unitatis Redintegratio*):

Christ summons the Church, as she goes her pilgrim way, to that continual reformation of which she always has need, insofar as she is an institution of men here on earth. Consequently, if, in various times and circumstances, there have been deficiencies in moral conduct or in Church discipline, or even in the way the Church teaching has been formulated – to be carefully distinguished from the deposit of faith itself – these should be set right at the opportune moment and in the proper way. (UR 6)

These two aspects are brought together in a paragraph of *Dialogue and Proclamation*:

This means that, while entering with an open mind into dialogue with the followers of other religious traditions, Christians may have also to challenge them in a peaceful spirit with regard to the content of their belief. But Christians too must allow themselves to be questioned. Notwithstanding the fullness of God's revelation in Jesus Christ, the way Christians sometimes understand their religion and practise it may be in need of purification. (DP 32)

This very recognition of weakness leads to a deepening of inter-religious dialogue. It sharpens consciousness that dialogue is not simply about living in harmony and cooperating for the benefit of humankind, important though these goals may be, but rather is called to go deeper. There is a constant invitation to Christians and people of other religious traditions to live out to the full their religious commitment, to respond with greater fidelity to God's personal call. In this way relations between people of different religions can become truly a dialogue of salvation (cf. DP 39–40).

One way in which this can be done is by drawing inspiration from oriental religions and their methods of meditation. They can help lead to that stillness and recollection which allow for a deep contact with the divine mystery. Nevertheless a word of caution is appropriate. There is a possibility of mistaking certain physical sensations for spiritual experiences, and of interpreting a sense of oneness in a monistic fashion. Authentic Christian prayer always maintains the distinction between God and creature; it must always be 'in Christ', open to the power of the Spirit, and should be seen to have a positive effect in daily life.

There are some new religious movements which assure Catholics that their practices are in no way incompatible with the Christian faith. Here utmost caution is needed, for dual loyalty is hard to sustain. The most likely result of frequent association with a non-Christian group, joining in its prayers and rituals, is estrangement from the Church and from the Christian faith.

Yet a negative attitude on the part of Christians is not sufficient and could be counter-productive. There must also be a positive response to the needs of people: instruction in the ways of prayer and meditation, services for the healing of minds and memories as well as for physical healing, an increased sense of community. The riches are there, within the Christian tradition – and are being rediscovered, as for instance within the Christian Meditation community. The question is whether they are being made available widely enough.

One final question: can it be said that dialogue aims at conversion? This depends how one understands the term conversion. It does not necessarily mean a change of allegiance, though this can happen. What dialogue aims at is conversion in the biblical sense, namely 'the humble and penitent return of the heart to God in the desire to submit one's life more generously to him' (DM 37).

Conversion in this sense is open to all, to whatever religious tradition they belong. It is moreover a call addressed to all of us, in so far as we belong to a pilgrim people who have not yet reached their permanent dwelling.

To close this chapter, we can reiterate a conviction already stated. Today's world, with its increase in interreligious relations, calls for renewed reflection. An attempt must be made to make sense of all the facts in the light of revelation. This means working out a new synthesis. Yet it is unlikely that any synthesis will prove wholly satisfactory. New situations will call for new reflection and the shaping of yet another new synthesis. So the process will go on until our partial knowledge will give way to full understanding of God's plan. For 'at present we see indistinctly, as in a mirror, but then (at the end of time) face to face' (1 Cor. 13.12).

3

Religious pluralism in the USA today:
A Catholic perspective

JOHN BORELLI

'Religious pluralism' is no simple term. It has several usages, and we need to be clear what we mean by this term when we refer to religious pluralism today. I distinguish three general usages, which have different implications for Christian faith and life:

1 religious pluralism as a sociological term describing a particular kind of social relationship among participants of various religions in a given society;
2 religious pluralism as a political term defining the relationship between government and religious groups in the USA;
3 religious pluralism as a term used in theology and the academic study of religion to explain relationship among religions as ways or means of living in relationship with God or what others may hold to be of ultimate value.

Engaged religious diversity

Primarily religious pluralism refers to the interaction of religious groups. I say 'primarily' because in most cases, I believe, persons use the term to refer to a noticeable, even beneficial, multiplicity of religious groups in a given society. It indicates that in such a society, or set of societies, there is a variety of religious traditions and that persons identifying with these traditions actively interact with one another in such a way that the interaction influences and even changes the traditions themselves. In this usage, religious pluralism refers to more than a plurality of religions. It is not simply another way to say there are many religious traditions observable in a society, for it signifies more than the fact of religious diversity. While it is true that the existence of many religions with their specific differences create a religiously diverse society, religious pluralism refers to a richness that is greater than the sum of the various components. Thus, more precisely, religious pluralism in this sense means engaged religious diversity. Unless religious persons engage with one another across religious lines as religious persons, sharing their thoughts and attitudes on what is of ultimate concern to them, religious pluralism is not a matter of their concern.

When we study large religious families, like Christians, Muslims, Buddhists and others, we come to realize that they have a great deal of diversity among themselves. This might seem truer of some than of others in particular ways, for religious diversity can take several forms, for example, cultural or doctrinal, to name two. Muslims as a single group may be less doctrinally diverse but more culturally diverse than Jews. Christians share the same core beliefs but have different ways of structuring their communities. Differences in structure may reflect differences on doctrines, and Christians, in spite of having a single Scripture and ancient creeds everyone accepts, do have serious differences on some matters of faith and morals. Buddhists and Hindus vary significantly both culturally and doctrinally although there are certain basic ideas in each of the traditions. Unlike Buddhists and Hindus, many Christians feel a strong compulsion to restore unity in matters of faith. The ecumenical movement seems unique to Christians. Unity is an important value for them although how they define that unity will vary. Jews and Muslims value unity too but are not compelled in the same way that Christians are to restore unity. My point is that religious pluralism, engaged religious diversity, applies to relations among religions as well as within religious families.

Religious pluralism, as engaged religious diversity, was first true of the USA when the country was established and most citizens thought of it as Christian. There were a few Jews in some cities, some Muslims among African slaves, and the scattered population of Native Americans. Most of these were not on the minds of those who pondered the rich diversity of Protestants living side by side in relative harmony, compared with Europe. Catholic numbers have gradually increased such that the single largest Church in the USA is the Catholic Church (over 67 million by one recent count or 23 per cent of the population). There are still more Protestants than Catholics, but no single Church larger than the Catholic Church. This was not a situation the founders of the republic anticipated in 1789.

One recent study indicates, 'The percentage of the [US population] that is Protestant has been falling and will likely fall below 50 percent by the mid-decade and may be there already.'[1] Baptists make up the second largest family of Churches, with the Southern Baptist Convention as the second largest Church. Actually, the convention is the largest collection of Baptist Churches. There are black Baptists of several Churches and fellowships of moderate Baptists who do not belong to the conservative Southern Baptist Convention, which numbers fewer than 20 million. Methodists constitute the third largest family of Churches, with the United Methodist Church the third largest Church in the USA with about 9 million. There are three black Methodist Churches and a few independent Methodists. The existence of distinctively black Churches, even among the major denominations, is a legacy of slavery, which ended with the Civil War in 1865, and segregation, which ended officially in 1964. There are distinctively American Protestant Churches. One example is the Christian Church or Disciples of Christ, which arose on the frontier in western Pennsylvania and in Kentucky in the early 1800s, as a movement to unify Christians. It came into being in Kentucky in 1832. Disciples of Christ claim no official doctrine or dogma, but they clearly hold to core Christian beliefs and practices. Adult baptism with a statement of faith is the way one enters the Church. They describe themselves as thoroughly ecumenical and participate in various councils, consultations and dialogues with other Christians. There are fewer than one million.

In 2001, the Hartford Seminary Research Institute released its study *Faith Communities Today*, a survey of 14,000 congregations of 41 religious communities.[2] One interesting set of facts involved the size of congregations. The 'mega-church' phenomenon is still something of an anomaly, for less than 10 per cent of US congregations have more than 1,000 members and 25 per cent have fewer than 50 participating adults. Mainline Protestant churches remain heavily concentrated in towns and rural areas. Half the religious congregations in the USA, that is all congregations including synagogues, mosques and other religious centres, remain rooted in rural areas and have fewer than 100 participating adult members. In the USA, most people who are religious will identify themselves as members of congregations. The study also found that 62 per cent of the congregations responding felt they have a distinct 'denominational' identity. The USA is a nation of believers and of small religious congregations. The opportunities for interaction among religious groups are enormous.

President Lyndon Johnson (1963–68) accomplished much in creating the society that we have today in the USA. He succeeded the popular John F. Kennedy, who was not successful in guaranteeing civil rights for African Americans, and Johnson accomplished that task in less than a year. In 1965, he signed the Immigration and Nationality Act, which lifted restrictions on immigrants. The USA had open immigration until in the late 1880s when laws were passed excluding Asians in large numbers. The Supreme Court of the USA declared that anyone ineligible for citizenship could not immigrate to the USA, and a 1790 statute declared that only 'free white men' were those envisioned by the framers of the Constitution.[3] All that changed in the wake of legislation during the Johnson presidency.

All religious traditions seem to place some requirement on themselves to take account of their neighbours' faiths, but for Christians in the USA this was particularly important as the numbers of Muslims, Buddhists, Hindus and others began to increase with immigration. Christians had already developed national institutions to bridge differences or bring their resources together for civic and other projects. Christians among themselves need to discuss religious pluralism even in this sense as engaged religious diversity.[4] Recognition of a sizeable Jewish presence and invitations to Jews to join with Christians in national and civic organizations were already happening. The National Conference of Christians and Jews was founded in 1927. In 1955, Will Herberg published the now classic essay in American religious sociology, *Protestant – Catholic – Jew*.[5] Herberg's general point was that American society is not one giant melting pot but perhaps, or at least, three. The USA today still has the largest Jewish population in the world, and New York may still be the city in the world with the largest Jewish population (or, if not, it is just behind Tel Aviv). The number of Jews remained around 6 million for almost two decades, a figure that has stood as an unofficial benchmark for other religious groups.

The Muslim population is now larger than the Jewish population. African Americans, with their unique history, and South Asian

Muslims constitute the two largest groups of Muslims. African-American Muslims have a longer heritage in the USA than most Christians have. Arabs, Iranians, North Africans, South-East Asians, Europeans, Turks, Sub-Saharan Africans and other groups of Muslims now reside in the USA. Buddhists are here in large numbers and could even be approaching that 6 million benchmark. Japanese, Chinese, South and South-East Asian, Korean, Tibetan and any number of schools, lineages and forms of Buddhism now exist and many include practitioners with a Euro-American background. Hindus, in smaller numbers than Buddhists, are also in the USA, representing the range of practices and forms one finds in India. A majority of Native Americans are Christian, but many have now recovered traditional practices, incorporating these into their lives, and among those who have remained traditionalist, a major effort is underway to convey the wealth of their practices to a younger generation. Smaller religious groups are here too – Sikhs, Zoroastrians, Baha'is, new religious movements. Some may still look upon the USA as a 'godless nation' but, in fact, religiosity defines American society more accurately.

Separation of Church and state

Religious pluralism also has a political and legal meaning referring to the fact of the American experiment in democracy. By this I mean the separation of Church and state whereby no particular religious group or set of groups legally represents the minds, hearts and interests of the citizenry. This is the religious pluralism guaranteed in the initial two phrases of the First Amendment to the Constitution of the USA: 'Congress shall make no law respecting an establishment of religion, or prohibiting the free exercise thereof . . .' To some, on the one hand, the acceptance of this fact of equality before the law or even the lack of a religious preference or privilege for one religious group implies too much concession. For example, equal acknowledgement of rights before the law implies that, in the eyes of the law, doctrinal disagreements are opinions with no legal standing except when touching upon self-evident truths necessary for civil society. Equal recognition on the basis of representative democracy implies to others, on the other hand, an acknowledgement of equality of religious standing. Our founders agreed on one concern about religion: they did not want to see the bloody religious wars and persecutions among

Christians in Europe repeated on this continent. That was their context for amending the Constitution in a way that led to our present situation of the separation of Church and state.

Even how we phrase the issue of 'secular democracy', namely the separation of Church and state, is a Christian way of stating the relationship of the government to religious differences. This indicates how the founders of this democracy viewed the question. They wanted peace among the various Christian groups. Again, the increase in religious diversity has led to a different situation today, a more varied but still institutionalized religious pluralism, which policy-makers in the USA would like to see throughout the world.

In such a situation, all groups have the potential to thrive today, but to get to the point where we are now was not an easy process. In many ways, Catholics bore the brunt of the transition from religious pluralism, defined as Protestant diversity, to something larger that included them, Jews and others as full partners. In 1789, there were Anglicans, Presbyterians, Methodists, Congregationalists, Dutch Reformed, Quakers, Baptists and others. Despite differences, they had joined together in opposition to England in the Revolution. Most used the same English translation of the Bible, the King James Bible. Schools were either supported by local governments or were private schools, but school days usually included readings from the King James Bible.

With the non-establishment clause of the First Amendment, no single Church spoke for the majority of the population; rather, a generalized Protestant vision prevailed with toleration for the free expression of others. A number of factors combined – ordering the world according to God's plan so that Church and government reflect the same values, toleration, recognition of the sufficiency of the local congregation coupled with the willingness to see division into Churches as not wrong in itself provided believers agreed on essentials, and the creation of a public theology based on the convinced rightness of the moral and spiritual qualities of the USA. So while there was no religion established, American Protestants, the majority of the population, voluntarily established the public theology of service and support for the American system. The system needed the diversity of Protestant groups to mediate the diversity of cultural and linguistic groups but allowing a certain competitiveness in the social sphere, which, at times, worked against moral purposes. Councils of

Churches came into being to aid cooperation amidst diversity for common moral causes. This situation of Protestant denominationalism dominated the American scene until after the Second World War. While there was a legal separation of Church and state, in actual fact the values of Protestant Christianity permeated most American institutions. President Eisenhower, one of the heroes of the Second World War, had declared in the 1950s, 'Our government makes no sense unless it is founded on a deeply felt religious faith – and I don't care what it is.'[6]

Jews and Catholics as minority communities assimilated but kept their distinctive identities. They developed their own institutions – schools, hospitals, retirement homes, orphanages – and struggled with public schools and other institutions when they felt their religious identity was seriously threatened. Denominationalism promoted a great deal of individualism, based on choice. The institutions which Jews and Catholics developed aided a stronger personal affiliation with the whole group. They developed thriving subcultures, which for Catholics included greater attention to papal authority than perhaps for their European counterparts.

Dialogue

Finally, there is a theological and philosophical use of the term 'religious pluralism', which is the claim, stated in its radical form, that each religious tradition as such is a valid way in itself for addressing the human condition and connecting those who pursue that way with the ineffably Real and Infinite Being, by which Christians mean God.[7] This view is now espoused by several in the fields of history of religions, theology of religion or philosophy of religion. They represent what they feel is the result of decades of research bringing to light, for Europeans and Americans especially, the richness of the variety of religious traditions in the world and the development of methods to explore these traditions based upon religious experience. The methods of history of religions or philosophy of religion have revealed much to us about the meaning and content of religious beliefs and practices and have advanced our understanding in the general field of religious studies. Acceptance of these methods does not imply that one has to accept the metaphysical foundation on which this view of religious pluralism rests, namely that all religions are ultimately valid in themselves. Some criticize this view because it reduces the diversity of various religions to a single essence or meaning for the term religion and therefore that this is not a view of true religious pluralism, that is, an equality of really distinct religious traditions.[8] James Fredericks summarizes the shortcomings of this version of religious pluralism for Christians:

> Pluralism, despite its claims for itself, is not helpful for Christians interested in responding to religious diversity in new and creative ways today. By rendering religious differences theologically uninteresting, pluralist theories do little to encourage Christians to learn more about non-Christian religious traditions on their own terms. Since radically contradictory religious beliefs are in reality differing interpretations of the same transcendent absolute, the encounter between religious believers is rendered less dangerous, but also less interesting than it would be otherwise. Pluralism fails the second of the two criteria for an adequate theology of religions. It does not assist Christians in responding creatively to the fact of religious diversity today. What about the first of the two criteria? Are the pluralist theories in keeping with the demands of the Christian tradition?[9]

One might perhaps argue for a sort of 'partial' religious pluralism from a Christian point of view that renders religious differences more interesting. I am thinking for example of a Christian understanding of how people of other religions, responding to God's grace and call through their own religions, share in the reign of God, the kingdom of God, present in history, of which they live according to who and what they are, in their own right as it were.[10] With this suggestion, we are at the cutting edge of speculation regarding religious pluralism and Christian faith from a Catholic point of view.[11] There is no consensus among Christians on the ultimate value of other religions in relationship to Christianity, and one finds a range of views among Catholics.

A Catholic perspective

Forty years ago, in the summer of 1964, the bishops of the Catholic Church were preparing to return to Rome for the third of four sessions of a Church-wide assembly of bishops, the Second Vatican Council, which met from 1962 to 1965. Catholics call these

Church-wide assemblies of all bishops 'universal councils', 'ecumenical councils' or 'general councils', and they consider these meetings the highest authority in teachings and practice. There have been 21 general councils from a Catholic perspective.

Bishops meet in council or synod from time to time. In the build-up to the great jubilee year 2000, Pope John Paul II summoned several such synods by geographical regions: Africa, America (north and south), Asia, Oceania and Europe. Unlike Vatican II, they were not universal assemblies of bishops. Not all the bishops of the region attended and most participants were from one continent or region. Also, unlike Vatican II, these synods of bishops did not issue any major statements other than notices or communications and a set of propositions. Pope John Paul II would take into consideration the propositions and proceedings and eventually, within a year or two, issued an apostolic letter, which is a particular kind of document from the Pope, concluding that particular synod. By contrast, Vatican II issued 16 documents, all passed by the assembled bishops from all over the world with the Pope (John XXIII in the first session and Paul VI in the last three sessions) presiding over the assembly. There is an often-quoted passage in the documents of the Second Vatican Council that sums up well one of John XXIII's stated purposes for the council: *aggiornamento* or adaptation of Church discipline and teaching to the needs and conditions of the times. The passage appears in the final document of Vatican II, The Pastoral Constitution on the Church in the Modern World (*Gaudium et Spes*): 'At all times the Church carries the responsibility of reading the signs of the time and of interpreting them in the light of the Gospel, if it is to carry out its task' (GS 4).

Dialogue is the primary way through which Catholics are urged to address the religious pluralism encountered in their daily lives. Vatican II's Declaration on the Relation of the Church to Non-Christian Religions (*Nostra Aetate*) urged the sons and daughters of the Church 'to enter with prudence and charity into discussion and collaboration with members of other religions' and 'while witnessing to their own faith and way of life' let them 'acknowledge, preserve and encourage the spiritual and moral truths' in the religions, cultures and social lives of others (NA 2).[12] Dialogue is now part of the fabric of Catholic identity. It was the Second Vatican Council that formally recognized interreligious understanding and broadened it to include interreligious dialogue as an explicit teaching with universal status. This was a new development for the Catholic Church.[13]

By promoting genuine interreligious dialogue, the Catholic Church did not intend that contact with people of other religions should be a one-way conversation of Catholics proclaiming to them the good news of Jesus. The language of *Nostra Aetate* is clear that Catholics were to share their beliefs, values and teachings while preserving the spiritual and moral truths of others. Twenty-five years after the council, in his encyclical on missionary activity, Pope John Paul II asserted that, although this dialogue is a part of the Church's evangelizing mission, it is a means for mutual knowledge and enrichment and is not in opposition to missionary activity (RM 55).[14] In the same passage, he also gave one of the most positive Catholic teachings about other religions up to that time when he wrote that religions are the main and essential expressions of the spiritual riches of whole peoples and God speaks to them through their religions.

Catholic teaching is serious when it encourages people to engage in interreligious dialogue as the mode of living with religious pluralism. It demonstrates both a strong encouragement for interreligious dialogue and a theological position that it is through Christ that God reveals the fullness of truth and the means of divine communion. On the one hand, Christianity is one among the religions, which are the means God uses to draw all people to their divinely prepared destiny, and, on the other hand, Christianity offers the fullness of this truth. By not espousing a theological position of religious pluralism, at least in the radical form that gives no priority to a single religion, if that is at all possible, does Catholic teaching undermine the reality of dialogue as mutual exchange and enrichment?

More recently, and in circumstances when the Catholic Church's commitment to interreligious dialogue was doubted, Pope John Paul II sought to clarify this seemingly ambivalent position.[15] In his weekly public audience of 29 November 2000, he traced briefly how God offers salvation to all nations through the various covenants with Adam, Noah, Moses and Christ as revealed through Christ and taught in Scripture and tradition. On this occasion he cited several passages in the Old and New Testaments, his first encyclical (*Redemptoris Hominis*) and the second-century teacher Irenaeus. He then observed that 'the sacred books of other religions, however, are open to hope to the extent that they disclose a horizon of divine communion, point to a goal of purification and salvation for history, encourage the search for truth and defend the values of life, holiness, justice, peace and freedom.' Through 'profound striving' and 'religious experience' all people are open to the divine gift of charity and its demands. He then added, 'The interreligious dialogue which the Second Vatican council encouraged should be seen in this perspective.'[16]

Religious pluralism, understood as engaged religious diversity, in its most profound sense, calls for this kind of dialogue as spiritual sharing. Pope John Paul II used the term religious pluralism in this way in his first letter of the new millennium, issued on 1 January 2001:

> In the climate of increased cultural and religious pluralism which is expected to mark the society of the new millennium, it is obvious that this [interreligious] dialogue will be especially important in establishing a sure basis for peace and warding off the dread spectre of those wars of religion which have so often bloodied human history.
>
> (*Novo Millennio Ineunte* 55)[17]

4

Pluralism and the parish

A changed scene

The parish where I was born and brought up was in Walsall, a leather town in what used to be South Staffordshire and now is part of the West Midlands. Catholics were in the minority, though there was a good group living around our parish church, St Patrick's. Most, like myself, were of Irish origin, though there were also a couple of Italian families, ice-cream sellers. In the town, I do not remember ever meeting someone who belonged to another religion, either at school or in other circumstances, not even among the patients who came to see my parents, both general practitioners, in the surgery at our house. There were no Jews, as far as I can remember, and certainly no Muslims or Sikhs or Hindus.

Then came the years of immigration and a note of pluralism entered into our area of the Midlands, including Walsall. First there arrived individuals, then families, then communities. The increase during the late 1950s and 1960s was noticeable, every time I came home for holidays. Around 1960 my parents, with retirement in view, moved from the centre of the town to a quieter house. They changed parishes, and were now in the 'posh' parish of St Mary's the Mount. Yet, lo and behold, all the houses around the parish church began to be occupied by newcomers from Pakistan. The sights and the smells were different. Some people were uneasy at this, but I remember my mother saying that the women in saris brought a dash of colour to our rather drab Midlands town. Gradually also the skyline changed. Not only were there the usual churches of different denominations, but now you could see a purpose-built mosque, one of the first in the country I believe, a Hindu temple, a Sikh gurdwara. Pluralism had come to stay.

This is a pattern familiar to many, I am sure, though the spread of these communities throughout England and Wales is not even.

There are areas of high concentration of other faith communities: Leicester, Bradford, Birmingham, Dewsbury, certain areas of London (Southall, Tower Hamlets). I was interested to discover recently that Harrow, in North London, is one of the boroughs in London with the highest number of Asians and that the Zoroastrian community has received planning permission to build, on the site of a former cinema, their fire temple. There are, of course, other parts of the country where it would be hard to come across a Hindu or a Muslim, let alone a Zoroastrian. Given the greater mobility of our times, parishioners may well be working in other areas where they do come into contact with people of different religions. There is also the upward mobility of some, though not all, of the members of these communities, so that you will find Muslims and Sikhs among the students at the universities, and also among the staff. And where would the National Health Service be without the doctors from other countries, many of whom are not Christians? Finally, there is the international scene, which makes it imperative to know something about other religions, and in particular about Islam.

Parish reactions to pluralism

A number of parishes adopted an open and generous attitude to the first wave of migrant workers. They could offer them help in different ways: material help, assistance in dealing with local authorities, acting as mediators, sometimes providing instruction in language skills. Parish halls or other premises were put at the disposition of these communities for their feasts, for weddings and at times even for prayers. This generosity may have been accompanied perhaps by a certain condescension, but it usually sprang from a good heart.

As the different faith communities grew, so did hesitation on the part of the Catholic community. The demands of these faith communities, particularly of the Muslims, increased, and their voices seemed perhaps to become more strident. Now it was less a matter of borrowing places for worship, but acquiring them, so the question arose about selling surplus Catholic property. There were questions too about what attitude to take towards children belonging to other religious traditions who were attending Catholic schools. What religious instruction should be given? What Catholic practices should all take part in? As the local authorities, in their own way, came to terms with religious pluralism, the embarrassment of Catholics only grew. Some local authorities, aided and abetted by the mass media, seemed to go overboard to show that they respected all traditions – except Christianity. So lights could go up for *Diwali,* but not for Christmas, and no Christmas cribs please. Special mention would be made of Ramadan and 'Id, but no attention to Lent and Easter. Hot cross buns were out, *chapatis* in. All this helped to generate a sense of frustration among staunch Catholics, and perhaps even a feeling of resentment that others should be given special treatment. So there may have been the growth of a more inward-looking parish community.

In recent years, particularly with the events of September 11, 2001, and the Madrid train bombings of 11 March 2004, there has appeared a new note of fear. There is the threat of terrorism, connected with a certain type of Islam. Various events have lent justification to this apprehension. So the attitude to Islam and to Muslims tends to be one of suspicion. Yet there is another aspect to take into consideration. There is the realization that people belonging to other communities generally have more children than do Christians, including Catholics. So the balance of faith communities is changing. Moreover, the other communities often appear to be livelier than our parish communities. Added to this is the fact that some Muslims do not hide their desire to win Europe over to Islam, seeing this religion as the solution to the perceived moral decadence of the West. Does not all this create a defensive attitude among Christians today?

Is this the right attitude? Can it be justified by the teaching of the Church? Would it not be good to go back to the vision of the world presented by the Second Vatican Council and see how it applies today? This I would like to do now, through a rereading of the Declaration *Nostra Aetate* on the relations of the Church to the people of other religions.

Respect for other religions

It is interesting to note that *Nostra Aetate* does not immediately focus on the differences between the Catholic faith and other religions, but concentrates first on what they have in common and on the fundamental unity of the whole of humankind. In a nutshell, the teaching based on Scripture, and especially on the Acts of the Apostles, is that all peoples are created by God, come from one stock and share the common destiny that God has prepared for them. John Paul II repeated this many times, including when reflecting on the Day of Prayer for Peace, held in Assisi on 27 October 1986. On that occasion he referred to the common origin and common destiny of humankind, but added that in the in-between period 'we must learn to walk together in peace and harmony, or we drift apart and ruin ourselves and others'.

The common origin means that, despite the evident differences, there is a basic unity. It could be said that this reflects the very nature of the human person, *homo religiosus*, who is faced with the same fundamental questions: the meaning of life, the origin of suffering, how to understand death, where is true happiness to be found. People have turned to religions for the answers to these enigmas. Perhaps in our day some distrust the established religions and wish to create one of their own which would suit them better. This New Age tendency still reflects nevertheless the basic religious drive of the human person.

Nostra Aetate, after mentioning some of these religious responses, including Hinduism and Buddhism, states that

> the Catholic Church rejects nothing of what is true and holy in these religions. She has a high regard for the manner of life and conduct, the precepts and doctrines which, although differing in many ways from her own teaching, nevertheless often reflect a ray of that truth which enlightens all. (NA 2)

I would like to emphasize the words 'high regard', repeated in the next paragraph with reference to Muslims. The Church's attitude is one of respect for the followers of other religions, based on the values to be found in them.

Something should be added here, for *Nostra Aetate* is not to be taken in isolation but together with all the other documents of Vatican II. There could have been a cross-reference to *Dignitatis Humanae*, the Declaration on Religious Liberty, though this was only given solemn approval over a month after *Nostra Aetate*. The Declaration teaches that 'the right to religious freedom is based on the very dignity of the human person' (DH 2). There is an obligation to search for the truth, but the individual has the right to be free from coercion and to be respected with regard to individual choice concerning religious matters. Moreover this individual freedom is to be extended to communities, since religion has a social dimension to it. *Dignitatis Humanae* declares that to deny 'the free exercise of religion in society, when the just requirements of public order are observed, is to do an injustice to the human person and to the very order established by God for humankind' (DH 3).

The attitude to the various religions cannot therefore be dismissive, or one of mere tolerance. There must be a deep respect for people. To repeat what John Paul II said: despite the differences, we must learn to walk together. *Nostra Aetate* therefore follows its teaching on respect with the exhortation to the members of the Church 'to enter with prudence and charity into discussion[1] and collaboration with members of other religions' (NA 2).

Discernment

The fact that other religions may reflect 'a ray of the truth which enlightens all' does not imply that everything is light in them and that there are no shadows. We would acknowledge that, although the Church is Holy, the members of the Church are weak and inclined to sin, and hence the Church is *semper reformanda*. There is no reason why the same should not apply to other religions. Some people tend to be Manichaean, seeing things starkly as either black or white. Hinduism is either sheer idolatry or an immensely creative response to the Divine. Buddhism is just an ego-trip or else it is the most profound philosophy of life. Islam is a creation of the Devil or it is the only religion that can bring sanity and sanctity into today's world.

Is not the truth somewhere in between? *Nostra Aetate*, it must be admitted, points to the positive elements of the different religions, rather than to their negative aspects. It speaks of the recognition of the Supreme Being in the traditional religions, and the deep religious sense with which life is consequently imbued. It refers to 'the limitless riches of myth and the accurately defined insights of philosophy' in Hinduism, and the Buddhist way to 'perfect liberation'. With regard to Islam, some of the beliefs held in common with Christians are referred to, as also elements of practice, such as prayer, almsgiving and fasting. A completely objective and exhaustive examination of religions would have to point also to their defects. Traditional religion often imposes taboos that restrict human freedom, or enjoins practices that go against basic moral principles, such as the rejection of twins in some ethnic groups and their exposure to death. The iniquities of the caste system have been consolidated, not eliminated, by Hinduism. Buddhism seems to encourage a concentration on the problem of the individual, although it must be said that there is a growing movement of socially engaged Buddhism. Islam, by way of contrast, would be seen to emphasize the communitarian aspect of religion to the detriment of the individual's freedom, and one could also point to certain inequalities in the treatment given to men and women, though the passages in the Qur'an on which these are based can be given a reasonable explanation in relation to the culture of the time.

These shadows are mentioned to show that we should not be afraid to take a critical stance with regard to other religions, as long as we are ready, at the same time, to acknowledge the many beautiful and noble elements that they contain. Similarly, we should not be unduly offended if others find fault with Christianity, particularly in the way it is practised, but we would hope that they could also appreciate the depth of its riches. What must be avoided, at all costs, is the comparison of the ideals of one religion with the defects of another, or rather with the defects of its followers. One of the components of respect is to be true and just in one's appreciation of the other and the other's religion.

How does the parish react to this? It is now time to be more specific and to attempt to suggest a programmed response to pluralism.

The inclusive parish

Though the concern is with the parish and the pastor, it may be well to start off with a word about the bishop. Vatican II's Decree concerning the Pastoral Office of Bishops in the Church, *Christus Dominus*, states:

> Bishops should devote themselves to their apostolic office as witnesses of Christ to all men [*sic*]. They should not limit themselves to those who already acknowledge the Prince of Pastors but should also devote themselves to those who have strayed in any way from the path of truth or who have no knowledge of the Gospel of Christ and of his saving mercy, so that ultimately all (men) may walk 'in all goodness, justice and truth' (Eph 5:9).   (CD 11)

This text reminds the bishop that his pastoral care extends to all people living within the area of his diocese. He cannot confine his attention to Catholics only, even though they may rightly claim priority in his pastoral activity. He will be called to relate to other Christians, and also to people who belong to other religious traditions. These latter are not to be neglected on the pretext that there is too much to do already in looking after the members of the Catholic fold. The bishop is called to be a witness of Christ to all. His ministry is inclusive.

The question naturally arises as to how this witness is to be given in relation to people of other religions. A later paragraph goes some way to answering this question:

> Since it is the mission of the Church to maintain close relation with the society in which she lives the bishops should make it their special care to approach men [*sic*] and to initiate and promote dialogue with them. These discussions on religious matters should be marked by clarity of expression as well as by humility and courtesy, so that truth may be combined with charity, and understanding with love. The discussion should likewise be characterized by due prudence allied, however, with sincerity which by promoting friendship is conducive to a union of minds. (CD 13)

Much could be said about the spirit in which relations are to be developed, but what I should like to emphasize is that the bishop is not to be passive with regard to society, only reacting when necessary, but is called to initiate and promote dialogue.

What then of the parish priest? Canon Law states that 'The pastor exercises pastoral care in the community entrusted to him under the authority of the diocesan bishop *in whose ministry of Christ he has been called to share*' (Can. 519, emphasis mine). If the bishop has the care of all people within the territory of his diocese, can it not be said that the parish priest has likewise care of all who live within the bounds of the parish, whether they be Catholics, other Christians, people belonging to other religions, or modern-day people with no religion? Will he too not be expected to take the initiative to establish contact with the different categories of people in the parish?

What forms of contact could there be? Here are a few suggestions.

- House visitation (if this is still done); when visiting a Catholic family would it not be possible to greet briefly the neighbours who just happen to be Muslims or Sikhs?

- Something similar could be said about hospital visitation, offering a greeting to the people of other religions who are in the same ward as Catholic patients.
- Paying a visit to the different places of worship, particularly when the people there are celebrating a feast, in order to bring them greetings.
- Meeting the religious leaders of these communities in extended clergy fraternals; there will surely be a need to maintain strictly ecumenical contacts, but from time to time the network could be widened. The contacts established may prove exceedingly valuable if tensions break out, since channels of communication with the other community will already have been established.
- Participation in interfaith meetings organized by the local authorities.

Some parish priests may ask: How can we be expected to do all this when we do not have time to do everything our Catholic flock expect of us, let alone leaving periods free for reading, reflection and writing? A partial answer to this objection can be found in the final words of Canon 519, which says that the parish priest is to carry out his ministry 'with the cooperation of other presbyters or deacons and with the assistance of lay members of the Christian faithful'. The parish priest does not have to do everything himself. He can involve others in his ministry.

- There may be parishioners who would be willing to go on house visitation, including calling on families that are not Christian.
- Religious and laypeople may be part of the hospital visitation team.
- Delegations from the parish could go to greet other communities when they are celebrating their feasts.
- An assistant priest (an endangered species?) or a deacon might take part in the meetings of religious leaders held according to the pattern of clergy fraternals.
- A member of the parish council might be delegated to attend the interfaith meetings convoked by the civil authorities.

What would still be necessary would be feedback to the parish community. Everybody should be informed about who is in the parish, and particularly if newcomers have arrived in the area. If people are told about contacts made, they might become more interested to take part themselves. There is nothing like exposure and experience to break down prejudice and arouse a sense of mission. The bidding prayers might reflect not only international events but also the needs that exist on the doorstep.

Education for parish service

If the priest and people are to reach out to other faith communities, they will need to know more about them.

If you want to bring greetings to the Muslims for 'Id al-Fitr, the breaking of the fast after Ramadan, or 'Id al-Adhā, the Feast of the Sacrifice held in concomitance with the Hajj, the Pilgrimage to Mecca, then you have to know when the feast will take place in any particular year. The same goes for Vesakh of the Buddhists, or Diwali of the Hindus. And what festival are the Sikhs celebrating?

It is easy to lump all the Muslims into one, and not to realize that they belong to very different traditions. It would be useful to have an inkling about what they hold in common, and how they differ. Similarly with the Buddhists. That monastery in the suburbs of the town, to which group does it belong? Is the Dalai Lama really a sort of Buddhist pope? One could go on and on with such questions. And the more one learns, the more one realizes how little one knows.

The lack of knowledge can produce a reaction of fear, and inhibit contacts. The reluctance to engage someone of another faith community in conversation may come from ignorance not just of their beliefs, but also of one's own. Many people do not know how to answer the questions that are put to them, and so they prefer to avoid contact. There is an opportunity lost for witness, whether it be in the context of dialogue or of proclamation.

Can anything be done to provide such knowledge? Where there is a university, there will be probably some sort of extramural course on world religions. In fact if one searches there are many resources available. These would include the various offerings on the Internet. Yet there would need to be a complement to private study, a group that meets for discussion to stimulate understanding and assimilation, a guide as a point of reference. What would also be important would be to accompany the study of another religion or of other religions with a deepening of one's own faith. Moreover people have different levels of intellectual baggage, and the courses on offer are not suitable for everyone. Could anything be provided at the parish level, a talk, a meeting with someone who has experience of dialogue in a certain domain?

Do parishes today have lending libraries? Would it be possible to make books on the various religions available? Do people have access to the series of leaflets that were prepared by the Committee for Other Faiths? Or if people do not read any more, then what about videos on dialogue? There are a number that have been made. They could sometimes be seen together by a group, and be used as a starting point for a discussion.

So far I have been talking about adult education, equipping people for the various tasks they might take on in the service of the parish's outreach. Yet the children should not be forgotten. All sorts of questions arise with regard to the children in Catholic schools. What type of religious education is to be given? Is it a knowledge of religions as a cultural fact, with special emphasis on Christianity since this has been the main influence on the culture of this country, or is it an education in the faith? If it is the latter, what happens to the children who belong to other faith communities? Will they have to do maths problems, as I did when I was a boy attending the non-Catholic grammar school? Or will instruction in their own religion be provided? Can the parish community, rather than the Catholic school, provide the faith education and the preparation for the sacraments? What sort of understanding of other religions are young children given? Will they grow up with sympathy for the Muslims, Hindus and the Sikhs that they meet, or will prejudices be formed or strengthened? Will there be too much emphasis on the others, so that the Catholic children end up knowing little or nothing about their own faith? It is easy for me to list these questions, but the answers cannot be given by 'the expert'; they have to be worked out to suit the local context.

RCIA

There is a special type of education that is given in the parish, and that is the instruction given to adults who are to be received into the Church. The Rite of Christian Initiation of Adults has proved to be a valuable instrument for this purpose. It presupposes a period of pre-

catechumenate, which is expected to be a time of primary evangelization, in which the essential elements of the *kerygma* are conveyed.
Some of the people who present themselves during this period may
be interested inquirers, 'sympathizers', but others may already be
firmly committed to going forward to baptism. At this stage, but also
later, the instruction should be adapted to their circumstances.

Are there among the enquirers and candidates for baptism people
coming from other religions? It is said that in France about 10 per
cent of the catechumens come from a background of Islam. Several
questions arise here. Are Catholics ready to reach out to people of
other religions and to invite them to join the Catholic community?
Do we, as individuals, bear witness to our faith in such a way that
others may become interested in knowing 'what makes us tick'? Are
our communities attractive so that people would want to join them?

These questions might seem inappropriate in a book dedicated
to dialogue. Yet the Church can never forgo its mission to proclaim
Jesus Christ as Lord and Saviour. Dialogue cannot take the place of
proclamation. Both tasks have to be carried out. It is all a matter of
discernment. What I am advocating is not a hard sell, publicity drives
for the Church and even worse 'crusades'. Yet we should be ready to
talk about our faith. As Peter says to the first Christians: 'Always have
your answer ready for people who ask you the reason for the hope
that you all have' (1 Pet. 3.15). The questions may spring at first from
pure curiosity, but then, with the help of the Holy Spirit, there may
develop a growing sense of commitment. So the answers may
progress from a mere imparting of information to a sharing of experience of Jesus Christ.

What is important is that when people of other religions do come
to enquire about the faith they are accepted as they are, with all the
riches of their respective backgrounds. Much will depend on their
degree of belonging to their original tradition. It is not for us to force
people to be Muslims, or Hindus, or Buddhists, if they have only been
so sociologically, without any real practice. Yet care should be taken
not to take an antagonistic attitude towards these religions, but rather
cultivate a readiness to build on the values that are already enshrined
in them.

You often hear it said that there can be no conversions from Islam.
This is not true, though it is certainly hard for citizens of majority
Muslim countries to change their religion, since there is in most cases

not full religious freedom in this sense. Yet conversions do take place, and particularly in countries where there is true freedom of religion. A confrère of mine, Jean-Marie Gaudeul, has written a book entitled *Called from Islam to Christ. Why Muslims become Christians.*[2] He has studied the published stories of Muslims who have become Christians and has examined their motivations for taking this step. For some it has been the attractiveness of the person of Jesus, already as he is portrayed in the Qur'an. Indeed to some Jesus has appeared in dreams. Others have been led by a thirst for the truth, and have found that the Christian message fulfils their longings. The element of forgiveness in the gospel message is felt to be powerful, as also a new sense of freedom and of a personal relationship with God as Father. The sense of community has often been an important factor, a community that is not oppressive but welcoming and freedom giving. Some are looking for 'an Islam beyond Islam', a more spiritual religion beyond precepts. I remember Gaudeul saying once that the first New Testament text that should be explained to Muslims is Paul's Letter to the Romans, since there Paul emphasizes freedom over the rule of the law.

Gaudeul does not only describe the different ways to Christ and to the Church. He adds a series of useful reflections that apply also to converts from other traditions besides Islam. He asks what kind of welcome do people need. Here is his answer: 'The reception accorded to the converts is to be determined by their personal spiritual needs before and above the interests of the group. The offence in proselytism, as in rejection, is that the persons are not considered in themselves.'[3] He goes on to say that the candidates for baptism must have the opportunity of explaining themselves. Really they must be led to the realization that they are not choosing their new religion, as they would choose a new style of clothing, but that they are responding to a call.

Once a person is baptized, that is not the end of the journey. There is a need for the person to be welcomed into the community, to be invited to take an active part in the liturgy, to share in parish activities. There is above all a need for friendship, since the move from one religion to another can be accompanied by a break from one's former family and friends. Are our parish communities ready to play this role?

Mixed marriages

In today's pluralistic societies men and women belonging to different religions are almost bound to meet and some will want to share their lives in marriage. Some people tend to exalt such marriages as being the ideal way to interreligious dialogue, just as some would see inter-church marriages as the truest form of ecumenism. Others may be radically opposed, seeing interfaith marriages as a real danger to the faith. There probably has to be a realistic middle way. At some stage Catholic youngsters should be told that the difference of religion might possibly bring additional strain to a relationship that is to last for the rest of one's life. Yet when a mixed couple come to see the priest and say they want to get married, it is usually too late to get them to change their minds. Their freedom has to be respected.

Sometimes one gets the impression that the question of mixed marriages is reduced first to the problem of whether a dispensation is going to be granted, and then to what type of wedding to have. This is surely not sufficient. Preparation of mixed couples for marriage presents a similar problem to the presence of converts from other religions in the RCIA group. It will have to be judged whether they can join with other couples taking the preparatory course, where such a course exists, or whether it would be better for them to pre-pare alone. They will certainly need special attention. They should be led to look squarely at the possible difficulties ahead. The major ques-tion will be the religious upbringing of the children. The Catholic partner has to promise that the children will be brought up as Catholics, and the non-Christian partner needs to be aware of this promise. This does not mean that the children are not to be taught to appreciate the religion of the non-Christian partner, nor does it mean, if it happens that the children are not in fact baptized, that the Catholic partner should give up any idea of teaching them about the faith. They will need encouragement to do this.

Just as with catechumens, pastoral care should not end once baptism has been administered, so concern for mixed couples should not end with the wedding. There needs to be aftercare. Even Catholic couples need this, and movements such as Marriage Encounter and Teams of Our Lady can be a great help. Perhaps people in mixed marriages need the support of a group even more. Young couples will be able to share their difficulties with others who have had the same experiences and receive advice from them, or at least encouragement and strength. It seems to me that such groups should not be confined only to those couples who have married according to Church law, but could also include those who were refused a dispensation or did not ask for one. Surely the Catholic partner in such a marriage has the right to receive support from the Catholic community.

Joint action

One form that interreligious relations can take is the dialogue of action, people of different faith communities working together on behalf of their fellow men and women. Such action may be at the local level, organizing a car pool, setting up a play centre for children, initiating various youth activities. It may be a common involvement in concerns of a national nature, the right attitude towards immigrants, the need to combat racism, pro-life issues. The perspective may be international, regarding debt relief and fair trade, action for peace and reconciliation, ecological concerns. These actions may in some cases be purely secular, with religion playing no part. Yet there are interfaith movements where the respective religions provide the motivation for commitment in action on behalf of those who are suffering and in need.

How can such active dialogue be encouraged? Our Catholic communities have perhaps a tradition of going it alone. Ecumenical endeavours are difficult, let alone interfaith cooperation. It is often easier, and quicker, for the community that has seen a problem to tackle it and try to solve it, without waiting to get others involved. The dialogue of action is a real form of dialogue, since it supposes that people agree on the goals they are setting themselves, that they are happy about the methods to be used, the way these goals are to be achieved, and that they are clear about how responsibility is to be shared, including financial responsibility. All this can take time, hence the temptation of going it alone. Yet would it not be more profitable if others were to become involved? Is there not a sort of instinct, an ecumenical instinct or an interfaith instinct, to be aroused, so that what can be done together will be done together?

Interreligious prayer

Would it help in creating this spirit of cooperation if people of different religions prayed together? Are parishioners to be encouraged to engage in such prayers? Should Catholic chaplaincies be to the fore in organizing prayer events? There are many questions that arise regarding this form of interreligious relations, and I have said more about them elsewhere.

I would like to mention here a book written some years ago, *Encounter in the Spirit. Muslim–Christian Meetings in Birmingham.*[4] In it, Andrew Wingate, an Anglican priest, described the shock he received when the Muslim Imam with whom he had become friendly asked if he could pray for Andrew's father who was sick. He had to ask himself whether he believed in the prayers of someone of a different religion. After some soul-searching he answered in the affirmative and, as he says, 'praying together has been central to the friendship'. As long as each respects the identity of the other, there should be no difficulty in sharing prayer.

There are occasions when people of different religions desire and feel the need to offer prayers together in public: at times of crisis, whether natural disasters, terrible accidents, or in times of war. There are also civil occasions, such as Commonwealth Day, when prayer together seems appropriate. We in the Catholic tradition have the example of John Paul II's initiatives, the ecumenical and interreligious gatherings in Assisi in order to pray for peace, in 1986, in 1993 (for peace in Europe and particularly in the Balkans), and in 2002 as a response to the events of September 11, 2001. On the latter occasion, encouragement was given to arrange similar gatherings for prayer in different parts of the world.

It may be possible to find some texts to which no one will object – the prayer attributed to St Francis is one such – but this unity is obtained at the expense of the riches of diversity. If a unified expression is sought, it may be better to have recourse to symbolic actions, such as the lighting of candles or lamps, which often speak louder than words. Nor should one forget the powerfully unifying force of silence. Whether in the multireligious type of prayer or in the united interreligious prayer, careful preparation is needed, and as far as possible this should be common preparation together with the members of the other faith communities. In this way springing unexpected things on people, perhaps causing embarrassment, can be avoided. It is perhaps better to err on the side of prudence.

Parishioners could and should be encouraged to participate, with prudence and charity, in interfaith prayer. Chaplaincies could take the initiative in this field. Praying together, being present before God together, is surely one way of helping people to grow together in confidence and thus encouraging cooperation.

The parish as a school of prayer

If Christians are to pray with people of other religious traditions, they should first be familiar with prayer according to their own tradition. Are the people in our parishes, the young Catholics who frequent the chaplaincies, finding the help they need to discover their spiritual roots? In a recent piece in *The Tablet*, Sue Delaney notes that 'in recent years, many Christians have turned towards the meditation practices of Hinduism and Buddhism. Contemplative meditation, formerly practised only by monks and nuns, is now being adopted by increasing numbers of laypeople, including the mothers of families, often with little or no guidance. This can lead to problems'.[5]

Why is there little or no guidance? Let me refer to an older article by the Irish Jesuit, Michael Paul Gallagher, entitled 'Isn't there anything except the Mass?' Is it not true that the Eucharist has tended to monopolize the prayer life of the parish, leaving little room for other forms of devotion or types of prayer?

Perhaps this is unfair. You may say that meditation is essentially a private exercise, to be practised in one's private room with the door shut (cf. Matt. 6.6); that there do exist charismatic prayer groups, Bible sharing groups, Taizé prayer groups; that people have the opportunity of practising centring prayer, or of belonging to the World Community of Christian Meditation launched by Fr Laurence Freeman continuing the teaching of Dom John Main. Well, happy are those who have this possibility. Can any provision be made for others?

Those who are in contact with people of other faith communities, especially Buddhists and Hindus, may be attracted by their tradition of meditation. On a visit recently to a small Hindu ashram in Argentina, I was surprised to find that nearly all the people gathered were in fact Catholics. Will they find anyone to talk to about what they are experiencing, and also who might share with them the riches of the Christian spiritual tradition? Catholic monasteries, especially those in which the monks and nuns are active in Monastic Interreligious Dialogue, could be expected to provide this spiritual nourishment and guidance. It would be an asset to Catholic life if at least some parishes were able to give similar assistance.

Conclusion

Some parish priests may feel they are expected to be like those Hindu gods, with so many arms and legs, capable of busying themselves with many different undertakings all at the same time. What can I say to these? First, I do not think that answers can be given from on high. Principles can be reiterated, but they have to be applied in concrete circumstances, and it is those on the ground who know these circumstances.

Second, who said that the priest has to do everything himself? In this field of the relations of the Catholic community to other faith communities there is room for much cooperation. It is a question of discovering talents and tapping them, of encouraging people to develop their interests and use their gifts. The bishop cannot be expected to carry out the whole pastoral plan of his diocese alone, so why should a parish priest try to do this in his parish? If laypeople are involved in all the areas touched upon – educating people about other faith traditions, assisting with the RCIA programme, giving support to those engaged in mixed-faith marriages, fostering common action with people of other faith communities, helping to organize joint prayer meetings when the occasion arises, contributing to the parish becoming truly a school of prayer – will not the parish be a happier and a more lively place?

5

The role of the laity in interreligious dialogue

Laity indispensable

'Each member of the faithful and all Christian communities are called to practise dialogue, although not always to the same degree or in the same way', stated John Paul II. He added immediately: 'The contribution of the laity is indispensable in this area' (RM 57). We can see this contribution, or this involvement, according to the different forms dialogue can take: the dialogue of life, the dialogue of shared action, the dialogue of specialists and the dialogue of religious experience.

Dialogue of life

As we have seen, this 'dialogue of life' refers to a form of relationship 'where people strive to live in an open and neighbourly spirit, sharing their joys and sorrows, their human problems and preoccupations' (DP 42). It may be objected that this is not 'dialogue', that it is just 'living together'. Yet surely it includes communication, through a greeting, or a friendly enquiry, or just a smile. Dialogue does not consist only in formal discussions.

We can see that this form of dialogue, in the neighbourhood, at school, in the workplace, concerns everybody and therefore in a major way laypeople. It is within the capacity of all. It does not require any special training, but calls on qualities of the heart such as sympathy, respect, patience. Of course it may lead us to want to know more about our Muslim or Sikh neighbours, and so we start reading books or asking for talks to be given. We may even pluck up the courage to ask the Muslims and Sikhs, Buddhists and Hindus to tell us about themselves.

Though dialogue of life may appear to be spontaneous, it does require an effort – the definition quoted above uses the word 'strive'. It is easy to close in on oneself and ignore the other, especially if that other belongs to a rather closed community, which apparently does not want this dialogue. It requires perseverance to overcome the barriers of diffidence and suspicion.

How are we to rate this dialogue of life? What value is to be attributed to it? I think that if we remember the parable of the Good Samaritan we shall rate it very highly and place it well up on the dialogue scale. Love of God and love of neighbour go together as the way to eternal life. Once again, this dialogue cannot be taken for granted; it has to be worked at all the time. Otherwise outside influences can come into play and break up the existing harmony.

In this context, interreligious marriages should not be forgotten. Here laypeople have a particular responsibility and a special role to play in the pastoral care they need. In fact dialogue groups of mixed couples, especially in the case of Christian–Muslim marriages, have proved to be an important form of pastoral action and an opportunity for a deep dialogue.

Shared action

Good neighbourliness also means giving and receiving, rendering mutual service. This may be sporadic, like taking a sick person to the hospital, or agreeing to mind the children, or more organized, for instance setting up a neighbourhood play group, or care of the handicapped, which we could include as dialogue of shared action. This may be at the local level, or on a wider scale through cooperation between national or international organizations. Here again there is a vast field for lay involvement, since special skills are required which clergy usually do not possess. This is indeed dialogue, and religious attitudes have to be understood, even when the project is not explicitly religious.

This dialogue also has a profound theological value. To work for the integral development of human beings, to strive to liberate people from unjust structures of oppression or poverty, is to share in the building up of the kingdom of God. Laypeople who engage in this dialogue in action are truly instruments of God's love, helping to fulfil the prayer 'Thy Kingdom come'.

Dialogue of experts

In any type of formal discussion laypeople take an active part, reading papers, acting as discussants, or simply joining in the exchanges. Whether it be education, or journalism, or ecology that is being discussed, it is important to have real experts in these fields, and more often than not they will be laypeople. Nor should one forget that more and more laypeople are studying theology, and can therefore make an informed contribution to theological dialogue. Their presence in such formal meetings is, to my mind, of great significance. It helps to give a witness to what the Church really is, not just a clerical body but the people of God.

Here it would be good to note that women have a special role in dialogue. They often have a less threatening way of meeting people than men, and so can discuss delicate questions which may otherwise be avoided. This is certainly true with regard to Christian–Muslim relations and also perhaps in the Asian cultural context in general. Women's meetings can thus be very productive, but of course women also have their contribution to make in the dialogue as a whole, and men have to be open to their gifts.

What value is to be attached to this formal dialogue? It is best seen, I would suggest, in the light of the first part of a definition of dialogue given in DM 13: 'walking together towards the truth'. Through honest presentations of our views, through discussion, and above all by listening to one another, we can come to a better appreciation of our respective traditions. This can help to remove prejudices, to create understanding, and thus encourage both the dialogue of life and the dialogue of action.

It will be helpful if such meetings are conducted in a spirit of prayer. This will serve as a reminder that the truth is larger than ourselves, larger even than our own tradition.

Dialogue of religious experience

Dialogue can also go deeper, allowing believers to share their spiritual experience. This can of course be done spontaneously, in private conversation, but it can also be carried out more formally in what is known as the dialogue of religious experience. There can be the joint study of religious texts, the holding of joint prayer meetings or simply the presence at one another's worship. All this requires great care, a sense of profound respect for other traditions, and thus the avoidance of any semblance of syncretism.

Here, laypeople have a particularly valuable contribution. Spirituality is not restricted to priests, monks and nuns, and members of religious congregations. More and more laypeople are studying spirituality, engaging in retreat giving, offering their services for spiritual direction. Such people, firmly rooted in their own religious traditions, are well suited to this particular form of dialogue. Perhaps in this, as in other fields, they only need encouragement.

The role of the laity in religious education

The contemporary world is marked by religious plurality, as well as by technological progress, the unevenness of economic development, the impact of globalization, even of terrorism, the appearance of new political alignments – and the list could be continued. It is within this context that religious education takes place, a field in which laypeople are particularly involved.

Religious instruction/religious knowledge

The question now arises: how is religious education to be provided? It may be useful to distinguish between religious instruction (RI) and religious knowledge (RK). It should be emphasized that this is by no means an official distinction, but simply my own attempt to clarify ideas and highlight the different aims of religious education. The purpose of RI is to educate someone in a particular faith. This is not confined to conveying knowledge, a series of truths, to be understood and stored up in the memory, like facts of history or mathematical formulae. It is also transformative, bringing about a change in life as the truths of faith are enacted through ritual and translated into practical life. In fact it could possibly be called more appropriately religious formation. This process supposes a community of faith. The person giving the instruction or formation must be committed to that which is being handed on.

RK can approach religion in a more detached way. It will include the transmission of the essential elements of belief of a particular religion, or indeed of a number of religions. The rituals of these religions may be described, as also their ethical content. Here the aim is to bring about understanding, but not necessarily commitment. So for RK community of faith is not required. It is possible to teach something about a religion without belonging to that religion. In this case religion is being treated as a part of culture.

Characteristics of sound religious instruction

In a believing family, RI will start almost from birth, or at least from a very tender age. Religious instruction, given in the family, will largely be by example, and from within a community of faith, from within a tradition, where the parent or teacher shows that what is being handed on is part of personal conviction. This allows the young child to develop strong roots in the tradition, which ideally will assist in withstanding the period of doubt, of questioning basic truths, which is almost inevitably bound to occur at a later age.

The imparting of knowledge needs to be accompanied by personal involvement in both prayer and practice, and liturgy is important. In the Catholic tradition much of RI is, or should be, accomplished through the sermon or homily during the Sunday Eucharist. In more systematic fashion there comes the preparation for reception of the sacraments. Furthermore, there will need to be instruction in prayer, from the learning of simple formulas or traditional prayers, to a prayerful use of the Scriptures, and even introduction to different types of silent prayer and meditation.

With regard to living the faith in daily life, RI should not only convey moral principles and elements of the social doctrine of the Church, but should also encourage different types of service and reflection on experience. It is here, in learning how to live a Christian life in society as it really exists, that there will be opportunities for an interreligious dimension to RI. Christians are to be prepared for contact with people belonging to other religious traditions. A growing realization that the gift of Christian faith is precisely that, a gift, will encourage the ability to see how God is working in the lives of people who do not share this faith. This needs to be taught perhaps as much by example as by formal instruction, since it is a question of developing the right attitude and encouraging a spirit of respect and cooperation.

Characteristics of sound religious knowledge

Religious knowledge (RK) is a discipline that will be catered for in school, not only in the early years, but ideally throughout the whole process of education. More attention may be given to the religious tradition that is predominant in a particular area, but all religions that exist in that area should be covered, and RK should provide some information about the various religions of the world, both in the past and in the present.

One of the aims of RK should be to impart an appreciation for religious values. This is particularly important in a society where several religious traditions exist side by side. RK may well adopt a gradual approach. In the first years of school it may be necessary to give more attention to the religion of the majority of the pupils, while inculcating respect for those who do not belong to this religion. For instance, in a school where most of the pupils are Christians, feasts such as Christmas and Easter could be occasions for special lessons. At the appropriate time attention could be called to the holy days of other religions, such as Yom Kippur for the Jews, 'Id al-Fitr and 'Id al-Adhā for the Muslims, Vesakh or Hanamatsuri for Buddhists, Diwali for Hindus.

For older pupils it will be necessary to teach something of the history of the origins and development of different religions, an outline of essential beliefs and practices, perhaps also something on the way the different religious traditions attempt to respond to the problems posed by modernity. At times a thematic approach may be adopted, seeing how the different traditions view such questions as the use of the world's resources, marriage and the family, violence, war and peace, and many other questions that exercise the minds of people today. A critical stance towards various religious traditions is not to be excluded, but an attempt should be made to place all affirmations or texts that raise difficulties within their proper context.

RK is a proper subject for examination, like science or the history of art. The difficulty comes when RK is not accompanied by RI, whether in the school or outside. There is then the temptation of treating religion as just one subject in the school curriculum, something that has to be got through and can then be abandoned. This is the real reason for the distinction between RI and RK that I am using here. Since RK in a pluralistic context will often make use of a comparative method, it will be almost inevitable that teachers will have to present traditions that are not their own. This should not really create any difficulty, provided that the presentation is accurate, fair and respectful. This of course pinpoints the need for the training of such teachers.

One final point may be made concerning RK. If the teaching involves not only classroom work but also other activities, care must be taken to respect the integrity of each religious tradition. For instance, it may be useful to visit places of worship belonging to different religions, and even perhaps to be present at the time of worship, but without of course taking part. Attention is to be paid to the sensitivity of the host community and above all to the conscience of each individual.

Collaborative effort

However valid the distinction may be between RI and RK, it is obvious that there is a certain overlapping between the two. The formative aspect of RI cannot exclude the acquisition of knowledge. At the same time the people engaged in RK, whether teachers or pupils, may have a living commitment to a particular religious tradition. This points to the need for collaboration rather than competition. RI cannot be expected to have the breadth of RK, nor RK the depth of RI. The two should be seen as complementary.

As always in education, the parents have the prime responsibility with regard to their children. This is particularly evident in relation to RI. They will nevertheless look to the school and to religious institutions for help. If the school belongs to a particular religious tradition, it may well provide RI. Nevertheless such a school would also be expected to provide RK. It may well be the religious institution, church, mosque or temple that takes the responsibility for RI at different levels. It will be helpful if there is frequent contact and constant exchange between parents, teachers and religious personnel.

Let me conclude by quoting some recommendations from a consultation paper prepared a few years ago for the Catholic Bishops of England and Wales, *Catholic Schools and Other Faiths* (1995):

> That the relationship between Catholics and people of Other Faiths be an area of formation and education for priests, teachers and catechists and indeed for the Catholic community at large, so that the Catholic

community can be informed partners in the work both at parish level, and in particular as parents of pupils in schools and also as governors and prospective governors.

That the bishops encourage dialogue and partnership with national representative bodies of the major world faiths represented in Britain concerning the spiritual development and support of pupils of Other Faiths in Catholic schools and colleges.

That individual dioceses and school governing bodies develop this process of dialogue and partnership with their own local Other Faith communities and their representatives.

Part II

CHRISTIAN–MUSLIM RELATIONS

6

Christian–Muslim dialogue: Developments, difficulties and directions

Introduction

The second section of this book concentrates on Christian–Muslim relations. The reason for this particular attention is not merely that my own background and expertise lie especially in this field, but also, as will be explained below, the objective importance of the meeting between the followers of these two religions.

Over 40 Muslims took part in the Interreligious Assembly held in the Vatican City, 25–28 October 1999. They came from many different countries: Jordan and Lebanon, Turkey and Iran, Algeria and Morocco, Ghana, Nigeria and Congo, Bangladesh and Malaysia, USA and Canada, France and Switzerland, Kazakhstan and also Bosnia–Herzegovina – and this list is by no means complete. Some were official government figures. Some represented organizations. Others came as individuals. There were men and women, of different ages, professions and outlook.

This strong representation of Islam contrasted with the rather timid Muslim presence at the first major Vatican initiative in the field of dialogue, the Day of Prayer for World Peace, held in Assisi, to which Pope John Paul II had invited religious leaders in October 1986. A few years later, when John Paul II invited Jews, Christians and Muslims to return to Assisi in order to pray for peace in Europe, especially in the Balkans, there was a significant Muslim response. Notable was the presence of a mixed delegation from Bosnia–Herzegovina, including the then Rais al-Ulema.

It would seem to me true to say that the increasingly positive response of Muslims to invitations from the Catholic side, and also from other Christian bodies, shows a growing confidence in the process of dialogue in recent years. It has also been my experience, since my appointment in 1987 as Secretary of the Pontifical Council for Interreligious Dialogue, that initiatives have not been confined to the Christian side, but have also been taken by Muslims.

Before saying a word about recent developments in Christian–Muslim relations, I would like to present briefly the foundations for this dialogue. Honesty requires also that the difficulties be acknowledged. In the light of recent developments it will be possible to suggest some directions that relations between Christians and Muslims could take.

Foundations for dialogue

Various reasons can be given for the importance of Christian–Muslim relations and for the necessity of engaging in dialogue. These can be categorized as sociological, pragmatic and theological.

The sheer numbers of Christians and Muslims in the world make Christian–Muslim dialogue imperative. We are dealing here with the two largest of the world's religions. Christians of all Churches and communities are held to constitute about one third of the world's population. Catholics would count for somewhat over half of that number. In recently published statistics, they have been slightly outstripped by Muslims.

It is of course very difficult to give accurate figures for religious adherence. To take but one example, who could state with accuracy the number of Christians or Muslims in mainland China today? Figures are always changing. Nevertheless they can be taken as a rough guide. So, with these necessary provisos, it can be said that Christians and Muslims together make up about one half of the inhabitants of the world. It is obvious that relations between these two groups will be important not only for them but also for the rest of the world.

Christianity and Islam are not only religions with numerous followers; both religions also have a universalist outlook, and have spread worldwide, while modern movement of population means there is hardly any country on the globe where Christians and Muslims are not living side by side.

There is often talk about Islam and the West, but the terms used are ambiguous. Majority Muslim countries, whether in the Arab world or in Africa, in the subcontinent of India or in South-East Asia, contain significant numbers of Christians. Some of these belong to ancient communities that were in place long before the rise of Islam. Others, for instance in Saudi Arabia and in the Gulf, are present as migrant workers. The same is true, in the opposite direction, of Europe, America and Australia. Some countries of Europe, as in the Balkans, have long-established communities of Muslims. Others, such as my own country, the UK, have seen an influx of Muslims in the last decades, first single men, then their families, so that now flourishing communities exist.

It is surely in the interests of society at large that members of different religious communities should live together respecting each other and observing society's norms. While they claim particular rights, they must also respect those of others, including the right to religious freedom. This will include the right of assembly, of places of worship and, together with all citizens, of freedom of expression.

Apart from religious rights, which are fundamental, there are many other different aspects to the meeting between people of different religious traditions. For the purpose of ensuring good neighbourliness there is need of fostering greater knowledge of the cultural and religious traditions of different groups. Such knowledge will help in overcoming prejudices and racial or religious tensions. It can lead to greater openness and a willingness to cooperate. Hence the need to cater for the intercultural and interreligious dimensions of education. Hence also the need for appropriate structures that may support the work of dialogue and the building up of good relations.

Theological reasons

Good neighbourliness has just been mentioned. For Christians this could evoke the parable of the Good Samaritan. After telling this story of the man who was willing to help someone who did not belong to his own group, just because that person was in need, Jesus said: 'Go, and do the same yourself' (Luke 11.37). For Jesus, relations should go beyond cultural boundaries, beyond caste and creed.

Indeed one could say that the Christian foundation for dialogue is love, God's love which embraces the whole of humankind, but which is made manifest in a perfect way in Jesus Christ. God, becoming man in Jesus Christ, has entered into a relationship with every member of the human race. Each human person has been created in the image and likeness of God, and so is deserving of respect. Yet the fact that the Word of God has become flesh, has entered into human history, has enhanced beyond measure the dignity of the human person. Here are the grounds for opening up a dialogue with every fellow human being in order to establish a respectful relationship.

It is because God, the Creator, wishes the salvation of all – that is he wishes all to share in his life and glory – that he has sent his Son into the world to be the saviour. For Christians, Jesus is the gateway to the Father. The Gate is a narrow one. It means passing through the straits of death into new life. Jesus' teaching emphasizes death, not only the physical separation of body and soul, but also death to one-self, to one's own egoistic tendencies, in order to live for others. Jesus himself showed the way. The teaching of the Catholic Church holds that the Spirit of God can, in ways known to God, lead all people to share in this mystery of death and resurrection to new life.

Witness is an essential part of dialogue, but it is first witness to God before being witness to a particular religious faith. Dialogue should allow for mutual witness, a sharing of deep convictions, but always in a spirit of respect. For Christians the words of Peter are always relevant: 'Simply reverence the Lord Christ in your hearts, and always have your answer ready for people who ask you the reason for the hope that you all have. But give it with courtesy, and respect, and with a clear conscience' (1 Pet. 3.15).

A Muslim writer has affirmed that 'in virtue of the demands of Revelation itself the Muslim is by definition already open to dia-logue'.[1] It should be remembered that Muhammad preached in a society which included Jews and Christians, not all of whom accept-ed his message. It was therefore necessary for him to come to terms with this plurality. Passages in the Qur'an echo this situation:

Call thou (Muhammad) to the way of thy Lord with wisdom and good admonition, and dispute with them (i.e. the Jews) in the better way.
(16.125)

Dispute not with the People of the Book (i.e. the Jews and the Christians) save in the fairer manner, except for those of them who do wrong, and say: 'We believe in what has been sent down to us and what has been sent down to you. Our God and your God is one, and to him we have surrendered.' (29.46)

We could say that in these texts there is a command to invite to Islam, a call to mission such as is found also in Christianity, but there is also the recognition of a God-given truth which provides a meeting-point. There is a consciousness of holding something very precious in common which makes dialogue possible and saves it from becoming a double monologue.

The Qur'an recognizes the existence of different communities. Meditating on the condition of the human race, it points to a contrast between its original unity and present diversity:

> Had thy Lord willed, he would have made mankind one nation.
>
> (11.118)

> Had God willed, he would have made you one nation, but that he may try you in what has come to you. So compete in good works; unto God shall be the return, all together; and he will tell you of that whereon you were at variance. (5.48)

There are, it must be acknowledged, other passages in the Qur'an which indicate a more belligerent attitude towards Jews and Christians and towards unbelievers. Yet the texts referred to here, which are often quoted by Muslims, can provide a foundation for dialogue. More could be said on this point, but it is really for Muslims themselves to develop their own theology of dialogue.

Difficulties in dialogue

The more belligerent passages in the Qur'an remind us of the difficulties facing those who wish to engage in dialogue. Reference is often made to an affirmation such as the following: 'You are the best nation ever brought forth to men, bidding to honour and forbidding dishonour, and believing in God' (3.110). This is held to indicate that Islam contains a built-in discrimination based on religion. While it could be countered that this text does not necessarily imply superiority, but rather indicates a mission to bear witness in words and deeds, where discrimination exists it is very difficult for dialogue to develop. For good relations to flourish there is need of a certain equality between the partners.

Another difficult passage is the 'Verse of the Sword':

> Fight those who believe not in God and the Last Day and do not forbid what God and his Messenger have forbidden – such men as practise not the religion of truth, being of those who have been given the Book – until they pay the tribute out of hand and have been humbled. (9:29)

Here the attitude of domination is uppermost. The presence of such verses in the qur'anic message cannot be ignored. They have provided the basis for *jihād* against non-Muslims but also, and perhaps even more frequently, against those held not to be true Muslims, as with the civil strife in Algeria.

It should not be thought that only the Qur'an presents difficulties for dialogue. The Christian Scriptures, although not inculcating an aggressive spirit, can be understood in such a way as to lead to a closed mentality. Much will be made of the missionary mandate given by Jesus to the apostles: 'Go, therefore, and make disciples of all nations, baptizing them in the name of the Father, and of the Son, and of the Holy Spirit, teaching them to observe all that I have commanded you' (Matt. 28:19–20).

There are Christians who teach that unless a person believes explicitly in Jesus Christ that person cannot be saved, though I would hasten to add that this is not the Catholic position. It is perhaps not surprising, therefore, that some Muslims wonder whether there is not an incompatibility, at least at the practical level, between a declared missionary intention and real commitment to interreligious dialogue.

Other obstacles to dialogue

Dialogue will be impossible, or at least extremely difficult, where minds are closed. If there is a conviction that only I have the truth, and that the other person is completely in error, then there can be no true meeting of minds. Such a closed mentality will have to be overcome. This does not mean that I have to give up my own convictions. The Christian will believe that the fullness of revelation is given in Jesus Christ, but this does not exclude the presence of 'rays of the Truth', of what the early Christian Fathers have called 'seeds of the Word', in other religions. The Muslim will believe that the Qur'an is the final revelation, superseding all others. Yet this does not prevent the recognition of earlier revelations, which, in some measure at least, can still be valid. To my mind the experience of dialogue, meeting people whose sincerity and goodness cannot be denied, is the best way of broadening one's horizons and of coming to recognize God's action in people.

It is obviously extremely difficult to engage in dialogue if one does not enjoy the freedom to practise one's own religion openly. There will be a fear to reveal one's convictions. Criticism, or anything that might even be remotely construed as criticism, will be avoided so as not to put in jeopardy the limited freedom that may exist. A defensive mentality is created. People living in what is experienced as a hostile society will be tempted to treat their religious communities like clubs, as places where they can relax and be themselves. This is understandable, and yet it leads to a privatizing of religion and a dichotomy between religious life and public life. The element of witness, which, as has been said, is part of dialogue, becomes neglected.

Even where there is freedom, people may really know very little about one another. Recent immigrants are looked upon as strange, but there may be no wish to find out more about them and their traditions. Similarly the newcomers may not be inclined to learn about the history and cultural riches of their newly adopted country.

There is here a delicate task for present-day societies, a task that can only be accomplished through dialogue and cooperation. There is a need to provide educational programmes and materials that will allow the different components of society to know and appreciate one another better.

It is certain that insufficient knowledge of the other's religion and indeed of one's own religion is an impediment to dialogue. Ignorance about the other can lead to questions that can be considered offensive, to stereotyping and to the growth and persistence of prejudices. Ignorance about one's own religion can lead to a lack of openness to speak about religious topics for fear of being put in an embarrassing situation. This underlines the need to learn about other traditions and acquire better knowledge of one's own.

Tensions can occur between different religious groups as they do between members of the same family, and conflict may follow if there is no structure available for dealing with the difficulties. If the religious leaders of the different communities do not know one another, they do not know to whom to turn. Where councils of religious leaders exist, they can play a very important role in maintaining peace and harmony among their followers.

Dialogue has to be supported. There is a place for a network of committees and councils, of institutions and study centres, whether of one religion or joint ventures. There is a need for publications both popular and more learned. Many such bodies, institutions and publications exist, fortunately, but there is room for greater efforts in this field. Dialogue will remain precarious where commitment to it does not take an organized form.

Recent developments

It would probably not be wrong to say that modern dialogue between Christians and Muslims dates from the late 1960s and early 1970s. The Second Vatican Council, with its Declaration on Religious Liberty and the Declaration *Nostra Aetate* on the relation of the Church to people of other religions, provided a firm foundation for this dialogue. The mid-1970s were notable for a series of organized dialogues, in the Lebanon, in Spain, in Libya. For some these official meetings were unsatisfactory. It was felt that their public nature inhibited real exchange. Of this dissatisfaction was born a private group, the Groupe de Recherches Islamo-Chrétien (GRIC), which still meets to discuss theological questions, and has published some of its results in useful books.

In recent years certain bodies within the Muslim world have taken the initiative to arrange regular meetings. The Al Albait foundation, in Jordan, conducted separate dialogues with Anglicans, Orthodox, Roman Catholics and German Lutherans. The World Islamic Call Society, which has its headquarters in Tripoli, Libya, has engaged in a series of meetings with the Pontifical Council for Interreligious Dialogue. The Centre for Dialogue in Teheran, depending on the Council for Islamic Culture and Communications, has organized encounters with the Orthodox Church of Greece, with the Catholic Church and with Protestants. The published acts of these meetings provide a wealth of material on dialogue.

A further forum of dialogue which has been developing is that of university exchanges. To speak only of the Catholic universities in Rome, academic agreements have been signed between the Pontifical Gregorian University and the University of Ankara, between the same

Pontifical Gregorian University together with the Pontifical Institute of Arabic and Islamic Studies and the University Al-Zaitouna in Tunis. The first agreement has given rise to a regular exchange of professors and also to the occasional colloquium. The second agreement mentioned has confined its attention so far to arranging scientific colloquia in Rome and in Tunis alternately. Such colloquia benefit not only the professors who take part but also the students who are invited to listen.

Dialogue has been facilitated by the liaison committee set up between the Institute of Al-Azhar and the Pontifical Council for Interreligious Dialogue. The agreement constituting this committee was signed in Rome in May 1998. It is therefore a young body, one which has still to find its way. The setting up of this committee followed an earlier initiative, in 1995, establishing a joint Catholic–Muslim Liaison Committee. It brings together staff members of the Pontifical Council for Interreligious Dialogue with representatives of various International Islamic Organizations. Its annual meeting provides a forum for discussing matters of mutual concern and for monitoring the state of Catholic–Muslim relations around the world.

The impression should not be given that only from Rome is there activity in the field of Christian–Muslim relations, or indeed that initiatives are confined to the Catholic Church. There is much going on in different parts of the world, in Bangladesh and Pakistan, in Ghana and Sierra Leone, in the USA, in France and Germany and the UK. The Greek Orthodox, at the initiative of the Ecumenical Patriarchate, have organized meetings in both Brussels and Bahrain. From the Anglican side, Lord Carey as Archbishop of Canterbury, was instrumental in setting up the Alexandria Conference, a trilateral venture to contribute towards a peaceful resolution of the Israel–Palestine conflict. Another initiative of the Archbishop was the 'Building Bridges' series of Christian–Muslim conversations held in Lambeth, Qatar and Georgetown. In the two latter meetings, emphasis was placed on joint reading of the Scriptures.

Mention should also be made of the commitment to dialogue of the World Council of Churches, the Middle East Council of Churches and the Conference of European Churches, which together with the Council of Episcopal Conferences of Europe formed its own 'Islam in Europe' committee. There are interreligious bodies such as the World Conference on Religion and Peace. There is much happening in the scene of Christian–Muslim relations, but some of it needs to be related to local communities. This leads us on to consider some directions Christian–Muslim dialogue could take in this new millennium.

Future directions

It is difficult to predict how relations between Christians and Muslims will develop during the new century and millennium. There are those who pay attention to the fault-lines of society and foretell a conflict of cultures, in particular between the world of Islam and the Western world. Yet it would seem wiser to look for those elements, already existing, which can be counted on to produce greater understanding and cooperation. Here let me mention some of the things that I, personally, would like to see strengthened.

First, structures. Often these are weak because there are not enough people qualified to engage in the work of promoting dialogue. From the Catholic point of view it is encouraging to see that some Churches, even in Europe, are making sure that they have people trained to work in the field of Christian–Muslim relations. Yet in comparison to the work to be done, their number is few. Sometimes they are diverted to other tasks, which may be a sign that not enough importance is attached to relations between Christians and Muslims.

It would be good for each Church to have its own commission for Christian–Muslim relations, or at least an expert who might belong to a broader structure, a commission for interreligious dialogue, or a commission for ecumenism and interreligious relations. The role of the expert is not to do everything personally, but to advise others and help them to take the necessary initiatives.

The 'Islam in Europe' committee gives the example of ecumenical cooperation. It seems to me that it would be healthy if more initiatives could be taken at an ecumenical level. Often different Churches are trying to accomplish the same thing, each on its own. A pooling of resources would be a source of strength.

Another hope is that the number of Muslims trained in Christian studies might increase. In recent years the Nostra Aetate Foundation, set up by the Pontifical Council for Interreligious Dialogue, has been able to give grants to a certain number of Muslims for study or research in Rome. Some universities in predominantly Muslim countries have been sending their young lecturers to Catholic universities in order to perfect their knowledge of Christianity. This is a hopeful sign. The presence of lecturers formed in this way in faculties of theology or religious studies would guarantee a serious formation of the students. It goes without saying that there is need for Christians to study Islam in the same way. The hope would be that more Islamic universities would be open to receiving students who are not Muslims.

With the help of well-trained experts it might be possible to go further in strictly theological exchanges. Apart from the GRIC, and one of the Catholic–Muslim groups in the USA, there is practically no work being done in this field. It must be made clear that the purpose of theological dialogue is not to attempt to arrive at a unity of expression on particular questions. Here interreligious dialogue is very different from the inter-Christian ecumenical dialogue which does have as its aim the restoration of unity among all Christians. Christians and Muslims can never be united with regard to certain fundamental tenets of their respective creeds, yet they can clarify the questions, eliminate false problems, arrive at a better understanding of the different positions. It would be good to see new groups started in order to tackle theological issues.

Dialogue however is not confined to discussions. It can also take the form of action. In certain countries Christians and Muslims are working together to face up to problems of society. One thinks of the Muslim involvement in basically Christian pro-life movements. There are also instances of dialogue associations engaging together in advocating human rights, social reforms, care of the environment. Yet it would be very healthy, and would contribute to promoting good relations between Christians and Muslims everywhere, if there could be more concerted action. When disasters strike, floods or famine, earthquakes or tidal waves, religious groups or religiously motivated groups could be encouraged to cooperate more closely. Cooperation requires clarity in aims and transparency with regard to the methods used. For this to come about, and for responsibility to be shared, a great deal of dialogue is needed.

One final direction that may be pointed to is the move from bi-lateral to multilateral relations. Already structures such as the World Conference on Religion and Peace, or the International Association for Religious Freedom, bring together people of many different religious traditions. Local structures, such as the Inter Faith Network in the UK, or Marseille Espérance, now followed by Roubaix Espérance, in France, provide a forum for leaders of the different religious communities. It would be helpful if such structures could be multiplied in other parts of the world. This does not mean that bilateral dialogue is to be abandoned. It will always be necessary in order to clarify issues that affect particular religions and their relations. Yet bringing matters to a wider forum can often help to reduce tension. In our increasingly pluralistic world there will be a need for multireligious structures that reflect the true nature of society.

Conclusion

In the Interreligious Assembly held in October 1999 in the Vatican, people of many different religious traditions pledged themselves, in their Message, to work together in facing up to the problems of today's world. They insisted that such collaboration entailed respect for each one's identity and implied the rejection of fanaticism and extremism, which lead to violence. They underlined the importance of education for dialogue. While appealing to all leaders to refuse to allow religion to be used for inciting hatred and violence or for justifying discrimination, and exhorting them to respect the role of religion in society at all levels, they appealed to all their brothers and sisters to promote reconciliation, to commit themselves to overcoming the gap between the rich and the poor, and to work for a world of true and lasting peace. The applause that greeted the reading of this Message showed that it surely conveys people's aspirations and is truly a sign of hope for the new millennium.

7

Recent Muslim–Catholic dialogue in the USA

JOHN BORELLI

While teaching undergraduates in the early 1980s, I once told a class of students that the material we were then taking up on Islam would figure significantly in their lives. As my generation was sent off to Vietnam, their generation, I predicted, would serve in the Middle East and would have to think about Islam. I had no special insights at the time about the future role of Iraq in American history.

If we think about events of recent years and months that have shattered our sense of security in the USA, two stand out: the Oklahoma City bombing on 19 April 1995 and the events of September 11, 2001. These particular dates have a very personal meaning for me. My wife and I have three adult children. On September 11, two were in lower Manhattan. They saw the second tower collapse with their own eyes and, I am sure, will never forget what they saw that day. Our middle child, our older daughter, was in Oklahoma City on 19 April 1995, one mile north and in the direction of the blast that devastated the Murrah Building. When the so-called experts on terrorism showed up in the media soon afterwards observing that the bombing in Oklahoma City looked like the work of Middle East Arab terrorists, they made Arab and Muslim Americans additional victims of that bombing. Their misreading of a crime, soon shown to be perpetrated by white supremacists against controls by the federal government and global attitudes, was irresponsible. Tragically, the events of 9/11 were the result of terrorists from the Middle East, but innocent Middle Easterners and Muslims died in the conflagration

The USA invaded the Middle East, belligerently entering Iraq for the second time in 12 years. It is still too early to say what will be its outcome, but the events of 9/11 and the aftermath, especially this war and the reactions among so many in the world today, both positive and negative, constitute the world in which the present generation of graduate students in theology will conduct their professional work. These defining events will shape their attitudes and how they approach the world. Many in my generation were shaped in our youths by a considerable optimism inspired by John F. Kennedy and his youth and idealism, the civil rights movement, the war on poverty, and, as Catholics, the fresh air flowing in through the windows of the Church. With the Second Vatican Council, we laypersons began to see that this was just as much our Church as it was the Church of the clergy, and we learned to define the Church as the people of God.

John XXIII not only called the council but struggled to make it a council open to the modern world. He died after the first session, and Paul VI was elected his successor. In his first address to the council as pope, he made it clear that he was going to move the agenda of John XXIII forward. Here is an excerpt from that address that directed the assembled bishops to ponder the field of interreligious relations:

> The Catholic Church looks into the distance, beyond the confines of the Christian horizon; how could she place limits on her love, if this very love is to be that of God the Father who showers his favors upon everyone (cf. Mt 5:45), and who so loved the world that for it he gave his only Son (cf. Jn 3:16)? Look therefore beyond your own sphere and observe those other religions that uphold the meaning and the concept of God as one, Creator, provident, most high and transcendent, that worship God with acts of sincere piety and upon whose beliefs and practices the principles of moral and social life are founded.[1]

This paragraph represents the beginning of official Catholic reflection on religious pluralism in modern times.

The present society in the USA is far more consciously pluralistic in religious terms than it was a generation ago. In my youth, in the 1950s and 1960s, religious pluralism in America was defined as 'Protestant, Catholic, and Jew'. Few thought about the small religious minorities, and sadly this meant that few took account of Native Americans as religious peoples. Today, one of our great strengths as a nation is our religious pluralism, although there are some who are unwilling to admit it. One of the contemporary challenges for theology is religious pluralism, a term which is used in a number of ways. In this context, I mean by religious pluralism nothing more than the fact that there exists a variety of religious traditions and that persons identifying with these traditions interact with one another in such ways that the traditions themselves are affected by this interaction. Thus more precisely religious pluralism, as I am using it, means engaged diversity. Christians among themselves have much to discuss about religious pluralism in this sense of engaged religious diversity.[2] John Paul II used the term religious pluralism in this way, for example, in his first letter of the new millennium, *Novo Millennio Ineunte*:

> In the climate of increased cultural and religious pluralism which is expected to mark the society of the new millennium, it is obvious that this [interreligious] dialogue will be especially important in establishing a sure basis for peace and warding off the dread spectre of those wars of religion which have so often bloodied human history.[3]

I began with a 1963 quotation from John XXIII, the motivator for the Catholic Church to respond to the modern world. Here is a quotation from another author of that time:

> If it becomes evident that Islam possesses or is capable of solving our basic problems, of granting us a comprehensive social justice, of restoring for us justice in government, in economics, in opportunities and in punishment . . . then without doubt it will be more capable, than any other system we may seek to borrow or imitate, to work in our nation.[4]

These words were written in 1959, the time of John XXIII's papacy, by Sayyid Qutb, about whom it has been written, 'few Muslim thinkers have had as significant an impact on the reformulation of contemporary Islamic thought as him'[5] and who has been called 'the nonpareil exemplar of collective protest against those deemed to be the enemies of Islam.'[6] Writing for *The New York Times Magazine*, Paul Berman entitled his article on Qutb, 'The Philosopher of Islamic Terror'. Here is a key paragraph from Berman's article:

> Qutb's analysis was soulful and heartfelt. It was a theological analysis, but in its cultural emphases, it reflected the style of 20th-century philosophy. The analysis asked some genuinely perplexing questions about the division between mind and body in Western thought; about the difficulties in striking a balance between sensual experience and spiritual elevation; about the steely impersonality of modern power and technological innovation; about social injustice. But, though Qutb plainly followed some main trends of 20th-century Western

social criticism and philosophy, he poured his ideas through a filter of Koranic commentary, and the filter gave his commentary a grainy new texture, authentically Muslim, which allowed him to make a series of points that no Western thinker was likely to propose.[7]

Sayyid Qutb was hanged by President Nasser of Egypt in 1966.

My reference to Sayyid Qutb is not to stir up animosity against so-called Islamic fundamentalists; rather I want call to mind that a desire for modernization or updating, *aggiornamento*, as Pope John XXIII called it, for a more authentic and socially responsible religious life has been a significant theme in both Christianity and Islam in recent decades. One area of theological dialogue between Catholics and Muslims involves our relationship as people of faith to the contemporary world. *Pacem in terris* and the Second Vatican Council mark a beginning for Catholics in addressing the modern world. Sayyid Qutb also represents an initial voice of Islamist reflection on the modern world. Here in the USA, protected as we are by the religious pluralism guaranteed by the Constitution, we have an ideal situation for engaging in this discussion. We need, first of all, to ensure that respect for religious freedom and human rights remains a principle of our democracy and then to make use of this advantageous situation for interreligious dialogue, particularly on topics with difficult political and social implications.

Theology and questions of revelation and other religions

For Catholics, the Second Vatican Council will always be the most remarkable example of revitalization and change. A spirit of renewal and updating took hold of the assembled bishops in 1962–5 and major steps were taken in numerous areas of public life. One such step concerned interreligious relations. In the history of the Church there had been nothing like the council's Declaration on the Relation of the Church to Non-Christian Religions (*Nostra Aetate*). Yet this document cannot be taken by itself as marking a revolution in Catholic teaching on this point; it should be read together with the Dogmatic Constitution on the Church (*Lumen Gentium*) and with Pope Paul VI's encyclical on the Church, *Ecclesiam Suam*, which appeared in 1964.

Relations with Muslims, therefore, are understood within the context of a Catholic understanding of the Church and the ministry of service to all humanity in building the reign of God, in establishing justice for all, in ministering to the needs of all, and in fulfilling every true desire for union with God. *Nostra Aetate* specifically names Jews, Muslims, Buddhists and Hindus as well as noting the 'deep religious sense' among all peoples whose way of life is religious.

In *Nostra Aetate*, the bishops said the following about Islam:

> The Church has also a high regard for the Muslims. They worship God, who is one, living and subsistent, merciful and almighty, the Creator of heaven and earth, who has also spoken to people. They strive to submit themselves without reserve to the hidden decrees of God, just as Abraham submitted himself to God's plan, to whose faith Muslims eagerly link their own. Although not acknowledging him as God, they venerate Jesus as a prophet, his virgin Mother they also honor, and even at times devoutly invoke. Further, they await the day of judgment and the reward of God following the resurrection of the dead. For this reason they highly esteem an upright life and worship God, especially by way of prayer, alms-deeds and fasting.   (NA 3)

A whole series of theological questions follows from these statements. Muslims believe that Muhammad is a messenger, that is, a prophet to whom God gave guidance, and the Qur'an is 'Revealed Guidance in Divine Words', as our Muslim partners in dialogue tell us. We can at least say that Muhammad was prophetic, like many public leaders, in that he heard God's words and acted in such a way that his life was an example of the justice that God wills for the world. That is not enough for our Muslim friends; they would like us to say more to satisfy their understanding of Muhammad as the last of the prophets and seal of divine revelation. They say that Jesus received guidance, embodied in the gospel (*injīl*), and we, of course, explain that their understanding of the gospel as a book and our understanding of the gospel as preached word of God are not the same. We need to go beyond mutual correction to a deeper level of discussion. The goal of interreligious theological dialogue is not to urge our partners to change their beliefs to match ours. Such dialogue is not debate or argument. There is a need for each side to comprehend as much as possible and understand correctly the beliefs of the other side in their own terms. That is a first step beyond mutual correction.

Then by understanding their views of revelation and prophecy, to name two overlapping categories in both Islam and Christianity, we can pursue the deeper goal of understanding our own views, and theirs too, through unexpected or neglected insights through mutual exploration.

This is what we were doing in our Midwest regional dialogue. For several years, we at the US Conference of Catholic Bishops (USCCB), with the assistance of diocesan staff, set up 'regional dialogues' with Muslims. The main purpose of these dialogues on a regional basis was to connect with both national and local Islamic leadership and thereby engage the diversity of the Muslim population in the USA. We would identify an Islamic organization or association in a certain region to be our partner in planning and setting up a dialogue in the city where that organization is located. Working with our Islamic partners, we would invite Catholics and Muslims from cities within a manageable commuting area to be part of the dialogue. We depended on diocesan staff to co-host meetings with an Islamic partner and to identify Muslim partners to attend the dialogue.

Regional dialogues met annually in a retreat environment for two or three days. The first of these began in Indianapolis in 1996 with the Islamic Society of North America (ISNA). Bishop Kevin Britt, Bishop of Grand Rapids and now deceased, served as the Catholic co-chairman, and Dr Sayyid M. Syeed, secretary-general of ISNA, was the Muslim co-chairman for most of the meetings. After an initial meeting, we settled on the topic 'the word of God'. We Christians spoke of Christ as the Word of God, and Muslims spoke of the Qur'an as the 'Words of God'. Jesus is also called 'the word of God' in the Qur'an, but this name indicates how he came into existence. God spoke Jesus into existence. The real parallel is between Christ and the Qur'an. We expanded our discussion to the broader topic of revelation, and we prepared a tool for introducing Muslims and Christians to one another through the core beliefs regarding revelation.

We learned something important. Muslims were willing to acknowledge that most of the themes of the New Testament that we highlighted in our discussions resonated with them. We disagree of course on the incarnation, and they remain suspicious of our explanation of one God and three persons. The warnings in the Qur'an against the Christian beliefs in the incarnation and the Trinity are just too strong to be set aside. Together we agreed that both the Bible and

102

the Qur'an can be abused in the sense that they can be interpreted to suit personal purposes. Interpretation is a communal, and by that I mean traditional, effort. Muslims locate texts within the whole of the Qur'an, interpret words and passages in the context of the prophet's life, in the order of the qur'anic passages as they were received, and what the commentaries have said about these passages through the ages. We Christians have our methods of interpretation too. There is much to be explored between Christian and Muslim scholars on methods of scriptural interpretation.

Another topic that arises from this discussion is the nature of revelation itself. At present, we Christians would not place the Qur'an in the same categories as the Hebrew Scriptures and the New Testament. We understand the fullness of revelation coming through Jesus Christ, a fullness that sheds light on the revelation given to Israel through the ages. When we meet a Scripture whose content is similar in many ways to that of the Bible and to our understanding of God and God's interaction with humanity, we are faced with a question about the nature of divine revelation itself. Muhammad lived more than five centuries after the apostolic Church. What can we say about his experience of God, the experience that he mediated to the Arab tribes who gathered around him, and his role in the lives of Muslims to the present? The Qur'an offers a unique challenge to us as we reflect on divine revelation. We can ignore it, as we have pretty much done for 14 centuries, or we can finally address these challenges.

Theological discussion, not debate and confrontation

After learning that the regional model could work in the Midwest, we turned to the Mid-Atlantic region and the Islamic Circle of North America (ICNA), with its headquarters in Queens, New York, to explore the possibility of a second regional dialogue. ICNA has served American Muslims of South Asian origin although its membership is gradually including a more diverse population. Bishop Ignatius Catanello co-chaired this dialogue. It has met annually since 1998 in the New York City area, apart from one year at St Charles Seminary in Philadelphia. This dialogue studied various aspects of marriage and family life with the hope of a publication in a few years, which will outline our values and practices.

Finally, in 2000, we established a regional dialogue on the West Coast. Bishop Carlos Sevilla, the bishop of the Diocese of Yakima, co-chaired this dialogue, and our partner was a collection of West Coast Islamic *shura* or advisory councils. We met in Orange, California, and we started by examining the theme of surrender/obedience to God. We concluded our fourth meeting in February 2003 and issued a statement after that discussion. We had settled on the theme of John Paul II's 2002 World Day of Peace message in which he had said there is no peace without justice and no justice without forgiveness. Our dialogue concluded with these points of consensus:

1. We, Catholics and Muslims, believe that God is the source of peace and justice, and thus we fundamentally agree on the nature of peace and justice and the essential need of all to work for peace and justice.

2. Our rich teachings and traditions of peace and justice serve as a resource and inspiration for all; however, our immediate and present actions to work together are often wanting. The need to work together for peace and justice is a pressing demand in these troubled times.

3. We believe that it is God who forgives and that as Catholics and Muslims we are called by God to offer forgiveness. Forgiveness is an important step to moving beyond our past history if we are to preserve human dignity, to effect justice, and to work for peace.

4. We may disagree on certain points of doctrine, even as we respect the others' rights to believe in the fundamental integrity of their teachings, and affirm all their human and religious rights. With love and in the pursuit of truth, we will offer our criticisms of one another when we believe there is a violation of integrity of faith in God. We must avoid demonizing one another and misrepresenting one another's teachings and traditions.

5. When we meet in dialogue and discuss matters of peace, justice, and forgiveness, while being faithful to our traditions, we have experienced a profound and moving connection on the deepest level of our faith, which must take effect in our lives.[8]

A document entitled *Friends and Not Adversaries: A Catholic–Muslim Spiritual Journey* was completed in December 2003 and posted on the USCCB website. It indicates the progress of this dialogue and significant points of consensus. The report encourages Muslims and Christians to investigate spiritual themes in ways that are mutually beneficial.[9]

After September 11, 2001, time was set aside to discuss reactions to these tragic events. In two of the dialogues the topic of religion and violence was addressed. Building upon trust and good will already in place from previous meetings, we drew closer together in candid and sincere conversation about this single topic, which had been the source of so much ill will and animosity between Christians and Muslims.

After 16 years at the USCCB, what have I learned from my Muslim friends and the experience of dialogue with Muslims? My reflections can be distilled into ten points:

1 For too many centuries, from the beginning of the encounters between Arab Muslims and the Christians outside of the Arabian Peninsula, Christians have made outlandish statements about Islam, Muhammad and Muslims in general. Muslims feel compelled to lecture Christians about the basics of Islam in order to correct our mistaken views. They are particularly eager to tell Christians that Islam is not a new religion and that they venerate all the prophets, including Jesus and his mother Mary.

2 Muslims and Christians have a tendency to generalize about other religious groups. Muslims may offer praise or criticism of these other groups. What they are truly looking for in religious individuals is God-consciousness or fear of the Lord, which Christians might call virtue. This is what is important for Muslims, and this is what they expect to see in Christians.

3 Christians and Muslims often use the same religious terms. We often talk past one another because we presume the other understands the words being used. Clarity is needed to ensure understanding of terms like revelation, the word of God, son of God, begotten and gospel.

4 Muslims generally look upon Christians as one group. There are few who are aware of the variety among Christians, just as there are few Christians who can distinguish different groups of Muslims. Consequently if a Christian says or does something negative with regard to Islam, Muslims expect other Christians to

correct that person. Silence is taken as an expression of agreement. Christians may not think they need to dissociate themselves from a Christian who is not even remotely related to their own Church. The same applies when a Muslim says something negative about Christians or Christianity.

5 Muslims expect Christians to live according to their moral standards, taking care of the needy, to be honest, faithful, not to steal, not to kill, etc. The reason for this is that in their understanding God's guidance is a moral message, whether in the Torah, gospel or Qur'an.

6 Muslims are particularly eager to tell Christians about their respect for Jesus, and cannot understand why Christians can be negative or distrustful towards them.

7 The word 'mission' functions in the same way among Muslims as the word 'jihad' does among Christians. Both words have beautiful meanings but they carry connotations of violence, intolerance and disrespect. The problem for Christian–Muslim conversation is that in a thorough discussion these words are difficult to avoid using.

8 Christianity is a highly structured religion. Whether we are Catholics, Presbyterians, Anglicans, Orthodox, Baptists, Lutherans or whatever, we have identifiable instruments of authority and communion. This kind of structure is not so prominent in Islam. There are authoritarian structures among both Christians and Muslims, but they function in different ways.

9 On the level of everyday experiences, Muslims and Christians can and do relate very well. Women's groups continue to meet in spite of political developments because they share experiences and concerns. In a retreat environment Christians and Muslims relate together well when they maintain their prayers and reflect together on issues of mutual importance.

10 Christians and Muslims often judge one another by their extremists. This can happen between any two groups, but because of the particular history they have had and the way strife has been promoted as a way of dealing with one another, they each make the mistake of judging the other's worst by their own best. They often let the extremists do the talking and thus capture public attention.

I would add some further considerations of a general nature.

Interreligious dialogue is by no means based on compromise whereby parties negotiate a common ground, each giving up a little, to reach a mutually beneficial position. Compromise is important for society to work as well as it does, but giving up essential doctrines and practices is not what interreligious dialogue is about: there is no attempt to reduce two sets of belief to one or to harmonize irreconcilable differences. Nor is interreligious dialogue a debate or argument over who is right and who is wrong.

On the contrary, interreligious dialogue refers to a religious attitude that encompasses both obedience to truth and respect for freedom of conscience. Participants are free to speak what they believe is true in matters of faith and morals and seek to understand and respect the perspective of others as much as is possible. Second, interreligious dialogue involves both witness of one's faith to another and mutual exploration of religious convictions. Third, the environment for interreligious dialogue is one that promotes holiness. Prayer and religious practices accompany the sharing of beliefs and the common search for the truth. Fourth, among the several goals of interreligious dialogue are these that are distinctively religious: mutual understanding and respect for one another as religious persons; common action for accomplishing what one's religious faith considers to be true and good; and spiritual growth and a deeper understanding of one's beliefs and those of another.

In an interreligious dialogue between Christians and Muslims, the partners clarify for one another how they understand God's revelation. Christians and Muslims know they have very great differences on matters of theological faith but they do not seek to minimize these nor explain them away. Together they seek to understand the mystery of the oneness of God and the meaning of divine revelation to humanity. Christians and Muslims can agree that God calls them to interreligious dialogue and that it is through God's guidance that they come together to do the will of God.

Dialogue remains a new experience for many Christians and Muslims, despite the fact that many in their communities have been attending dialogues for a number of years. On the Christian side, it is difficult to avoid making comparisons. Ecumenical dialogues seem to function as orderly partnerships in cost sharing, planning, arrangement and agreement on goals. This is not the case for Christian–Muslim dialogues. They follow their own logic and depend on different circumstances. Many on both sides need to be convinced of the need for dialogue even if they understand that it does not involve the compromise of beliefs. Many Christians and Muslims are too aware of the wounds of the past to expose their feelings through dialogue.

Interreligious dialogue can offer profoundly enriching moments. In the Midwest dialogue, after we had spent some time on the nature of revelation, we began to explore more carefully how we live and venerate the message of Scripture. For example, we compared *lectio divina*, the Christian spiritual practice of attentive reading of Scripture, and the art of chanting the Qur'an. We also looked more carefully at prayer in Scripture, and compared brief exegeses of gospel passages on 'the Lord's prayer' and the *fātiha*, the opening *sūra* of the Qur'an, which is prayed many times a day by Muslims. The West Coast dialogue shared views comparatively on peace, justice and forgiveness, and we reached such a level of a consensus on these three important themes of spirituality that we issued publicly our agreement, as quoted earlier. Many on the dialogues found these exchanges, comparative exercises and prayerful exchanges very moving and convincing of the importance of Christian–Muslim relations in the present.

I began this essay by suggesting that that we are at the beginning of a new period, both for Christians and for Muslims. My initial references were to two voices, one Catholic and one Muslim, in the mid-twentieth century urging their co-religionists to come to terms with the modern world. We are now in a post-9/11 world in which a new generation of scholars will work. If Christians and Muslims are to move beyond their confrontations and their bafflement with one another, then we must begin where we are now. We Christians begin first with ourselves and learn about Islam to move beyond generalities and stereotypes. We hope that Muslims will do the same, to move beyond what they have heard said about Christianity to understand us better.

With our Muslim friends in the USA, we have taken steps towards dialogue. We have built trust to move beyond suspicion and caricatures. Our theological dialogues, small steps that they may be, are only a start. As theologians, we are only at the beginning of a task with many exciting possibilities.

8

From heresy to religion:
Vatican II and Islam

While it is perhaps not pleasant to look at past opinions of Christians regarding Islam, it will help us to see how long the journey has been to where we are today if we examine a few of these.

Some past opinions on Islam

A 'monk of France', probably Hugh of Cluny (1049–1119), wrote to the Muslim king of Saragossa, Muqtadir Billah, a letter inviting the ruler to embrace Christianity. In it he spoke about Islam as a deception, attributing it to the work of Satan. He stated: 'Satan . . . deceived the children of Ishmael in regard to the Prophet whose mission they acknowledged and thereby drew many souls to the punishment of Hell.'[1] Though the tone of the letter is otherwise fairly friendly, this way of seeing Islam as something devilish and the Prophet of Islam as an instrument of Satan obviously produced a strong reaction. The ruler did not reply himself, but entrusted this task to a scholar, Abū l-Walīd Sulaymān ibn Khalaf al-Bājī, known for his skill in polemics. Al-Bājī gives all the main arguments of Islam against Christianity and ends, in his turn, by appealing to his correspondent to be converted to Islam; with little success, one would be inclined to think. From the Christian side, Islam was seen as something diabolical since it prevented God's saving work from being accomplished. This was an opinion quite common in missionary circles up to the Second Vatican Council.

An earlier writer, George Hamartolos, this time not in the West but in the Byzantine Empire, compiled a history of humankind from its origins to the middle of the ninth century. He dedicates one chapter, chapter 235, to Islam. He compares Islam unfavourably to Christianity, stating that it is a religion that springs from a false prophet. 'These foggy-minded and stupid men', he writes, 'refuse openly to examine the truest faith, sacred and guaranteed by God, while these hardened wretches accept the forgery to which this swindler gave the appearance of true religion'.[2] At least this writer does not invoke the influence of Satan, but he does give evidence of prejudice born of ignorance. As Gaudeul remarks:

> George (Hamartolos) did not know Islam, understood no Arabic, repeated what his predecessors had said but with such hatred, contempt and self-righteousness, that his readers took it for granted that what he said was true and passed it on to future generations.[3]

This attitude is unfortunately still found in polemical booklets from both sides.

Turning to someone who did have direct experience of Muslims and Islam, John of Damascus (675–753), we see that in the first century after its rise Islam was treated as a breakaway from Christianity. Muhammad was said to have been influenced by Christians. John says that Muhammad 'supposedly encountered an Arian monk' (other authors, with greater likelihood, speak about encounters with a Nestorian) and 'formed a heresy of his own'.[4] John, living under Muslim rule, shows that his information about Islam is generally correct and gives evidence of knowledge of the Qur'an. Yet each element of the religion is taken separately and not evaluated within the context of the religion as a whole. In fact it could be said that Islam is not described in itself at all, but is only considered in its relationship to Christianity. It is certainly unjustified to consider Islam as a Christian heresy. As defined by Canon Law, heresy is 'the obstinate post-baptismal denial of some truth which must be believed with divine and catholic faith' (Can. 751). To become a heretic one must first belong to the Church. This obviously does not apply to Muhammad.

Another categorization of Muslims, as unbelievers, is found in the writings of Thomas Aquinas. He was naturally inclined to reserve the term 'believer' to one who shared the Christian faith. Thomas, as a Dominican friar, was requested to compose a work to help those of his order who were preaching to Jews and Muslims. This was the origin of his *Summa contra gentiles.* He admitted that he knew very little about Islam, so he concentrated mainly on the way of presenting the elements of Christian faith to people who did not accept the authority of the Christian Scriptures. In the first three sections of this work, dealing with God in himself, God as Creator, and with the moral life as the way to God, Thomas uses rational arguments for he is speaking about truths accessible to human reason. Only in the final section, when treating the specifically Christian mysteries, are the Scriptures used, for these truths can be known solely by revelation. It should be noted that Thomas is not trying to prove these truths, but rather to demonstrate that they are not contradictory.

Thomas outlines this method explicitly in a shorter treatise, *De rationibus fidei contra Saracenos, Graecos et Armenos ad Cantorem Antiochenum*. He writes:

> First of all I wish to warn you that in disputations with unbelievers about articles of the Faith, you should not try to prove the Faith by necessary reasons . . . Just as our Faith cannot be proved by necessary reasons, because it exceeds the human mind, so because of its truth it cannot be refuted by any necessary reason. So any Christian disputing about the articles of the Faith should not try to prove the Faith, but defend the Faith.'[5]

What is to be observed here is that Thomas is not treating Islam as a corrupt version of Christianity but, implicitly at least, as a separate religion. In fact his writings could be considered the foundation for the position that classifies Islam as a natural religion.

In contrast to Christianity with its mysteries and dogmas, Voltaire exalted Islam as a natural religion accessible to all. He considered Muhammad to have been a great philosopher. Similarly Thomas Carlyle presented Islam as the work of a genius. This is surely reductionist, an over-simplification. Yet some Catholic theologians are also inclined to treat Islam as a natural religion. What they probably mean is that this religion remains, in its approach to God, at the level of what can be known by reason alone. George Anawati has qualified this assertion. For him Islam can be said to be a natural religion in so far as the truths it professes are accessible to reason, and yet, for Muslims at least, it is a revealed religion since they adhere to these truths as being received from God.[6] This would seem to correspond exactly to the Islamic view. Muslims do indeed say that Islam is a natural religion, the religion of *fitra*, that is the religion given by God to humankind at their very creation. The prophets have been sent simply to remind them of this religion. This prophetic mission culminates in Muhammad establishing Islam as the definitive universal religion.

Some positive appreciations of Islam

Not all past opinions of Islam have been so negative. The position adopted by the Catholicos Timothy I in Baghdad (728–823) is well known.[7] Asked explicitly by the Caliph Al-Mahdi to give his opinion about Muhammad, Timothy's reply was 'Muhammad is worthy of praise by all reasonable people, O my Sovereign. He walked in the path of the prophets, and trod in the tracks of the lovers of God'.[8] Timothy's reasons for this affirmation are that Muhammad taught his followers the doctrine of the unity of God, detaching them from idolatry and polytheism; he drove people away from bad works and brought them to good works; he also taught about God, His Word and His Spirit.

Coming to more recent times let me mention Louis Massignon (1883–1962). This distinguished Islamicist, having recovered his own Christian faith through contact with Islam, devoted his life to presenting the true faith of Islam to the West. He will be considered in the chapter on 'Prophets of dialogue', but here it can be noted that he certainly helped to bring about a new vision of Islam in Catholic circles although his own position, as we shall see, was not adopted by the conciliar texts.

The teaching of Vatican II on Islam

Vatican II marks a radical change in attitude of the Church towards other religions, and in particular Islam. Its references to this religion are found in two documents, *Lumen Gentium* and *Nostra Aetate*.

It has often been said that the Second Vatican Council spoke about Muslims but not about Islam. This is true in so far as the council did not intend to give a full description of Islam, or to enter into a detailed discussion of what could be conceived as positive and negative aspects of this religion. The statement in *Lumen Gentium* is very succinct and thus can be quoted in its entirety:

> But the plan of salvation also includes those who acknowledge the Creator, in the first place among whom are the Muslims: these profess to hold the faith of Abraham, and together with us they adore the one, merciful God, mankind's judge on the last day. (LG 16)

In some ways paragraph 3 of *Nostra Aetate* could be considered an extended commentary on these lines, going on to draw out some practical consequences for relations between Christians and Muslims.

It should be noted, nevertheless, that *Nostra Aetate* does speak about religions, and these general affirmations should be held to refer also to Islam. The religions, as has been said, provide answers for the fundamental questions of human existence (cf. NA 1). Nothing that is true and holy in religions is rejected by the Church. Consequently the Church gives encouragement to its members to enter into a dialogue of exchange and collaboration with the members of other religions (cf. NA 2). On this basis then an examination can be made as to what the council says, at least by way of implication, about Islam as a religion.

Islam as a monotheistic religion

It is not surprising that recognition should be given to Muslims' belief in the one God, and thus to the monotheistic nature of Islam. After all, this belief is a fundamental characteristic of Islam, forming the first part of the profession of faith and constituting the main burden of Islamic theology as is shown by its name, *tawhīd* (establishing or defending the oneness of God). What is significant is the additional note in the text of *Lumen Gentium* according to which Muslims *together with us* adore the one, merciful God. Such a statement could be attacked by both Christians and Muslims.

Some Christians do not wish to admit that Christians and Muslims adore the same God. Our God, they say, is essentially different since we believe in a Trinity of persons, which Muslims reject. The council, although its documents are replete with trinitarian references, does not go into this question here. It is content, in both its texts on Islam, to refer to some of the Beautiful Names of God according to the Islamic tradition: the Living, the Subsistent, the Merciful and Almighty, thereby showing that the way Muslims understand God is not unidimensional. The affirmation *together with us* remains; though Christians and Muslims understand God differently, we do not worship different divinities, since God is one. Our religions are monotheistic.

Some Muslims may also object to the statement of *Lumen Gentium*. There are Muslims who attack the Christian claim to monotheism. There is a qur'anic basis for this attack, since the Qur'an contains a reference to a Trinity consisting of God, Jesus and Mary (cf. Q. 5.116). Christians may well reply that the Qur'an is denying a false Trinity; they will still be considered by some Muslims to be *mushrikūn* (associators) or *kāfirūn* (unbelievers). This may be the reason why certain Muslims prefer to keep the term *Allāh*, not translating it into other languages and thus attempting to mark an essential difference in their understanding of God – yet forgetting that Arabic-speaking Christians have no difficulty in giving a trinitarian connotation to the same term. The text of *Lumen Gentium* could be taken as a discreet appeal to Muslims to respect the unity of belief in the one God, despite the difference of understanding, though this was probably not the intention of the authors of the text.

Whatever may be the case, one often sees references to 'the three monotheistic religions', indicating Judaism, Christianity and Islam. That these are monotheistic religions is true, and the texts of Vatican II can be seen to bear witness to this fact. Yet to talk about *the three* monotheistic religions would seem to be an exaggeration. There are in fact other monotheistic religions. One has only to think of the Sikhs. If the three religions of Judaism, Christianity and Islam are to be brought together in a special way, another category has to be found.

The council's texts on Islam speak about belief in God as Creator and Judge. This is also something that Christians and Muslims have in common. It is not to be overlooked since it has practical consequences, providing an opening for dialogue on the common origin and common destiny of humankind. It can also lead to a joint evaluation of the role of human beings as viceregents (*khulafā'*) or stewards of God's creation, with implications for a more equitable distribution and respectful use of the earth's resources. Such a reflection is not going beyond the conciliar basis, since *Nostra Aetate* exhorts Christians and Muslims to work together to 'preserve and promote peace, liberty, social justice and moral values' (NA 3).

Islam as a revealed religion?

Besides talking about the three monotheistic religions, Muslims often use the term 'celestial' as applied to these same religions. They have a celestial origin because they claim to be based on revelation. Do the texts of the council encourage Catholic Christians to accept this terminology? In *Nostra Aetate*, after the reference to Muslims' belief in God who is one and the Creator, there is added 'who has also spoken to men'. As Caspar has written:

> This divine name, the God who reveals, is of capital importance for the religious and supernatural value of the Islamic faith. The Muslim does not merely believe in a God of reason, a 'God of philosophers' as Pascal put it, but in a living God, 'the God of Abraham, Isaac and Jacob', a God who has spoken to men, within their history, by men, the prophets, even if Christians and Muslims have a different idea of the identity and role of these prophets'.[9]

In fact no mention is made of prophets in *Nostra Aetate*. Obviously Christians do not recognize Muhammad as prophet in the way Muslims do – that is, as the final prophet bringing the definitive revelation – otherwise they would become Muslims. On the other hand Muslims have difficulty in accepting any type of qualified prophetic role that Christians would be ready to attribute to Muhammad. Therefore silence was preferred on this point, to the continuing disappointment, it must be admitted, of many Muslims.[10]

The Church's constant teaching is that after Jesus Christ there is no further need of revelation; for as Jesus said, 'Heaven and earth will pass away, but my words will never pass away' (Matt. 24.35). Accordingly Islam is not considered by the Church to be a revealed religion.

Nevertheless the words used in *Nostra Aetate* are significant since they underline the importance of faith for Muslims. It is a faith that flows into life for, as the declaration says, '(Muslims) strive to submit themselves without reserve to the hidden decrees of God'. This is the basic attitude of *islām*, which is by no means a fatalistic submission to a despotic divinity but the response of an adoring servant (*'abd*) to a transcendent God who remains wrapped in mystery.

Islam as a scriptural religion?

Muslims claim that the Qur'an contains the direct words of God, and their Scripture plays a central role in Islamic worship and life. Moreover Islam readily classifies Jews and Christians as 'People of the Book'. Christians, however, may well object to this classification since they consider themselves to be followers of a person, Jesus Christ, and not of a book. The notions of revelation and the role of the Scriptures are not the same in the two religions.

Nor is there the same relationship between Islam and Christianity as there is between Christianity and Judaism. Paragraph 4 of *Nostra Aetate* states:

> The Church of Christ acknowledges that in God's plan of salvation the beginning of her faith and election is to be found in the patriarchs, Moses and the prophets . . . On this account the Church cannot forget that she received the revelation of the Old Testament by way of that people with whom God, in his inexpressible mercy, established the ancient covenant.

Between Jews and Christians there exists therefore, as the same document expresses it, 'a common spiritual heritage'.

The link between the Qur'an and the Christian Scriptures, including the Old Testament, is much more tenuous. There are some references in the Qur'an to biblical elements, but the texts of the previous Scriptures are not retained as such – in fact the accusation is levelled that they have been falsified – and they are certainly not used in Islamic worship.[11]

So although Islam gives a place of primary importance to its own Scripture, the Qur'an, it is not recognized by Christians as a biblical religion. That there should be a difference of appreciation on this point is not surprising. Just as Christians cannot expect Jews to accept the New Testament as the authentic interpretation and fulfilment of their Scriptures, so Muslims should not expect Christians to accept the Qur'an as the authentic interpretation and definitive version of previous Scriptures.

Islam as an Abrahamic religion

Both texts of Vatican II link Islamic faith with Abraham. *Lumen Gentium* says that Muslims 'profess to hold the faith of Abraham'. *Nostra Aetate* states that Muslims submit to God 'just as Abraham submitted himself to God's plan, to whose faith Muslims eagerly link their own'. It must be admitted that these references to Abraham remain somewhat vague. Abraham's faith is recognized, but it is not said how he exemplified this faith. Muslims see Abraham as a champion of monotheism and attribute to him the rebuilding of the Ka'ba, the shrine in Mecca that has become the direction of Muslims' prayer. Christians insist on Abraham's response to God's call to leave his country for a promised land. By both religions Abraham is given as a model of submission to God's mysterious decrees. This spirit of submission was illustrated in a pre-eminent way in his readiness to sacrifice his son, an episode in Abraham's life exalted by Jews, Christians and Muslims, but with a different identification of the victim.

There is silence above all on the question of descent from Abraham. The first version of the text to be introduced into *Lumen Gentium*, following the line advocated by Massignon and his disciples, read: 'The sons of Ishmael, who recognise Abraham as their father and believe in the God of Abraham, are not unconnected with the Revelation made to the patriarchs.' This text also applies to Islam as a revealed religion or a scriptural religion. But in fact the reference to Ishmael was eliminated. Quite apart from the historical question of the descent of the Arabs from Abraham through Ishmael, a question that remains disputed, the silence on this point is quite consistent with the Christian position with regard to Abraham. Physical descent is unimportant; it is faith that counts. Paul, while referring to Abraham as 'the ancestor from whom we are all descended' (Rom. 4.1), declares that 'what fulfils the promise depends on faith, so that it may be a free gift and be available to all of Abraham's descendants, not only those who belong to the law (i.e. the Jews), but also those who belong to the faith of Abraham who is the father of us all' (Rom. 4.16). Elsewhere Paul argues that the promise made to Abraham and to his posterity is actually fulfilled in Christ (cf. Gal. 3.16).

There are profound differences in the way Jews, Christians and Muslims see Abraham, yet there is a common recognition of Abraham as a model of faith and submission. As long as there is a readiness to respect the different interpretations, the figure of Abraham provides common ground for the followers of Judaism, Christianity and Islam, which can be called with some justification 'Abrahamic religions', though this term does not describe them adequately or completely.[12]

This whole examination of what the Second Vatican Council said about Islam can be concluded with the words of R. Caspar:

> The Council affirms positively the minimum which is to be accepted. Islam is in the first rank of non-Christian monotheistic religions. If further studies concerning the theology of religions and in particular regarding the theological status of Islam allow one to say more, the Conciliar texts are not opposed.[13]

Consequences of respect for Islam as a religion

Islam is treated by Vatican II as a religion worthy of respect. This has certain practical consequences, some of which appear in the conciliar texts. There is an explicit recognition of the religious spirit of Muslims. There is mention of certain typical expressions of Islamic religiosity, prayer, alms-deeds and fasting. These are the three central 'pillars' of Islam. The first and fifth pillars, the profession of faith and pilgrimage to Mecca, are passed over, presumably because they are too strongly bound up with what is specifically Islamic.

As already mentioned, the council issued a special declaration, *Dignitatis Humanae*, on religious liberty. *Nostra Aetate*, which exhorts Christians and Muslims to work together to preserve and promote liberty, should be read in conjunction with this document. Its principles apply also to Islam. So freedom of worship is upheld, not only for individuals but also in its corporate expression. This implies the possibility for a community to have its own places of worship. There is also the right to teach about one's religion, thus in schools, but also through publications and through the media in general. In all this the civil authorities have the right to exercise a certain control but not to deny the public practice of religion.

One consequence of treating Islam as a separate religion, and not as a Christian heresy, is to be seen in the question of mixed marriages, codified in the new Canon Law, promulgated in 1983, which takes into account the vision of Vatican II. For such marriages a dispensation is required. A distinction is made between the dispensation of 'mixed religion' for baptized persons belonging to different Churches, and that of 'disparity of cult' for people of different religions. In the latter case certain conditions have to be fulfilled before the dispensation will be granted: there must be sufficient safeguards for the faith of the Christian partner who must also promise to do all in his or her power to have all the children baptized and brought up in the Catholic Church; the other partner must be informed about these promises; 'both parties are to be instructed on the essential ends and properties of marriage, which are not to be excluded by either party' (Can. 1125). In Christian–Muslim marriages this last condition needs to be verified carefully, since the Islamic approach to marriage allows polygamy (though in some countries this permission is restricted by statutory legislation) and also repudiation and divorce.

These considerations about Islamic marriage may explain why the council decided not to refer in *Nostra Aetate* to the moral attitude of Muslims not only at the individual level, but also at family and social levels, as had originally been proposed. They preferred to state simply that Muslims 'highly esteem an upright life'.

The recognition of Islam as a separate religion leads finally to an encouragement to dialogue and cooperation between Christians and Muslims. This is in fact the whole purpose of the declaration *Nostra Aetate*. When the amended document was presented to the council it was explained that it was 'not an exhaustive presentation of the religions and their faults and weaknesses but rather (it was) to point out the connection between peoples and religions which (could) serve as a basis for dialogue and collaboration'.[14] The definitive text contains a reference to 'quarrels and dissensions' and there is an appeal to 'forget the past' and make an effort to achieve mutual understanding. To forget does not mean to ignore, but rather not to let oneself be bound by the past. Pope John Paul II called for a 'purification of memories', a re-examination of the past that includes an acknowledgement of wrongdoing and repentance before God. When faced with questions from the past such as the Crusades and the Islamic conquests, colonialism, the slave trade in which both Christians and Muslims participated, there could be room for a common endeavour to ensure that the burden of history does not poison present relations between Christians and Muslims.

Developments since the Vatican Council

On the reflective level there has been very little change in the position of the Church with regard to Islam. One witness to this is the *Catechism of the Catholic Church* promulgated by Pope John Paul II in 1992. This official compendium of the teaching of the Church merely repeats *Lumen Gentium* 16, giving a reference in a note to *Nostra Aetate* 3.[15] In the teaching of the popes since Vatican II there are perhaps two aspects that have been emphasized which, if not completely new, strike a slightly different tone. The first of these is a reference to common bonds. John Paul II, addressing the Catholic community in Ankara in November 1979, appealed to them 'to recognize and develop the spiritual bonds that unite us'[16] (i.e. Christians and Muslims). Similarly in his discourse to young Muslims in

Casablanca, in August 1985, the Pope stated: 'The Catholic Church regards with respect and recognises the quality of your religious progress, the richness of your spiritual traditions. I believe that we, Christians and Muslims, must recognise with joy the religious values that we have in common, and give thanks to God for them.'[17] There is nothing grudging here, but rather a call to spiritual emulation.

The second note is that of brotherhood. Already Pope Paul VI, speaking to the Islamic communities of Uganda in 1969, had expressed his hope 'that what we hold in common may serve to unite Christians and Muslims ever more closely in true brotherhood'.[18] John Paul II, meeting Muslims in Paris in June 1980, greeted them as 'our brothers in faith in the one God'.[19] He made this even clearer in the Philippines the following year:

> I deliberately *address you as brothers*: that is certainly what we are, because we are members of the same human family . . . but we are especially brothers in God, who created us and whom we are trying to reach, in our own ways, through faith, prayer and worship, through the keeping of his law and through submission to his designs.[20]

This may not seem significant until we remember that traditionally the term 'brother' was reserved for fellow Christians. The World Council of Churches, in its documents, prefers to speak about 'neighbours of other faiths'. The use of the term 'brother' by the popes can be seen as a sign of openness and friendship.

In evaluating progress since Vatican II we should pay attention not only to the words of the popes but also to their actions. Paul VI went as a pilgrim to the Holy Land in 1964 and greeted Muslim leaders there. Ten years later he instituted, within the Secretariat for non-Christians, a special Commission for Religious Relations with Muslims. John Paul II made a point of meeting with Muslims on many of his journeys, and included Muslims in all his invitations to come together to pray for peace. In 1989 he took the unprecedented step of writing a letter to Muslims about the situation in the Lebanon; in 1993 after the Gulf War he himself addressed the annual message to Muslims on the occasion of the end of Ramadan. During the Jubilee of the Year 2000, John Paul II performed his own pilgrimage to the Holy Land, where he not only visited places connected with the life, death and resurrection of Jesus Christ, but went also to the Western Wall and to the Dome of the Rock, and he made a point of meeting with Jewish and Muslim religious leaders. The following year he completed his pilgrimage by following in the footsteps of Moses – taking the opportunity of visiting al-Azhar in Cairo – and in those of St Paul – which provided the occasion for entering the mosque of the Umayyads in Damascus. Later events did not alter the Pope's attitude of respect for authentic Islam.

Conclusion

Much more could be said about the practical development of relations between Christians and Muslims in the years since the Second Vatican Council. A complete survey would need to take into account the increase in diplomatic relations established between the Holy See and countries with Muslim majorities. It would have to record the work done by the Pontifical Council for Interreligious Dialogue both in the field of reflection and in actual encounters with Muslims. It would also take note of the academic agreements that have brought about cooperation between Catholic and Islamic universities. It would list the various publications on Christian–Muslim relations coming from Catholic Church authorities in different parts of the world and the actions they have undertaken to put relations with Muslims on a sound footing. In all of this it can be noted that the texts on Islam officially proclaimed by Vatican II remain not only a constant point of reference but also a source of inspiration.

9

Muslims in Europe:
A religious and cultural challenge
to the Church

Diverse communities

The exact number of Muslims in Europe is not known. There is no census giving accurate statistics, and indeed in many countries religious affiliation is not included in the census form. A report issued several years ago by the Islam in Europe Committee of the European Conference of Churches (KEK) and the Council of Episcopal Conferences of Europe (CCEE) put the figure at around 20–24 million for the whole of Europe including the Russian Federation.

It should be noted that there is some unevenness in distribution. In Western Europe the greatest number of Muslims are to be found in France (above 4,000,000), followed by Germany (about 3,500,000) and then the UK (perhaps 2,000,000). The Benelux countries have fewer Muslims in absolute numbers, but a higher proportion of the whole population. Portugal, Spain and Italy have smaller size communities in relation to their respective populations. Of course statistics often reflect only official residents, and so a large number of illegal immigrants would have to be added to obtain the total number.

Very often when Islam is mentioned it is thought of as a recent phenomenon in Europe, but there are communities that have a long history behind them. In the first half of the fourteenth century the Muslim Tartars of the Golden Horde, who had already penetrated into Russia, began invading Poland and established themselves on the borders of Ukraine. They even reached Finland. Similarly the Ottomans, who seem to have developed from a nomadic group in Asia Minor, crossed into Europe in 1357. They profited by the disunity of the Balkan Slavs, and the religious division between Orthodox and Catholics, to overrun a large part of the region. The

Muslim communities in this area thus have a history that goes back six centuries, and this holds good also for Bulgaria. Romania has a small Muslim population, a mixture of Tartars and Turks, whose origins go back to the same period.

This situation of a plurisecular Islamic presence is to be contrasted with Western Europe where it is only the last century that saw the introduction of Muslim communities. Immigration began after the First World War and intensified after the Second. The economic recovery called for an increased labour force. More recently political upheavals in different countries or economic difficulties have brought about new waves of immigrants, among whom are many Muslims. A number of these only transit through European countries on their way to North America, but others settle and augment the already existing Muslim communities.

A distinctive feature of the Muslim presence in Europe is the variety of its origins. This to a certain degree reflects the varying colonial experience of Western powers. Thus in France North Africans predominate, with those of Algerian origin being the most numerous on account of the closer ties between Algeria and France. Nevertheless there are also Muslims from West Africa (Mali, Senegal) and from the Comores, as well as a growing number of Turks. In the UK most Muslims trace their origins to the Indian subcontinent, although the Yemeni community, which is perhaps the oldest, should not be forgotten, nor the Turkish Cypriots and the many Arabs who live in London. The Netherlands has Muslims from its former colonies, particularly Surinam, and these have been joined by North Africans, mainly Moroccans, and some Turks. The latter two groups are found in Belgium and Luxembourg. In Spain too Moroccans predominate, but there are also considerable numbers from the Middle East. Italy has Eritreans and Somalis from its former colonies, but has also Moroccans, Tunisians and Egyptians, West Africans, and, more recently, immigrants from Albania.

It is significant that many of these Muslims are full citizens of the countries in which they reside. To these citizens of foreign extraction, or the second and third generation descendants, should be added converts to Islam. These would be statistically few, but their influence often goes beyond their numbers.

This almost bewildering variety in the European Muslim mosaic means that there is no single cultural identity. Islam brings certain

123

constant features, but the different underlying cultural substrata still remain influential. It will be necessary to take this into account when considering the cultural challenge to the Church of the Muslim presence in Europe.

In addition to the difference of origins attention must be called to the diversity of social situations. Whereas in the more ancient communities, for instance in the countries of ex-Yugoslavia, many Muslims are engaged in farming, the majority in Western Europe belong to the working class. Many are engaged in precarious employment, and unemployment, especially among young Muslims, is high. Yet in many places Muslims have established their own trades and businesses. They have opened shops and set up their own cafés and restaurants. There are also professionals, doctors, teachers and journalists. As the younger generations benefit by higher education, so the number of Muslims belonging to the professional ranks will increase. This also is bound to have its effect on cultural and religious relations between Christians and Muslims.

The contribution of Islam to European culture

The above outline has not included the earlier presence of Muslims in Western Europe. Very soon after its birth Islam, expanding fast, established itself in Spain, in Sicily, and to a lesser extent in Southern Italy. This presence lasted, in Sicily, until the end of the eleventh century, while in Spain the *Reconquista* was completed only at the end of the fifteenth century. Though the physical presence of Muslims came to an end, the contribution of Islam to European culture was not wiped out.

The role of the Arabs in transmitting Greek science to the Western world is well known. The development of the natural sciences and medicine, the mathematical sciences, astronomy and optics all owe much to the knowledge passed on by the Arabs and enriched by their own investigations and reflections. Their influence was felt too in the field of philosophy and thus also in that of theology, as can be seen in the work of Thomas Aquinas, despite the difficulties he ran into for using Aristotelian texts handed down by 'heretic' Muslims.

On another level Arab-Islamic influence can be seen in art and architecture, in literature (on the *Divina Commedia,* to give a well-known example), in music and even in the culinary art. The languages of Western Europe are replete with loan words from this Arab-Islamic cultural milieu. Although the Renaissance, with its glorification of all things classical, encouraged a return to the Greek originals, thus bypassing the translations and commentaries handed down by the Arabs, in the Post-Renaissance period there was a renewal of interest in the Arab world. As travels increased, so did a taste for the exotic, as can be seen in the success of the *Arabian Nights* and later in the poetry of Goethe.

The first European Synod, a meeting of Catholic bishops from the different countries of Europe, held in 1991, recognized the contribution of Islam to the making of Europe. When the question of the Christian roots of European culture was raised, attention was drawn to the presence of both Jewish and Muslim communities. The position paper presented by Cardinal Ruini took into account the various contributions to European culture, and saw the Christian faith as the crucible melding these together. The final document endorsed this view:

> European culture has drawn its force for growth from a multitude of sources. Greek finesse, Romanità, the acquisitions contributed by Latins, Celts, people of Germanic stock, Slavs, Hungaro-Finns, Hebrew culture and the influence of Islam have (all) played their role in the development of this complex whole. Yet no one can deny the decisive contribution of the Christian faith as the radical and permanent foundation of Europe.   (cited in Goncalves 1992, pp. 33–4)

The Synod was considering the past, but it may perhaps be expected, since cultures are never static, that the various communities present in Europe, including the Muslim communities, will bring their influence to bear on the evolving culture of Europe.

The social impact of Islam

There are other religious communities existing in Europe, Buddhists in France, for instance, or Hindus and Sikhs in the UK. One hears relatively little about these, whereas the presence of Muslims provokes much more comment. This is surely not merely on account of their far greater number. It stems from their attitude towards society. Whereas for the other religions it would appear to be sufficient that the communities enjoy the liberty of having their own places of worship, leaving behaviour as a private or family matter, for Islam the whole of life is to be shaped by obedience to the law of God. This means that Islam tends to have a greater impact on society. In Europe, where Muslims constitute minorities, the innate tendency of Islam to express itself socially may bring about tensions.

Before examining the demands that Muslims make, it would be useful to say a word about the legal status of Muslims in Europe. This differs from country to country. In Western Europe, Belgium was the first country to give official recognition to Islam, in 1974. Austria followed in 1979, although there was a legislative basis dating back to the Austro-Hungarian Empire. In Germany, the state maintains a position of neutrality towards religions. The different religious bodies can become 'publicly recognized corporations' (*Körperschaft offentlichen Rechts*). Once this is done the religion qualifies for an allocation of the special tax that the state collects. Islam has not yet succeeded in obtaining this recognition on account of its lack of internal unity. A similar situation obtains in the Netherlands where the 'system of pillars' (*verzuiling*) is applied. Islam is not recognized as a 'pillar' alongside the Catholic Church, the Reformed Church, the re-reformed communities and secular humanism, essentially for the same reason as in Germany. In Italy too Muslims have not yet succeeded in establishing an official agreement (*intesa*) with the state, which would enable them to benefit from the 8/1000 (0.8 per cent) of income tax which can be designated for a specific religious community. In the UK, where the Church of England (Anglican) is established in England, while the Presbyterian Church is established in Scotland, Islam is treated as any other non-established religious community. Muslim organizations can register as charities, thus acquiring tax exemption.

In each country there are Muslims of different origins, backgrounds and tendencies. Agreement among them is difficult, so no central Muslim organization has evolved. Yet governments, for the sake of law and order, naturally wish to be able to deal with recognized community leaders. Their absence has in some cases led the state to intervene.

In Belgium, for example, the government recognized the Islamic Cultural Centre in Brussels as the representative body for Muslims in the country. Since this centre depended on foreign embassies, the government decision was contested by a number of Muslims. The government was eventually led to create a 'Committee of Wise Persons', which evolved into a 'Constitutive Council'. This Council elected an executive body of 17 members, which has the authority to appoint teachers of religion and also spiritual assistants for hospitals and prisons. In this way the Belgian government has a channel through which to transmit financial assistance, while exercising a certain amount of control.

In France, too, the government strongly desired to establish a National Representation of Muslims, which would thus constitute a valid interlocutor. The difficulty was to know how such a body could be determined. The solution adopted was to concentrate on the organization of Islamic worship, and to base the selection of the representative body on mosques and mosque communities. This solution has been implemented, not without difficulties. Elections have been held and the Muslim Council has come into existence. It should be remembered, however, that only a maximum of 10 per cent of Muslims in France attend the mosque and were thus eligible to vote. The body is therefore hardly representative of all Muslims in the country.

Demands Muslims make of society

In the first years of the migrations, in the 1950s, religion was not the central concern of Muslims. These were generally young men looking for employment. Their primary need was to learn the language of the new country in which they found themselves. Decent accommodation was another concern, since they were often housed in special huts for *Gastarbeiter* (guest workers) or in derelict buildings earmarked for demolition. It was their material needs that dominated their attention.

It was only when these workers were able to have their wives and children join them that religious needs began to be felt. Premises of varying nature, garages or rooms in dwellings, were transformed into prayer rooms. The desire soon developed for purpose-built mosques, which could serve not only as houses of prayer but also as centres for education and social concerns. Often this natural development has met with obstacles. Local authorities have shown tardiness in granting the necessary planning permission, with bureaucratic delays often masking opposition. This may sometimes have been based on religious prejudice, but in other cases the extra-liturgical activities (Qur'an schools, clubs) have led to the mosques being suspected, sometimes as possible centres for the support of fundamentalist views or even terrorist movements.

Christian communities may be called upon here to play a mediating role. A religious community has, after all, the right to have its own places of worship. On occasions contacts with local authorities can be facilitated. Above all an effort can be made to create a favourable climate of public opinion, which will make the incoming religious community welcome in the neighbourhood. Thus, when the Rome Mosque was inaugurated in June 1995, Pope John Paul II, speaking at the General Audience that day, welcomed this new place of worship in the city, although he also mentioned that Christian communities throughout the world should enjoy the same religious freedom.

Muslims are not obliged to go to the mosque in order to perform their ritual prayer. Even the Friday prayer is an obligation incumbent on the community rather than the individual. A Muslim who prays five times a day would find it difficult to go to the mosque on each occasion, but in any case this is by no means necessary. The ritual prayer can be performed anywhere so long as it is possible to perform the ablutions beforehand and to create a sacred space by means of a carpet or its equivalent. Accordingly some Muslims request the possibility of performing their prayers during work hours. They point out that the time required is short, the equivalent of a break for a smoke. Sometimes such demands are found embarrassing; in other cases they can be accommodated without difficulty.

Some Muslims may also request special consideration during the month of Ramadan. In majority Muslim countries the month of fasting brings with it a change in the rhythm of life, whereas elsewhere a compromise has to be found between the demands of the fast, and the concomitant change in mealtimes, and the demands of work. There are also Muslims who would request that that their main feast days, 'Id al-Adhā (the Feast of the Sacrifice) and 'Id al-Fitr (the breaking of the Fast at the end of Ramadan) should be declared holidays, at least for Muslims.

Abstinence from alcoholic drinks and from pork does not usually present any great difficulty to Muslims living in a predominantly non-Muslim society. It may, of course, produce a degree of separation, particularly in those milieux where sociability is always connected with the consumption of alcohol. Muslims may have to make special efforts to avoid the impression of being unsociable.

The situation is rather more complicated with regard to meat in general. The basic requirement of Islam is that there should be no consumption of meat of an animal sacrificed to a divinity other than God. On this basis Islamic law has stipulated that animals should be ritually slaughtered in the name of God, with the head turned in the direction of Mecca, and the blood allowed to flow. While Muslims were present in a country on a temporary basis, they could avail themselves of the permission to buy meat from butchers without being concerned whether it was *halāl* or not. Where communities have been established, then the demand comes for meat from animals that have been ritually slaughtered. Here there can be difficulties with civil authorities, for the public abattoirs do not usually satisfy Islamic requirements. If Muslim communities take the matter into their own hands and start private slaughtering, for instance at the time of 'Id al-Adhā, this can raise serious health concerns. There can also be a type of culture clash, between Muslims adhering to a religious view of killing animals, and the supporters of 'animal rights'. In Sweden there has been a serious conflict between some Muslims and the civil authorities who hold the Muslim method of slaughtering to be completely barbarous.

It is above all in the field of education that Muslim communities express their concern. Many parents desire for their children an environment which is respectful of religion and which inculcates moral values. There is often considerable dissatisfaction with state schools, giving rise to the demand for the establishment of Muslim schools. A special need is felt with regard to girls, since mixed education is refused by some parents, if not entirely at least for certain activities, such as sport and swimming. Dress requirements for girls (and occasionally for boys who wish to grow beards in accordance with the tradition of the Prophet) can, as is well known, create difficulties. Usually these can be overcome as long as the distinctive manner of dressing is not motivated by pure ostentation or a desire to proselytize.

Educational systems differ from country to country, so that in some places it is possible for Muslims to open schools that will benefit from state subsidies, whereas elsewhere all such schools would have to be supported by private means. Even in the first case local authorities do not always give the necessary authorization, fearing

129

that the establishment of confessional schools would prevent the integration of Muslims into society.

In the absence of their own schools, a significant number of Muslim parents are turning to Christian educational establishments. They find the ethos of the Christian school appealing. Also in some countries there are still Catholic schools for girls. In certain urban areas over 50 per cent of the children in Catholic schools are Muslims. This obviously is a great challenge to those responsible for these schools, for respect has to be shown to these pupils while at the same time preserving the Catholic character of the establishment.

A final demand made by Muslim communities is to have their own cemeteries, or at least a special section in public cemeteries, in which to bury their dead. The reason for this is that Islamic tradition lays down that the graves should be oriented towards Mecca, and this is not always possible in municipal cemeteries. It would seem that much progress is being made in this respect. This demand is significant since it is a sign of the permanence of Muslim communities in their country of adoption. In the early years it was natural that the remains of a deceased person would be returned to the country of origin. Now questions of the expense of such transport, but also the presence of the family in the country of residence, strengthen the desire for burial in that country.

The outward expressions of Muslim piety, and the demands referred to, may create a sense of unease among the non-Muslim majority, and a feeling that the real purpose behind certain requests could be more to emphasize the Muslim presence than to satisfy a spiritual need. Yet Muslims' readiness to give public witness to their faith can provide a challenge to Christian individualism.

Challenges to Muslims in Europe

For those Muslim communities that are of more recent origin in European countries there is a challenge to show that they fully belong to the societies in which they are inserted. It may be said that while the first generation of Muslims in Western Europe were 'immigrants' and kept up the 'myth of return', the second and third generations have a very different outlook. They do not feel that they have to justify their existence. What they want is to be at the same time wholly Muslim and wholly British, or French or German. An example of this changed mentality is found in the *Islamic Charter* drawn up by the Central Council of Muslims in Germany (ZMD). This body by no means represents the totality of the Muslims in Germany, but it is one of the three leading Muslim umbrella organizations. The preamble to the Charter contains the following statement:

> The Muslims living in Germany, not only the 500,000 of German nationality, now feel at home there. In general they no longer consider themselves as immigrants in a guest country but as German citizens, or prospective ones.
>
> As an important minority in this country, Muslims are under the obligation to integrate themselves into German society, with an open mind, and to enter into dialogue about their faith and religious practices. In turn, the majority in the country is entitled to learn the position Muslims take towards basic issues like the Federal Constitution, the rule of law, democracy, pluralism, and human rights.
>
> (Troll 2002)

This introduces fundamental articles such as the following:

11. Whether German citizens or not, the Muslims represented by the Central Council (ZMD) accept the basic legal order of the Federal Republic of Germany as guaranteed by its Constitution, providing for the rule of law, division of power, and democracy, including a multi-party system, universal suffrage and eligibility, and freedom of religion. Therefore they have accepted as well everybody's right to change his religion, to have another religion, or none at all. The Qur'an forbids any compulsion or coercion in matters of faith.

13. There is no contradiction between the divine rights of the individual, anchored in the Qur'an, and the core rights as embodied in Western human rights declarations. We, too, support the intended protection of individuals against an abuse of state power. Islamic law demands equal treatment of what is identical and permits unequal treatment of what is not identical. The command of Islamic law to observe the local legal order includes the acceptance of the German statutes governing inheritance, and civil as well as criminal procedures. (Troll 2002)

Such articles, far-reaching in their general tenor, would need to be interpreted with regard to particular issues. The reference to German statutes governing inheritance would suggest that these would be followed rather than the stipulations of the Qur'an in this matter.

The same would hold good, a fortiori, with regard to accepting monogamous marriage, since the possibility of polygamy is based on a Qur'anic permission not an obligation. On the other hand, the mention of allowing unequal treatment of what is not identical might be applied to Muslim women who could still be prevented by their religious authorities from marrying non-Muslims.

Insertion into European society brings with it new demands in Islamic leadership. The desire of the state to have a unified interlocutor has brought about the creation of national councils and the need for greater cooperation among the different components of the Muslim community. New demands are made on the communities. In certain countries, Austria, Belgium and Germany, for instance, provisions exist for Islamic religion classes to be taught in schools, and funding is available for this. Yet there is often a lack of qualified teachers. The communities will have to see that enough people are prepared to teach religion according to the guidelines laid down by the educational authorities.

Muslim communities are also being called upon to provide chaplains in universities and other institutes of higher learning, in hospitals and prisons, and in the armed forces. This is a type of service for which traditional imams are not prepared since it is an entirely new role. Most imams are still 'imported' from the countries of origin of the various Muslim communities. They are not necessarily well adapted to the task that awaits them. There is an obvious need to reinforce or create establishments *in* Europe for the training of imams *for* Europe.

The response of the Church

European society, as we know, is ethnically, culturally and religiously plural. In every part of the continent people of different backgrounds are necessarily coming into contact. This can be seen as a threat, giving rise to a spirit of exclusion; or it can be seen as an opportunity, a source of enrichment. For Christians the parable of the Good Samaritan can be taken as a guide. Jesus teaches that we should not so much expect others to be neighbours to us, but rather that we should strive to be neighbours to them. This means taking initiatives, reaching out to people, trying to find ways to bring people together.

A number of Episcopal Conferences have commissions for inter-religious dialogue (often combined with ecumenism), and some have created or support particular institutions for relations with Muslims. Perhaps the oldest among such institutions is the Secrétariat pour les Relations avec l'Islam (SRI) set up by the French hierarchy in 1973. Nevertheless, the development of Muslim communities in Europe calls for expansion of the present structures.

Christian communities are looking for help in order to understand the Muslims whom they encounter. They wish to be able to call on experts who can enlighten them on various pastoral issues such as mixed marriages, prayer with Muslims and how to respond to Muslims who enquire about the Christian faith. There is therefore a need for formation of these experts if the necessary pastoral guidance is to be provided. Existing institutions, and those which should be created, need qualified personnel. At a time when there is a shortage of vocations to the priesthood, it is obvious that there is a role here for the laity. Indeed Christian–Muslim relations can be seen as an appropriate field for collaborative ministry. Of course the promotion of lay experts, both men and women, at the service of the Christian community in this field will require adequate financial investment.

An area in which such experts will be able to contribute is that of adult education. As we have seen, many Catholics wish to learn more about Islam, but courses on Islamics should be accompanied by reflection on the Christian faith. Another field is that of research. There is a constant need to keep abreast of the developments in the different Muslim communities, as well as to be aware of social, economic and legal factors which influence community relations. It would be useful to engage with Muslims in a reflection on European culture, on common values, and on relations between the continent of Europe and countries with a Muslim majority. The question of the right to religious liberty and its concrete application could be included in the topics for common reflection.

The role of the clergy remains vital. Today's pastors need to be acquainted with the Church's teaching on dialogue and proclamation, to have some knowledge of other religions and in particular of Islam, and to have developed the right attitudes conducive to fruitful encounter. All this indicates the need for adequate formation, both theoretical and practical, at the seminary level, and perhaps for on-going reflection at the level of deanery meetings or similar structures.

Openness to collaboration

There is an opportunity here for ecumenical cooperation. Such co-operation already exists, for instance at the level of the Islam in Europe Committee of the KEK and CCEE, to which reference was made at the beginning of this chapter. There are also regional bodies, such as the Churches' Commission for Interfaith Relations of Churches Together in Britain and Ireland, whose pastoral reflections on relations with Muslims can be a useful source for Catholic communities. There are also individual Churches, such as the Evangelische Kirche Deutschland or the Eglise Réformée in France, which have issued statements or published materials on Christian–Muslim relations. An ecumenical reflection on cultural development in Europe, in the light of the Islamic presence, could be very useful.

Increased cooperation with Muslim institutions could also be envisaged. Areas in which reflection would be useful are, for instance, the role of religion in society, the contribution of religions to creating a culture of dialogue and peace, the appropriate way to combat terrorism. There could also be joint reflection on cultural and political relations between Europe and other areas of the world, the role of Europe in the search for a solution to the Israeli–Palestinian conflict, the need to safeguard the rights of religious minorities. Closer to home, consultations could be organized on the formation of imams and clergy, the teaching of religion in schools, and on value education in general.

10

Dialogue and proclamation in the perspective of Christian–Muslim relations

The document *Dialogue and Proclamation* of 1991, already referred to several times, remains at a general level. It does not deal specifically with any one religion. It recognizes nevertheless the need for more particularized approaches: 'It is also important that specific studies on the relationship between dialogue and proclamation be undertaken, taking into account each religion within its geographical area and sociocultural context' (DP 88). In the present chapter I will try to respond to this need by reading this document in the light of relations with Muslims. My reflections will still remain general, however, since it is not possible to pay attention to all the different geographical and cultural contexts.

In showing a need for reflection on dialogue and proclamation DP first calls attention to 'a new awareness of the fact of religious plurality' (DP 4a). The same paragraph speaks about the 'clear evidence of revival' of certain religions. Both these observations apply to Islam. In the last decades the movement of populations has brought large numbers of Muslims into societies that are Christian, at least by tradition. Moreover many of the Muslims who have come to stay in Western societies are claiming the right to practise their religion to the full. This situation calls for renewed reflection on relations between Christians and Muslims.

The document speaks also about hesitation as regards to dialogue (DP 4b), perhaps because of the problems it raises (DP 4c). It could be noted that these hesitations have existed also among Muslims, but are gradually being overcome.[1]

The World Day of Prayer for Peace, in Assisi, 27 October 1986, was seen as having given a great impetus to interreligious relations (DP 5). It is true that there were not many Muslims present at that event.

On subsequent occasions, however, such as the Prayer for Peace in Europe, and especially in the Balkans, held in January 1993, and the Day of Prayer for Peace in the World, on 24 January 2002, Muslims responded much more readily to the invitation. This could be taken as a sign of greater confidence on their part and also of a recognition that they need to engage in dialogue with Christians and others.

All these factors could point to the utility of giving greater consideration to dialogue and proclamation within the context of Christian–Muslim relations.

A Christian approach to Islam

The section of DP dedicated to interreligious dialogue starts with important reflections of a theological nature. It summarizes the teaching of the Second Vatican Council and of the more recent official teaching of the Catholic Church, and then suggests some elements for discernment in the attitude to take towards the religions. The subheading at paragraph 14 reads 'Religious traditions are viewed positively'. This could be illustrated by what the council has to say about Islam.[2] I have already discussed this in a previous chapter (pp. 112–19).

After outlining the council's positive attitude towards religions, DP also acknowledges that the council stresses that the missionary activity of the Church is still necessary (DP 18). This has to be kept in mind also in relation to Muslims. The Church, in announcing Jesus Christ, and in proffering an invitation to join the community of believers in Jesus Christ, cannot exclude any category of persons. Yet this proclamation is to be accomplished in accordance with the principle of religious liberty as expressed in the Declaration *Dignitatis Humanae*. Here again there is an opportunity for dialogue, examining the concept and practice of both proclamation of the gospel and *da'wa* (the call to Islam), a dialogue which may not always be easy but which can be fruitful.[3]

Since the Vatican Council there has been little development in the official teaching of the Church about Islam, yet the popes have constantly encouraged an assimilation of the council's vision. This can be seen from the many addresses concerned with Christian–Muslim dialogue, but also from their own practical example. Paul VI, when visiting Uganda in 1969, celebrated Mass in Namugongo, the place where many of the young Martyrs of Uganda were burned to death.

Later, addressing the Islamic communities of Uganda, he stated: 'In recalling the Catholic and Anglican Martyrs, We gladly recall also those confessors of the Muslim faith who were the first to suffer death, in the year 1848, for refusing to transgress the precepts of their religion.'[4] It is interesting to notice this acceptance of a 'unity of witness' which anticipates, and in some measure even goes beyond, the 'ecumenism of martyrdom' which John Paul II emphasized.

The impact of Assisi 1986 has already been mentioned. The visit of John Paul II to al-Azhar, Cairo, 24 February 2000, and the warm reception he received there, led to this day being commemorated annually. The visit to the Umayyad Mosque in Damascus in the spring of 2001 was also of considerable significance, the first time a Sovereign Pontiff had entered a mosque for an official event. Important also was the invitation to the Synod for Lebanon in 1995 of representatives of the different Muslim communities, Sunni, Shi'ite and Druze, to attend as official observers.

DP had already drawn attention to the universal action of the Spirit (DP 17). John Paul II referred to this in a General Audience on 9 September 1998:

> It must be kept in mind that every quest of the human spirit for truth and goodness, and in the last analysis for God, is inspired by the Holy Spirit. The various religions arose precisely from this primordial human openness to God. At their origins we often find founders who, with the help of God's Spirit, achieved a deeper religious experience. Handed on to others, this experience took form in the doctrines, rites and precepts of the various religions.[5]

Though this statement remains general, it is significant since it would appear to be the first reference in official Church teaching to the role of founders of religions. Whether and to what extent it applies to Muhammad would remain to be investigated.

The fact that the presence of God can be seen in other religious traditions does not mean that everything in them is good. They have their limitations. Consequently,

> an open and positive approach to other religious traditions cannot overlook the contradictions which may exist between them and Christian revelation. It must, where necessary, recognise that there is incompatibility between some fundamental elements of the Christian religion and some aspects of such traditions. (DP 31)

Applying this to Islam, one would have to point to doctrinal differences, regarding the Trinity, the divinity of Christ, the death of Jesus on the cross and the redemptive value of his passion, death and resurrection, not to mention the different understanding of the relationship between human beings and God. There are also other points of contrast, for instance certain qur'anic prescriptions which would imply discrimination against women, or a different concept of religious liberty. Dialogue with Muslims cannot ignore such differences. It cannot be mere accommodation but must include a critical stance. Yet the challenge is not just one way: 'Christians too must allow themselves to be questioned. Notwithstanding the fullness of God's revelation in Jesus Christ, the way Christians sometimes understand their religion and practise it may be in need of purification' (DP 32).

Many Christians living among Muslims have experienced the purifying effect of contact with Islam. It is as if their faith is being scoured of accretions and brought back to its essential content. There can be a greater appreciation of the divine transcendence, but also of that great love which leads God to become man. There is less of a tendency to take the incarnation for granted. Christians can be challenged too by the firmness of faith of Muslims and their readiness to express their faith in public. Though he did not mention Islam by name, John Paul II probably had Muslims in mind when he wrote:

> It sometimes happens that the firm belief of the followers of non-Christian religions – a belief that is also an effect of the Spirit of truth operating outside the visible confines of the Mystical Body – can make Christians ashamed at being often themselves disposed to doubt concerning the truths revealed by God and proclaimed by the Church, and prone to relax moral principles and open the way to ethical permissiveness. (RH 6)

Nor did the Pope hesitate to suggest, in a talk to the parish priests of Rome at the beginning of Lent one year, that Muslims tend to take fasting more seriously than Christians.

Conversion

This section of DP ends with some reflections on the dialogue of salvation. It is because God has been in dialogue with humankind that the Church, and individual Christians, must be in dialogue with all (DP

38). So the aim of dialogue is not merely mutual understanding and friendly relations (DP 39). These should not be minimized, and remain a legitimate goal of dialogue. This is particularly so where Christian–Muslim relations are concerned, since these are so often fraught with tension. One of the tasks of dialogue will be to try to discover the causes of the tension, which quite often are not religious but rather economic, social and political, and then to build up confidence in order to remedy the situation.

Dialogue, however, can go deeper, leading to a strengthening of each one's religious commitment and a more generous response to God's personal call. This should not be understood as 'helping Muslims to be better Muslims'. It is rather an encouragement to a process of conversion to God. Of this a previous document had spoken:

> In biblical language, and that of the Christian tradition, conversion is the humble and penitent return of the heart to God in the desire to submit one's life more generously to him. All persons are constantly called to this conversion.   (DM 37)

It must be said that within the Islamic tradition there is a wealth of spiritual writings which emphasize this constant process of conversion, in the search for sincerity, in the elimination of anything that might threaten single-minded devotion to God. In fact the need for ongoing conversion could itself be a fruitful theme for Christian–Muslim dialogue.

The document just quoted continues, nevertheless, 'In the course of this process, the decision may be made to leave one's previous spiritual or religious situation in order to direct oneself toward another' (DM 37). It is important to keep open this possibility of conversion understood in this other sense as a change of religious allegiance. This is not something that Islam readily accepts. Apostasy (*ridda*), defined as 'an act of rejection of faith committed by a Muslim whose Islam has been affirmed without any coercion', has serious legal consequences such as dissolving a marriage or annulling inheritance rights, and can even put the life of the convert from Islam in danger.[6] Of course the Catholic Church does not acquiesce easily to departure from the Church, and applies the canonical sanction of excommunication to the apostate, i.e. to one who totally repudiates the Christian faith (Can. 751, 1364). Yet this does not entail civil consequences. The right to change one's religion, as part of the right to religious liberty, is one of the thorny questions that will keep returning in conversations between Christians and Muslims.

The forms of dialogue

The various forms of dialogue – dialogue of life, of action, of discourse and of religious experience (DP 42) – all exist in Christian–Muslim relations. It should perhaps be said that theological dialogue is difficult, given the fundamental differences in belief which have already been mentioned. There is a danger of defending one's own position and attacking that of the other by any means. Theological dialogue between Christians and Muslims will only be fruitful if it aims at clarification rather than refutation, and includes a real attempt to appreciate the logic of the other's position. In fact, however, formal dialogue between Christians and Muslims will often be concerned with social questions, such as the use of the earth's resources, the role of women in society, religious education, to mention only some of the topics discussed in colloquia in which the Pontifical Council for Interreligious Dialogue has been involved.

There is indeed a need 'to join together in trying to solve the great problems facing society and the world' (DP 44). There are examples of common action, such as a joining of forces to defend family values during the 1994 UN Cairo Conference on Population and Development. There have been joint statements condemning terrorism, put out by the Islamic–Catholic Liaison Committee and by the Joint Committee of Al-Azhar and the PCID, following the events of September 11, 2001. There is still room for more cooperation to promote integral development, social justice and human liberation.

A further context calling for interreligious cooperation is that of culture (DP 45). There is much to be done in the field of education, particularly since the increased religious plurality in society presents new challenges. There is a need to create a culture of dialogue, in order to prevent what might be the self-fulfilling prophecy of the 'clash of civilizations'. It is interesting to note that it was an Islamic country, Iran, that persuaded the United Nations to declare 2001 to be the Year of Dialogue among Civilizations.

Here it might be possible to point to something missing from the document *Dialogue and Proclamation*. When dealing with the different forms of dialogue the impression is given that it is always a question of *bilateral* dialogue, Buddhist–Christian, Hindu–Christian, Jewish–Christian, Muslim–Christian, though this is not said explicitly. There could have been some mention of *trilateral* and *multilateral* dialogue. Trilateral dialogue, Jews–Christians–Muslims, or the dialogue of the Abrahamic faiths, is not new, but is perhaps growing. The political realities of the Middle East render this type of dialogue difficult, but also underline how necessary it is, since understanding has to be created and respect and confidence restored. Because of the antagonisms that can be aroused in bilateral or trilateral dialogue, multilateral dialogue can prove useful by helping to soften the points of conflict. Here too there is a growth of interreligious organizations, responding to a felt need in today's society.

Dispositions for dialogue

All the dispositions for dialogue indicated by DP (47–9) apply to relations with Muslims. A balanced attitude is required. On the one hand there is the need to overcome prejudices: that Islam is fatalistic, legalistic, morally lax, fanatical; that it is opposed to change, a religion of fear;[7] or that all Muslims are terrorists. Muslims are very sensitive to what they term *Islamophobia*. On the other hand ingenuousness is to be avoided. As has been said above, some aspects of Islam are incompatible with Christianity. Moreover there are radical elements in Muslim societies, from which Muslims themselves suffer, and these should not be ignored.

A further condition for fruitful dialogue is religious conviction. Christians entering into dialogue with Muslims should not be afraid to give witness to their faith in Jesus Christ. Dialogue leads to mutual witness, but this cannot come about if one of the partners is unwilling to express their own convictions. Of course, as Peter says, this witness needs to be given in the right manner: 'have your answer ready for people who ask you for the reason for the hope that you all have. But give it with courtesy and respect and with a clear conscience' (1 Pet. 3.15–16).

The third condition is openness to truth. Because of their belief in Jesus Christ as the Son of God, Lord and Saviour of the whole of humankind, Christians may be inclined towards a sense of superiority. They should remember that

141

the fullness of truth received in Jesus Christ does not give individual Christians the guarantee that they have grasped that truth. In the last analysis truth is not a thing we possess, but a person by whom we must allow ourselves to be possessed. (DP 49)

It can be useful to try to convey this conviction to Muslims. They like to classify Christians as 'People of the Book', yet, as our name implies, we are followers of a person, Jesus Christ, who is the way, the truth and the life. Now Muslims too can develop a sense of superiority, based on their conviction that to them the final revelation has been given. Perhaps they would need to be encouraged to accept the radical meaning of their frequent invocation *Allāhu akbar*, God is always greater than anything we can ever conceive, and it is he who is calling us to himself. That is why dialogue can be described as a process in which we 'walk together toward truth' (DM 13).

Obstacles

DP is a realistic document and has no hesitation in mentioning difficulties that can arise in dialogue (DP 51–4). It is not necessary to deal at length with all these, but some have particular relevance to Christian–Muslim relations. There is mention of sociopolitical factors. These could include majority–minority relations. It is difficult to engage in dialogue if being in a minority situation leads to the adoption of a defensive attitude. Such a difficulty can only be overcome by ensuring freedom and respect for each person's rights. There is also mention of burdens of the past. These would include the Crusades and colonialism, but also the practice of slavery, which has aroused negative feelings towards Islam, especially among many peoples of Africa. The Declaration *Nostra Aetate* took cognizance of this: 'Over the centuries many quarrels and dissensions have arisen between Christians and Muslims. The sacred Council now pleads with all to forget the past, and urges that a sincere effort be made to achieve mutual understanding' (NA 3). It may not be possible to forget the past, yet there could be an attempt to reread the past together and so come to a better understanding and even to a 'purification of memories'.

Another obstacle mentioned is suspicion about the other's motives in dialogue. On the one hand, some Muslims tend to think that Christians enter into dialogue as a covert way of trying to bring about conversions to Christianity, just as they entertain the same suspicions regarding the charitable activity of the Church, its *diakonia*. From the Christian side there is a certain diffidence with regard to Muslims, the feeling that they are only entering into dialogue in order to strengthen the position of the Muslim minorities and bring about the eventual domination of Islam. This can be compounded when there is seen to be a lack of reciprocity, religious freedom demanded for Muslims in Western countries but not granted to Christians in certain Muslim majority countries. These questions themselves have to be tackled in dialogue. As is stated very clearly: 'Many of these obstacles arise from a lack of understanding of the true nature and goal of interreligious dialogue. These need therefore to be constantly explained' (DP 53).

Yet certainly progress has been made. Muslims have set up their own structures for dialogue, such as the International Islamic Forum for Dialogue, or the Permanent Committee of Al-Azhar for Dialogue with Monotheistic Religions. With the help of these structures it has been possible, as mentioned above, to make joint statements of Catholics and Muslims about such issues as terrorism, or the situation in the Holy Land. This is a sign of growing confidence.

Proclaiming Jesus Christ

The second section of the document *Dialogue and Proclamation* gives a summary presentation of the mandate given to the Church to proclaim Jesus Christ as Lord and Saviour. Much of this does not require any particular commentary from the point of view of Christian–Muslim relations, but some observations can be made.

There is an insistence on the urgency of proclamation (DP 66). However difficult it may be for Muslims to accept Jesus Christ as Son of God, Lord and Saviour, this does not dispense Christians from bearing witness to their faith, and inviting Muslims to embrace that faith if and when, in the Spirit, they discern that it is the moment to do this. As is made clear, the Church is to follow the lead of the Spirit (DP 68). This will give a particular quality to the manner in which the gospel is proclaimed: with confidence in the power of the Spirit, but also with humility and respect; in a dialogical and inculturated manner (DP 70), recognizing and making use of the values which those who are being addressed have received from Islam.

So obstacles to proclaiming the gospel to Muslims could be created by a lack of appreciation for their religious background and an attitude of superiority (DP 73). On the other hand, some difficulties may arise from outside the Christian community (DP 74), such as the circumstances obtaining in some majority Muslim countries. These could be restrictions with regard to religious freedom, limiting the possibility of presenting the Christian message or putting restrictions on the possibility of conversion to Christianity. In certain places there is an identification of belonging to a particular nationality or ethnic group and being a Muslim. In the light of this it is recalled that proclamation is not the only element of the Church's mission, and that

> in situations where, for political or other reasons, proclamation as such is practically impossible, the Church is already carrying out her evangelising mission not only through presence and witness but also through such activities as work for integral human development and dialogue. (DP 76)

It must be repeated that these activities, the social outreach of the Church and its commitment to dialogue, are not geared to proclamation but are ways in which the Church tries to express the respectful love of God for all people. Nevertheless the duty of proclamation remains: 'in other situations where people are disposed to hear the message of the Gospel and have the possibility of responding to it, the Church is in duty bound to meet their expectations' (DP 76).

Dialogue and proclamation taken together

The document ends with some reflections on the relationship between dialogue and proclamation. They are closely linked, for dialogue contains an element of witness to one's own faith, and proclamation is to be carried out in a dialogical manner. Yet they remain distinct, for the goal of each is different. They are both authentic elements of the Church's evangelizing mission, and in fact 'one and the same local Church, one and the same person, can be diversely engaged in both' (DP 77). This was my own personal experience in Northern Sudan, where the Catholic parish was preparing people for baptism and at the same time providing adult education with the help of Muslim teachers for all, Christians and Muslims, who wished to avail themselves of the opportunity, and generally cultivating good relations with the Muslim population. The need to attend to 'the particular circumstances of each local Church' (DP 78) is very relevant with regard to Christian–Muslim relations.

A reference is made to a 'spirit of emulation' (DP 79), encouragement given to all religious institutions and movements 'to meet, to enter into collaboration, and to purify themselves in order to promote truth and life, holiness, justice, love and peace' (DP 80). In today's increasingly pluralistic world there is a growth in multireligious movements. Christians and Muslims find themselves side by side, and together with people of other religious traditions, in trying to face up to common problems. They stimulate one another to greater efforts. John Paul II included interreligious dialogue in *Novo Millennio Ineunte*, his 'charter of action' for the Church in the current millennium:

> In the climate of increased cultural and religious pluralism, which is expected to mark the society of the new millennium, it is obvious that this dialogue will be especially important in establishing a sure basis for peace and warding off the dread spectre of those wars of religions which have so often bloodied human history. The name of the one God must become increasingly what it is: *a name of peace and a summons to peace.* (NMI 55)

DP ends with a brief meditation on Jesus as the model of dialogue (DP 85–6). Christians who are engaged in relations with Muslims can find new unexpected material for their meditation in the Islamic view of Jesus, not only according to the Qur'an and classical tradition, but also in the approach of certain contemporary Muslims.[8] Moreover the mystery of Jesus, though understood differently by Christians and Muslims, invites to further dialogue:

> Why did God wish to speak to humankind? What did he wish to say? How has he said it? How is his word to be received? Whatever may be the final identity that Muslims and Christians attribute to and recognise in Jesus, Son of Mary – and on this point, as has been noticed, there are profound differences – it remains true that he appears to both groups as someone who has a particular relationship with the mystery of the Word and the process of its transmission: he belongs to their spiritual patrimony and therefore cannot remain foreign to them. It is consequently desirable that, while respecting the final identity which each attributes to him, they may derive mutual enrichment from the values of faith and submission, of love and sacrifice, of which he remains for many the symbol, the witness and the model.[9]

Dialogue and Proclamation called for specific studies with regard to the different religions (DP 87–8). In this chapter I have attempted to heed this call, trying to show that although this document remains at a general level, the principles it announces and the guidance it gives are fully relevant to relations between Christians and Muslims. DP can be considered a faithful reflection on and application of the Conciliar Declaration *Nostra Aetate*. The events of the last decade and the entry into a new millennium have in no way diminished its importance.

11

Christians and Muslims together: Creating a culture of peace

We are living in difficult times. The terrorist attacks of September 11, 2001 have resulted in a 'war on terrorism' that has led not only to the bombing of Afghanistan but also to the war against Iraq. Despite the lack of authorization from the United Nations, and despite the appeals of Pope John Paul II and many other religious leaders, and considerable popular opposition to the war, the bombardment and the invasion of Iraq went ahead. It is too early as yet to estimate the effects of this war, whether as regards the number of lives lost, the destruction of Iraq's infrastructure, the impact on the region or the damage done to Christian–Muslim relations. Christians and Muslims have joined their voices to make it clear that Iraq should not be identified with Islam, and certain Western countries should not be identified with Christianity, yet the danger of such generalizations remains.

Already the events of September 11, 2001 had aroused fear of Muslims, particularly in the USA, but also in Europe. On occasions people have been badly treated because they were thought to be Muslims. This happened to some Sikhs, and also to people 'with Middle Eastern features'. On the other hand, interest in Islam increased. Those whose task it is within the Christian Churches to promote relations between Christians and Muslims were inundated with requests to speak to local communities. A need was felt to try to understand the true nature of Islam.

Moreover Muslims too were feeling the need to make it clear that Islam and terrorism are not interchangeable. They were eager to defend the good name of Islam, and they looked for the cooperation of their Christian partners in order to achieve this.

All these factors have brought Christians and Muslims together, perhaps more than ever before. New opportunities have been created for a constructive dialogue between the adherents of Christianity and of Islam. In this chapter I shall concentrate on what is required to create a culture of peace. We should remember that one of the aims of dialogue is to allow people to live in harmony and peace, despite their differences. The worth of this goal is not to be underestimated. It could be seen as an anticipation of the peace we believe will characterize eternal life. We are looking for, longing for, that fullness of life where there will be no rivalry, no conflict, where there will be no suffering and no tears. The Qur'an says that those who enter Paradise 'will not hear there any vain discourse, but only salutations of Peace' (Q. 19.62), and peace, a peace which is not of this world, is what Jesus has promised his disciples.

We know that we are far from this goal, but rather than dismissing it as something impossible to achieve, we should be striving to create already in this world a culture of peace.

Creating a culture of peace

Before outlining some of the qualities which would need to be developed, it may be as well to recall some of the obstacles. These can be of two kinds: internal attitudes and external factors.

The first internal attitude is one of self-sufficiency, which tends to make a person dismissive of the other, feeling that they have nothing to learn from someone with another viewpoint. Another is fear arising from a lack of knowledge, which inhibits any real discussion. A further obstacle is prejudice, usually acquired from parents or peers.

There is a further, external obstacle, already discussed under 'difficulties' of dialogue: the lack of freedom to practise one's own religion, which can lead to a defensive mentality and a fear of offering even constructive criticism. How can this obstacle be overcome? It surely requires the creation of public opinion favourable to religious plurality. It requires perhaps of majorities that they be sensitive and attentive to the needs of minorities. The exact system adopted may not be uniform. What is important is not the appearance of freedom, but real freedom.

If I am to come now to the positive attitudes that will help to create a culture of dialogue, and thus contribute to a culture of peace, I am inclined to start with that quality which is at the basis of all learning, *curiosity*. It is healthy curiosity that pushes the child constantly to ask why, sometimes to the despair of parents. Should we not have the same curiosity with regard to our neighbours who differ from us? Why do they not pray like us? How do they pray? Why are they celebrating a feast? What does it commemorate? How do they celebrate? Such curiosity – and of course the list of questions is never-ending – can lead to an attitude of *respect,* as the values in another religion become clearer.

Respect can then lead to *admiration.* There are certainly features of Islamic life and worship that provoke admiration: the emphasis on the family, the importance given to prayer, fasting and alms-giving.

Another attitude is that of *solidarity,* a willingness to give and receive help, a readiness to work together on behalf of humanity. This spirit can give rise to the founding of associations that bring together Christians and Muslims, for example to take care of the handicapped. The spirit of solidarity can be shown by cooperating in providing humanitarian relief, and there is surely need of such co-operation at the present time. It could take the form of upholding basic human values.

In the service of peace

The final statement by participants in the Interreligious Assembly, convened by the PCID in Rome in October 1999, underlined the need for the cooperation of people of different religions in the service of peace. It is often said that there will be no peace in the world until there is peace among the religions. A finger is pointed to religions as being at the origin of conflicts. It could be questioned whether this is wholly true. Of course, it must be admitted that religion has, in the course of history, produced conflicts, and can do so today. But such conflicts may have a multiplicity of causes, and so it is only fair to distinguish between those which are strictly speaking religious, taking their origin from differences of belief, and those which are based on non-religious motivations but take on a religious colouring.

Whether the causes are religious or not, the followers of different religions feel the duty to contribute to overcoming conflicts and to work for peace. I was heartened during a recent visit to Nigeria to find in Kaduna, a city that has seen much violence aggravated by religious differences, a group of Christians and Muslims who are cooperating in communicating skills in conflict resolution.

Christians and Muslims are conscious that peace is a gift from God which has to be implored, but which also has, in a sense, to be earned. It is this conviction that led Pope John Paul II to invite representatives of different religions to Assisi to pray for peace, first in October 1986, and again on 24 January 2002. On the latter occasion he said:

> If peace is God's gift and has its source in him, where are we to seek it and how can we build it, if not in a deep and intimate relationship with God? To build the peace of order, justice and freedom requires, therefore, a priority commitment to prayer, which is openness, listening, dialogue and finally union with God, the prime wellspring of true peace.
>
> To pray is not to escape from history and the problems which it presents. On the contrary, it is to choose to face reality not on our own, but with the strength that comes from on high, the strength of truth and love which have their ultimate source in God. Faced with the treachery of evil, religious people can count on God, who absolutely wills what is good. They can pray to him to have the courage to face even the greatest difficulties with a sense of personal responsibility, never yielding to fatalism or impulsive reactions.[1]

The representatives gathered in Assisi on that day made a solemn tenfold commitment to peace, each commitment being read out in a different language. The following are those which emphasize the need for dialogue among the religions.

1 We commit ourselves to proclaiming our firm conviction that violence and terrorism are incompatible with the authentic spirit of religion, and, as we condemn every recourse to violence and war in the name of God or of religion, we commit ourselves to doing everything possible to eliminate the root causes of terrorism.
2 We commit ourselves to educating people to mutual respect and esteem, in order to help bring about a peaceful and fraternal co-existence between people of different ethnic groups, cultures and religions.
3 We commit ourselves to fostering the culture of dialogue, so that there will be an increase of understanding and mutual trust between individuals and among people, for these are the premise of authentic peace.
5 We commit ourselves to frank and patient dialogue, refusing to consider our differences as an insurmountable barrier, but recognising instead that to encounter the diversity of others can become an opportunity for greater reciprocal understanding.[2]

The pillars of peace

Truth is the first pillar of peace, according to the teaching of Pope John XXIII in his letter *Pacem in Terris* of 1963. John Paul II recalled this anniversary in his message for the Day of Peace 2003, and brought to mind the four essential requirements for peace identified by John XXIII: truth, justice, love and freedom.

- Truth brings each individual to acknowledge his or her own rights, but also to recognize his or her own duties towards others.
- Justice leads people to respect the rights of others and also to fulfil their duties.
- Love goes beyond justice, for it makes people feel the needs of others as if they were their own, and this empathy leads them to share their own gifts with others, not only material goods but also the values of mind and spirit.
- Freedom, finally, is a factor in building peace when it allows people to act according to reason and to assume responsibility for their own actions.

John Paul II in his message for the previous year, 2002, had himself spoken of two pillars of peace: justice and forgiveness, which is a particular form of love. Human justice is always imperfect and needs to be complemented by forgiveness, thus allowing broken relationships to be restored, confidence to be regained and a new departure to take place. This holds good not only for individuals, but also for social groups, even states. It is the capacity to forgive that can create the conditions necessary to overcome the sterility of reciprocal condemnations and the spiral of increasing violence.

Permanent landmarks

It would be possible to go on and give concrete examples of the ways in which Christians and Muslims do relate together, whether in a spontaneous way at the level of daily life or more consciously in common ventures. Something could be said about formal dialogue, of a theological or spiritual nature, or concerned with social problems. We could speak about bilateral dialogue, which is confined to Christians and Muslims, or trilateral dialogue, when Jews are included, or also of multilateral dialogue in which representatives of all religions are invited to take part.

We can also point out that a culture of dialogue needs perhaps to have some permanent landmarks, in the form of structures and also of recurring dates. Structures are not ends in themselves, but they can serve to provide continuity. Where structures have been set up, by the religions separately or by both together, there is greater hope that when individuals move or are called to other functions the dialogue will survive. The PCID is one such structure. It is there to encourage local churches to action.

This brings me to the second point, the need for recurring dates. Our partners at al-Azhar have requested that the joint committee with the PCID should hold its annual meeting around 24 February. This is the date when Pope John Paul II visited al-Azhar. The desire is to keep this date alive in people's memories. There could be other dates: each country would have to find its own. Certain national holidays that are not religious in character provide occasions for creating a feeling of solidarity and common commitment to one another and to society as a whole.

12

Mary as a sign for the world according to Islam

It may surprise some readers of this book to learn of the place that the Mother of Jesus has in Islam. This in fact lies behind the statement in *Nostra Aetate* that the Muslims honour the Virgin Mother and even at times devoutly invoke her (NA3). One of the features of Mary in the Qur'an is that, together with her Son, she is considered a sign for the whole of humanity. I wish here to comment on some of the qur'anic texts which speak of Mary in this way.

The first passage I shall quote is *sūra* 21.91: 'And (remember) her who guarded her chastity: We breathed into her of Our Spirit, and We made her and her son a sign for all peoples.'[1] This *sūra* relates stories of biblical figures, Abraham, Noah, David, Solomon, Job, Zachary, before coming to this passage. Mary thus comes at the end of a long line of figures presented as models. The verb in parentheses, 'remember', is not actually part of the text, but it can be supposed as a command from God to Muhammad to mention in the book, or in the recitation, i.e. in the Qur'an, the person being described. Here the name of that person is not indicated, though it is well known that Mary is in fact mentioned by name 34 times in the Qur'an, the only woman to have this privilege. We must presume, then, that the reference to the one 'who guarded her chastity' would be easily understood. In other words, the story of Mary and the virginal birth of Jesus must have been well known. According to Mir Ahmed Ali's commentary (MAA), 'The reference is to (the) Virgin Mary being made to bear Jesus without any male partner in the parentage – see 19:16–35; 3:44; 4:171'. Yusuf Ali (YA) says of Mary 'Chastity was her special virtue: with a son of virgin birth, she and Jesus became a miracle in all nations.'

Before looking at the passages that relate the virgin birth, it may be well to examine other elements of the verse in question.

The 'We' is obviously God, this plural of majesty being frequent in the Qur'an. The Spirit (*rūh*) is a somewhat mysterious figure, and will finally be interpreted by the Qur'an itself, and by Muslim tradition, as a name for the Angel Gabriel. Yet the closeness to God, even something of the divine, remains. Jesus himself is said to be not only God's Word which He cast into Mary, but also a Spirit from God (cf. Q. 4.171). There is here, in any case, a reference to God's action bringing about the virginal birth of Jesus.

Mary and her son (whose name is not indicated either) are made 'a Sign' (*āya*). The same word can interpreted as miracle, as can be seen in the quotation above from Yusuf Ali. It is also the term used for a verse of the Qur'an, for each verse of the book is a sign from God for those who have understanding. It is to be noticed that the word here is in the singular. Mary and Jesus are not each of them a sign, but rather form together a single sign. It is 'for all peoples'. The Arabic term *al-ʿālamīn* means literally 'the worlds'. It is used in this sense in the Opening Chapter of the Qur'an, where God is said to be *rabb al-ʿālamīn*, 'The Cherisher and Sustainer of the Worlds' (in Yusuf Ali's translation). Jesus and Mary can be considered a sign for all times, all places and all people.

Let us turn now to the first text referred to above by Mir Ahmed Ali, the account of the Annunciation given in *sūra* 19.16–21. Though the passage is long it is worth quoting in full:

16. Relate in the Book (the story of) Mary, when she withdrew from her family to a place in the East.
17. She placed a screen (to screen herself) from them; then We sent to her Our angel, and he appeared before her as a man in all respects.
18. She said: 'I take refuge from thee to (God) Most Gracious: (come not near) if thou dost fear God.'
19. He said: 'Nay, I am only a messenger from thy Lord, (to announce) to thee the gift of a holy son.'
20. She said: 'How shall I have a son, seeing that no man has touched me, and I am not unchaste?'
21. He said: 'So (it will be): thy Lord saith, "That is easy for Me: and (We wish) to appoint him as a sign unto men and a mercy from Us": it is a matter (so) decreed.'

Certain features of this passage can be highlighted. Here Mary is mentioned by name. She is said to withdraw to a place in the east. Mir

Ahmed Ali understands this as being a reference to the eastern part of the synagogue where Mary used to go to pray in private, or a house of prayer on the eastern side of Jerusalem where Mary went to take a bath. For Yusuf Ali, Mary went 'to a private eastern chamber, perhaps in the Temple. She went into privacy, from her people and from people in general, for prayer and devotion.'

The word translated 'angel' is *rūh*, Spirit, who is here not breathed, but sent. 'The spirit was the Angel Gabriel ... the spiritual power of the Angel Gabriel caused Mary to see him in human form, otherwise the angel as a spirit remained only a spirit' (MAA). It is perhaps worth noting that in the parallel passage in *sūra* 3.42–3 the message is brought to Mary by 'angels' (in the plural). They first refer to her election:

42. Behold! the angels said: 'O Mary! God hath chosen thee and purified thee – chosen thee above the women of all nations.
43. O Mary! worship thy Lord devoutly: prostrate thyself, and bow down (in prayer) with those who bow down.'

The Qur'an definitely exalts the figure of Mary.

To return to *sūra* 19, Mary is frightened by the apparition of the angel, and takes refuge in God Most Gracious (*al-Rahmān*). *Al-Rahmān* is one of the most frequently used names for God, and one that is found in early Christian texts. The angel reassures her: his mission is to announce the gift of a son. 'God had destined her to be the mother of the holy Prophet Jesus Christ, and now had come the time when this should be announced to her' (YA). MAA follows the Arabic more closely: 'I am only a messenger (Angel) of thy Lord, so that I give to thee a son purified.' The second 'I' is obviously a reference to God, not to the angel himself, which explains the version of YA.

Mary questions the possibility of giving birth, as in the Gospel of Luke. She protests that she is not unchaste. The choice of this word, in a double negative, is probably commanded by the rhyme (*baghiyyan* to rhyme with *sharqiyyan*, eastern, *sawiyyan*, in all respects, sound, etc.). Yet the accusation that Jesus was the child of prostitution was part of Jewish polemic against Christians (cf. Q. 4.156). The angel's reply accentuates the power of God for whom all things are possible.

It is God's will to make Jesus a sign for all people (the term *nās* is general) and a manifestation of God's mercy (*rahma*, from the same root as the Divine name *al-Raḥmān*). How is this to be understood? Jesus is a sign, for 'his wonderful birth and wonderful life were to turn an ungodly world back to God'; he is a mercy, for 'his mission is to bring solace and salvation to the repentant' (YA).

> Jesus' advent in the wonderful way it took place, i.e. being born with-out a father, was to bring back to the people's mind the Omnipotence of God Who could act as He willed irrespective of the usual needs for the working of the natural phenomena in the birth of a man, and to allow respite to the people to earn the Mercy of the Lord by repen-tance and self-discipline by amending their faith and conduct accord-ing to the Ten Commandments given to Moses. (MAA)

The insistence on God's omnipotence is striking. It will be seen that this excludes all human participation. Mary does not have to consent to what is being announced to her. There could be no Muslim text equivalent to the homily of St Bernard where he im-agines the heavens and the earth suspended, waiting for Mary to pro-nounce her *fiat*. God has merely to say to something 'Be', and it is (cf. Q. 3.47). It is easy for him. It is a thing decreed.

If we continue reading *sūra* 19 we find that Mary, having con-ceived, retires to a remote place and gives birth to her son at the foot of a palm tree. She then comes, carrying her son, to her own people. It could be noted in passing that it would normally be the father's task to present the child to the family, but in this case there is no father; the fact of the virgin birth is once again emphasized. The family are astounded. Mary is criticized, but she does not defend herself. She had been commanded to keep a fast of silence in honour of the Most Gracious God. Such a vow is not unknown in monastic circles; one has only to think of the title given to the English edition of Thomas Merton's autobiography, *Elected Silence*. So Mary points to her child, and the people are astonished: 'How can we talk to one who is a child in the cradle?'

'What could Mary do?' comments Yusuf Ali. 'How could she ex-plain? Would they, in their censorious mood accept her explanation? All she could do was point to the child. And the child came to her rescue. By a miracle he spoke, defended his mother, and preached – to an unbelieving audience.' What Jesus says is again worth quoting in full:

30. He said: 'I am indeed a servant of God: He hath given me revelation and made me a prophet;

31. And He hath made me blessed wheresoever I be, and hath enjoined on me Prayer and Charity as long as I live;

32. (He) hath made me kind to my mother, and not overbearing or miserable;

33. So Peace is on me the day I was born, the day that I die, and the day that I shall be raised up to life (again)'.

Jesus in the Gospels refers to himself as the Son of Man, and there are obvious echoes of the Suffering Servant. Yet here the choice of the name 'servant of God' is in contrast to the Christian claim that Jesus is the Son of God. Jesus, for Muslims, is a prophet, and nothing but a prophet. He is to practise prayer (*salāt*) and pay the alms-tax (*zakāt*), two basic duties of any Muslim. It may be noticed though that Mir Ahmed Ali understands these in a broader sense, 'the soul being prayerful to the Lord' and 'purity of thought and conduct', adding 'the whole life of an apostle of God would naturally need to be ideally pure in word and action as a model to his followers.' Part of this good conduct is to be kind to his mother. Earlier the *sūra* relates the birth of John the Baptist (*Yahyā*) who was said to have been kind to his parents (Q. 19.14). The mention of only the mother of Jesus underlines once more the virginal character of his birth. Similarly the verse about peace is also said of John, so we should not jump to the conclusion that there is a reference here to the death of Jesus on the cross and his resurrection. As is well known, these mysteries of our redemption are denied by Muslims (cf. Q. 4.157–8). Mir Ahmed Ali sums up: Jesus was 'to vouch for his own position and to manifest that he was sent into the world as God's sign of his Omnipotence and Might'.

Let me refer to a further passage of the Qur'an in which Jesus and Mary are presented as a sign. It is *sūra* 23.50: 'And We made the son of Mary and his mother as a Sign: We gave them both shelter on high ground, affording rest and security and furnished with springs.'

What is this high ground? According to Yusuf Ali there is no need to search for it; it is the place where Mary withdrew to give birth. Mir Ahmed Ali is more precise. Mary 'was directed by God to take refuge in Bethlehem' where there was a date-palm and a spring of water. So this place was 'on the heights of Palestine nearby Jerusalem, surrounded by vineyards and fruit gardens and meadows with herds of cattle grazing in them.' He does, however, report also the opinion of two of the Shiʿite Imams, Muhammad al-Bāqir and Jaʿfar al-Sādiq, that the reference is to 'the fertile land on the banks of the Euphrates in Iraq'. It is certainly not, he says, Kashmir, a swipe at the Ahmadiyya who hold that Jesus was truly crucified, but that he did not die, but rather was taken down from the cross and cured, and then wandered all the way to Kashmir where he died and was buried.

For us Christians could this high ground be Golgotha? We do find Jesus and Mary united on this hill. The conquering of death through death and resurrection is the true source of rest and security. And the pierced side of the Son becomes a fountain of grace for the whole of humankind.

But this would be reading too much into the qur'anic text. It is better to be sober and accept the difference that exists between Christianity and Islam. Both the gospel and the Qur'an present Jesus as a sign in association with the Virgin Mary. In the gospel Jesus is essentially a sign of salvation: 'My eyes have seen the salvation which you have prepared for all the nations to see', says Simeon (Luke 2.30–1). Jesus is the sign of the irruption of God's love in the world, fulfilling the Old Testament prophecies (cf. Luke 4.18–19). John sums it up by saying: 'God's love for us was revealed when God sent into the world his only Son so that we could have life through him' (1 John 4.9). In the Qur'an this dimension of love is largely absent. The Qur'an insists much more on the power of God. God, who created the world simply by his word, has no difficulty in bringing about the virginal birth of Jesus. He who brought about this miraculous birth will also be able to bring about the new birth of humankind at the general resurrection. This is the essential message of the Qur'an: that there is one God, who is Creator and Judge, and that there is a life after this life on earth, that there will be a general judgement in which each will receive his or her due, the Garden of Paradise or the Fire of Hell. Of this Day of Judgement, of this Hour, Jesus is a sign: 'And (Jesus) shall be a Sign (for the coming of) the Hour (of Judgment): Therefore have no doubt about the (Hour), but follow ye Me: this is the Straight Way' (Q. 43.61). Indeed, for Islam, Jesus and Mary are united in the single sign of God's creative power.

The passage in *sūra* 19 on the Annunciation to Mary and the birth of Jesus concludes with a sort of commentary:

34. Such (was) Jesus the son of Mary: it is a statement of truth, about which they (vainly) dispute.
35. It is not befitting to (the majesty of God) that He should beget a son. Glory be to Him! When He determines a matter, He only says to it 'Be', and it is.

A little technical detail: the rhyme for these two verses is different, an indication that they have been added later. They form, as it were, a dogmatic statement. Jesus is the son of Mary. There is a positive side to this, the affirmation of the virgin birth, but also a negative side, the denial of the divine sonship. It is sobering also to see the reference to vain disputes. Jesus is a source of division, not only between Christians and Muslims, but among Christians. There is a real need for ecumenical endeavour so that Christians can give united witness to Jesus, son of Mary and Son of God, truly a sign for the whole of humankind.

Part III

WIDER HORIZONS

13

The witness of monotheistic religions

Some people tend to assert that Jews, Christians and Muslims do not adore the same God. This is not the teaching of the Christian Churches and certainly not of the Catholic Church. The Second Vatican Council, in its central document, the Dogmatic Constitution on the Church (*Lumen Gentium*), stated clearly that we all adore the same God (LG 16). This did not even have to be stated with regard to Judaism, for God's dealings with the chosen people form, as it were, the prehistory of Christianity and 'the Church cannot forget that she received the revelation of the Old Testament by way of the people with whom God, in his inexpressible mercy, established the ancient covenant' (NA 4).

Each tradition has a liturgical expression of this primary article of faith. Judaism makes use of the *Shemaʿ*: 'Listen, Israel . . . I am the Lord, your God, who brought you out of the land of Egypt, out of the house of slavery. You shall have no gods except me' (Deut. 5.1, 6–7). Christians proclaim *Credo in unum Deum*, I believe in one God. Muslims, at every ritual prayer (*salāt*), recite the *shahāda*: *Lā ilāha illā Llāh*: There is no divinity except God.

There are, of course, differences in the way of understanding this God. For the first of these religions, God has chosen one single people to bear witness before the world. For Christians, God has become incarnate, and in so doing has shown his solidarity with the whole of the human race that he has created. It is through the incarnate Son of God that the trinitarian nature of God comes to be known. For Muslims, such a trinitarian concept would seem to destroy the essential oneness of God. Moreover God's transcendence would exclude the possibility of incarnation. But God has raised up within each people a prophet to remind them of their primordial covenant with him. He has finally sent Muhammad to be the Seal of Prophecy and a mercy (*rahma*) for the whole of humanity.

We are dealing then with three distinct religions, and indeed the differences are to be found at the very heart of that which unites them, faith in the one God. Moreover these three traditions have seen their boundaries defined through historical development. Christianity did not set out to be a new religion, but it separated itself from Judaism, perhaps not without anguish. Islam discovered that Jews and Christians did not accept its message, and had to come to terms with the continued existence of their communities. So the three traditions have to coexist, leaving it to God to resolve their differences in his own good time.

Despite the differences in understanding, the common faith in the oneness of God remains. This means a refusal of any sort of *dualistic* vision of the world. Good and evil do certainly exist, but they are not two coequal principles that are eternally struggling one with the other. We know too that we cannot really divide good and evil into two distinct camps. We are conscious that in each one of us these two forces exist. Saint Paul has described in vivid terms this inward conflict:

> I cannot understand my own behaviour. I fail to carry out the things I want to do, and I find myself doing the very things I hate . . . The fact is, I know of nothing good living in me – living, that is, in my unspiritual self – for though the will to do good is in me, the performance is not, with the result that instead of doing the good things I want to do, I carry out the sinful things I do not want . . . In fact, this seems to be the rule, that every single time I want to do good it is something evil that comes to hand. (Rom. 7.15, 18–19, 21)

Yet Paul is also certain that there is a way out of this predicament. His cry is well known: 'What a wretched man I am! Who will rescue me from this body doomed to death? Thanks be to God through Jesus Christ our Lord!' (Rom. 7.24–5). Paul is here giving expression to the belief of Christians, but underlying this particularity is the general conviction that faith in the One Almighty God includes belief that, whatever appearances might suggest, the forces of evil will be overcome. Good will have the final word.

A further dimension of monotheism is naturally a refusal of *polytheism* where God would have to share his prerogatives with other divinities, and where indeed there could arise a certain rivalry between divinities jealous of their own spheres of influence. Our traditions are full of satirical arguments against such a conception of God. When the priests of Baal are unable to bring fire down to consume their sacrifice, Elijah mocks them, saying: 'Call louder for he is a god, he is preoccupied or he is busy, or he has gone on a journey; perhaps he is asleep and will wake up.' (1 Kings 18.20–40). The Christian author Minucius Felix, late second century, in his *Octavius*, criticizes the worship of idols: 'How much truer the judgement which the dumb animals pass instinctively on those gods of yours! Mice, swallows, kites, know that they have no feeling; they gnaw them, perch and settle on them, and (unless you scare them) build in your god's own mouth; spiders spin webs across his face and hang their threads from his head' (*Octavius* 22.6). In the Qur'an, Abraham smashes the idols of his people, and when they ask him if he is responsible for this deed, he says that this was done by the greatest of them: 'Ask them, if they can speak intelligently' (Q. 21.51–67).

Yet there are other forms of polytheism, or at least of associating something with God, which can insidiously creep into religion. Like the Little Prince who had to be vigilant lest baobabs should take root on his asteroid and completely take it over, so the one devoted to God has to beware lest the relationship become corrupted. It is necessary to act for God alone and, in seeking to do his will, to be careful not to associate with this worship our own desires and ambitions. Islamic spirituality has developed the idea of this fight against *shirk*, associating something with God, in ways that certainly have a resonance with Christians, and probably also with Jews.

Witness

Jews, Christians and Muslims, we are called to give witness to God in the world. Witness is a key concept in our three traditions and is worth examining a little more closely.

The law that God gives to his people, as an expression of his divine will, is inscribed on two tables. When Moses is instructed on how to build the sanctuary, he is told: 'Inside the ark you will place the Testimony that I shall give you' (Exod. 25.16). This is understood as a reference to the two tablets on which the Decalogue was written. It is there as a constant reminder to the people of their obligations. Now if the law is not observed, if the people abandon their God, then God will bear witness against his people. The prophet Micah presents

God as if he were conducting a trial: 'Listen, you peoples, all of you. Attend, earth, and everything in it. The Lord is going to give evidence against you' (Mic. 1.2). This witnessing *against* is always, however, in view of conversion and a return to God, for the prophet Ezekiel conveys the word of the Lord: 'As I live – it is the Lord who speaks – I take pleasure not in the death of a wicked man, but in the turning back of a wicked man who changes his ways to win life' (Ezek. 33.11).

In the Christian tradition, the good news of the kingdom, preached by Jesus, is destined to be 'proclaimed to the whole world as a witness to all the nations' (Matt. 24.14). This is why Jesus sends his disciples to be his witnesses 'not only in Jerusalem but throughout Judaea and Samaria, and indeed to the ends of the earth' (Acts 1.8).

In Islam the profession of faith takes the form of witness, but the witness of human beings is founded on divine witness: 'God testifies concerning that which he has revealed to you (Muhammad); in His knowledge He has revealed it, and the angels also testify. And God is sufficient as a witness [*shahīd*]' (Q. 4.166). Also in Islam this witness has a community dimension: 'Thus We have appointed you a middle nation, that you may be witnesses against mankind, and that the messenger may be a witness against you' (Q. 2.143).

This theme could be further developed, but I would like to suggest some ways in which a common witness can be given in the world today.

The primacy of God

Are we not called, as believers in God, to recognize that there is a truth which surpasses us? Is it not our duty to remind this modern society of ours that human beings cannot be their own measure? Human dignity has its source in the creative act of God, whether or not we would wish to go on and affirm that God has created the human person in his own image and likeness. This last-mentioned belief does in fact reinforce the requirement of respect for each human being. It is perhaps good to recall here the teaching of the final section of the Declaration *Nostra Aetate*:

> We cannot truly pray to God, the Father of all, if we treat any people in other than brotherly fashion, for all men are created in God's image. Man's relation to God the Father and man's relation to his

fellowmen are so dependent on each other that the Scripture says: 'He who does not love, does not know God' (1 Jn 4:8). There is no basis, therefore, for any discrimination between individual and individual, or between people, arising either from human dignity or the rights which flow from it. (NA 5)

To accept the will of the Creator is not to go against the interests of humanity but rather to promote them, helping humankind achieve its destiny.

As believers in God, are we not called to make our voices heard in society in this way? It is surely an obligation on our part to demand respect for the fundamental rights of human beings. There is a vast field here for common endeavour. We should remember that to show respect for our fellow human beings is also to show respect for God.

The responsibility of human beings

To insist on the primacy of God does not mean that the human being is reduced to the status of a pawn on the divine chess-board. On the contrary, faith in the Creator God leads to an acceptance of the role that he has entrusted to the human being, namely to be a 'co-creator', or, in Islamic terminology, God's *khalīfa*, his lieutenant or deputy. We are responsible for the created world and all it contains.

The very existence of evil becomes a challenge to the one whom God has placed in this world to take charge of it. As Paul has said, the whole of creation is groaning, waiting for liberation. We believers, in whom the Spirit is at work, are not exempt from this groaning, for we also aspire to true freedom (cf. Rom. 8.22–3). This does not mean waiting passively. It is our duty to cooperate with the Spirit of God, to work so that the kingdom of God may come.

Service to humanity

From human responsibility it is an easy step to the idea of service to humanity. Believers in God, we are called to bear witness to our faith in God but also to our faith in the human person.

We feel the need too for common witness in today's world. In October 1999 the interreligious assembly organized by the PCID, in which Jews, Christians and Muslims took part, in its final message declared:

We are conscious of the urgent need

- To confront together responsibly and courageously the problems and challenges of our modern world . . .
- To work together to affirm human dignity as the source of human rights and their corresponding duties, in the struggle for justice and peace for all.
- To create a new spiritual consciousness for all humanity in accordance with the religious traditions so that the principle of respect for freedom of religion and freedom of conscience prevail.[1]

They added:

We know that the problems in the world are so great that we cannot solve them alone. Therefore there is an urgent need for interreligious collaboration.

We are all aware that interreligious collaboration does not imply giving up our own religious identity but is rather a journey of discovery:

- We learn to respect one another as members of the one human family.
- We learn both to respect our differences and to appreciate the common values that bind us to one another.

Therefore we are convinced that we are able to work together to strive to prevent conflict and to overcome the crises existing in different parts of the world.

Collaboration among the different religions must be based on the rejection of fanaticism, extremism and mutual antagonisms which lead to violence.[2]

The conditions for a true dialogue

Dialogue is never easy. It is important to recognize that there are certain conditions required for it to be successful. The first of these is an open mind and a welcoming spirit. This means that two extremes are to be avoided: on the one hand a certain ingenuousness which accepts everything without further questioning, and on the other hand a hypercritical attitude which leads to suspicion. Impartiality is required. What is being sought is an equitable solution to the particular problem which is to be resolved.

Being open-minded does not imply being without personal convictions. On the contrary, rootedness in one's own convictions will allow for greater openness, for it takes away the fear of losing one's identity. It thus facilitates the understanding of the other's convictions.

Such an openness leads to the admission that the whole of the truth is not just on one side. There is always a need to learn from others, to receive from them, to benefit from their values and everything that is good in their traditions. Dialogue in this spirit helps to overcome prejudices and to revise stereotypes.

Returning to the concept of monotheism, it would seem to me that we are helped in this particular aspect of dialogue by our belief in a God who is truth. God alone is to be identified with absolute truth. We ourselves cannot pretend to attain this level. Without falling into relativism, we can readily admit that our view of things does not really attain to ultimate truth. For this reason in dialogue it is necessary not only to speak but also to listen to the other in order to receive what part of truth they can offer.

Openness includes the capacity to give and receive forgiveness. The teaching of Pope John Paul II, for instance his message on the Day of Peace in 2002, emphasizing justice and forgiveness as the two pillars of peace, is resolutely Christian, for Jesus taught that God is a Father who loves to pardon (cf. Luke 15). Yet surely this conforms to the image of God given in the First Testament. The Psalmist invites his soul to bless the Lord and to remember his kindnesses, 'in forgiving all your offences', for he is 'tender and compassionate, slow to anger, most loving' (Ps. 103.3, 8). The book of Nehemiah addresses God in a similar way: 'But you are a God of forgiveness, gracious and loving, slow to anger, abounding in goodness' (Neh. 9.17). In the Qur'an, God is constantly proclaimed *al-rahmān al-rahīm*, the Beneficent, the Merciful. He is also *al-ghafūr*, the one whose very inclination is to pardon. According to Islamic spirituality believers are to 'clothe' themselves with the attributes of God, so surely there is an encouragement to forgive as God is forgiving.

To conclude, we see that the monotheistic religions, in particular the Abrahamic religions, have much to contribute to peace. They will do so by upholding the dignity of human beings, by pursuing justice, but also by practising and appealing for the spirit of pardon.

14

Modern religious fundamentalisms

Introduction

Religious faith does not always feel happy in the modern world, with its secular outlook and emphasis on material goods. It is well to look briefly at the negative side of the reaction to modern life: what is often called fundamentalism. The following considerations rely heavily on the first volume of the Fundamentalism Project.[1] The volume runs to almost 900 pages, and is only the first of a series of six! It is obvious then that these reflections cannot hope to be exhaustive. They can only suggest some pointers which may help towards a greater understanding of fundamentalism in general and Islamic fundamentalism in particular.

The editors of *Fundamentalisms Observed* present certain features of fundamentalism which denote an active, not a passive, movement.

- Fundamentalism *fights back*. It is militant, reacting to that which is perceived as a threat to the core identity of the followers of the movement.
- It *fights for* a cause, defending a world-view which it has inherited, by force of arms if necessary.
- It *fights with* a certain number of key ideas which have been selected because they reinforce identity.
- It *fights against* all opposition, whether without or within. It is therefore inclined to be impatient with compromising moderates ('wets' in the political terms of the Thatcher era in Britain).
- It *fights under* a religious banner, i.e. under God or in the name of some transcendent reference. This is a source of great conviction in carrying out what is conceived to be a mission.[2]

It will be noticed that 'selectivity' is considered a mark of fundamentalism. It often includes an appeal to the past, as being the model for that which is genuine, but it is an idealized past. It has been suggested that this return to the original core of religion is easier in the case of 'prophetic' religions, which can refer to a sacred text. In other religions, whether they are considered pantheistic or polytheistic (Hinduism) or a-theistic (Buddhism), a much broader appeal has to be made in order to arouse a feeling of common commitment. A common element in fundamentalisms is seen to be the 'misuse of religion in public life'.[3] This, of course, can be construed in a positive sense, as a refusal to see religion relegated to the private sphere with no impact on society. The question will be what constitutes 'misuse'.

A further general remark can usefully be made. Fundamentalism is not to be equated with archaism. Though some adherents to fundamentalist groups may adopt an archaic style of living, others are quite willing to use all the latest technologies. Radio and television, videocassettes, computer programs, will all be pressed into the service of their ideals. This also gives an international dimension to fundamentalist movements which was absent in the past.

There is only space here to give a very brief outline of how this attitude manifests itself in the various religions.

Christian fundamentalism

In considering modern religious fundamentalisms it may be best to start with Christianity, since this is where the term takes its origin. Curtis Lee Laws, the editor of a Northern Baptist newspaper, *The Watchman Examiner*, wrote in 1920: 'A "fundamentalist" is a person willing to "do battle royal" for the fundamentals of the faith'.[4]

Nancy Ammerman discerns the following marks in North American Christian Fundamentalism. First evangelism, indicating an experience of being saved, of being 'born again'. The assurance for this religious experience is found in the Scriptures accepted with an unwavering faith in their inerrancy. The text, of course, has to be interpreted; hence the central role of Bible teachers and preachers who establish for the community authoritative meanings for different passages. A further feature of this fundamentalism is dispensationalism. By this is meant not only a strong expectancy for the End Times, and for the Rapture, that is the coming of Christ, but also an interest in discerning the signs of this coming. The approach can be 'premillennial', in which it is believed that Christ will come to inaugurate the struggle against evil and bring in a reign of goodness, or 'postmillennial', according to which Christ will come at the end of the period of preparation, when the world is ready for him. Whatever approach is adopted, the preparation for the coming strengthens the sense of belonging to a specially chosen group and thus leads to the final characteristic of this fundamentalism, its separatist tendency. 'Fundamentalists insist on uniformity of belief within the ranks and separation from others whose beliefs and lives are suspect.'[5]

Françoise Smyth-Florentin, a French Protestant biblical scholar, emphasizes the importance of the 'identifying factor'. The Scripture text is deemed to produce a conversion which in turn confirms the text. Smyth-Florentin considers this a 'vicious circle' in that it inhibits any exploration of the text in question. It thus contributes to another feature of fundamentalism, namely that it is characterized by a 'closed' mentality.[6]

Ammerman shows that there has been a revival of Christian fundamentalism on account of the social upheavals of the 1960s. This led on the one hand to increased organization, to the founding of academies for teaching sound doctrine and training pastors, to developing television programmes in order to reach as many people as possible, and on the other hand to an involvement in politics. This was the time of the formation of the Moral Majority, giving its support to the New Right.[7] Scott Appleby, in a paper read during a meeting in Asia on Christian–Muslim relations, draws attention to new alliances that have taken place in this regard. Pentecostals and Evangelicals, who were separate, now make common cause for political ends. The movement needs a well-defined enemy. It is reactive, thriving on confrontation. Here again there is no room for compromise. 'Their intolerance of tolerance is a pivotal strategy in demonstrating that their truth is absolute, self-contained, immune from error.'[8]

It will be understood that though the beliefs of Christian fundamentalists are specific to Christians, in particular their insistence on the experience of 'being saved' by Christ, the way they live out and defend these beliefs is by no means peculiar to them. Some of the same characteristics of fundamentalism will be found in other religions.

Jewish fundamentalism

The volume *Fundamentalisms Observed* gives two examples of Jewish fundamentalism that contrast quite starkly. One is *Gush Emunim*, the Bloc of the Faithful; the other is that of the *Haredim*, the ultra-Orthodox Jews whose name would appear to be taken from Isaiah 66.5, 'those who venerate – or tremble – at God's Word'.[9]

Gush Emunim was born at the time of the Six Days' War, either just before, in 1967, or slightly after, in 1968. The Haredim movement is older, being rooted in Hasidism but taking shape with the emigration of Jews from the Soviet Union to Israel and the USA after the Second World War.

For Gush Emunim the State of Israel is a fulfilment of the messianic ideal. It is as yet only a partial fulfilment, since it has to be carried through to the establishment of the State of Israel in the whole of the biblical lands. For the Haredim the present State of Israel is illegitimate. Secular Zionism is completely rejected, for it is seen to compromise with modernity while the Jewish tradition is held to be far superior to anything that is non-Jewish.

Gush Emunim has endeavoured to forward the expansion and consolidation of the State of Israel through symbolic gestures and actions that commit the government. It has been instrumental in the setting up of many of the settlements in the Territories. It has thus been trying to anticipate 'the shape of things to come'. Its activity is religiously motivated, and in this sense it competes with Zionism. Its radicalism can be seen at three levels. First, in working towards the Greater Land of Israel it disregards, as a matter of principle, Arab rights. Second, it too opposes secularism, trying to impose religious norms on society. Third, it broadens the traditional definition of Judaism to include nationalism, so that there can be no true Jewish religion without Zionism, and no true Zionism without religion.

The Haredim tend to be apolitical. They are nevertheless wooed by rival political parties and so can wield some influence, but generally they are not involved in the political arena. They stand for an absolute, and yet, existing in a pluralist world, their form of fundamentalism presents itself as an alternative. Gush Emunim, on the other hand, is political religion. It is constantly putting pressure on the Israeli government, and yet, in a sense, it is a separatist movement. With its own educational establishments, its own effective system of socialization, it has created a countersociety. It is said to operate alongside Israeli society, both dependent on it and independent of it, in fact competing with it and aspiring to lead it.

It may be that some aspects of these Jewish fundamentalist movements will have parallels in the Islamic world. But before turning to Islam some brief consideration could be given to Oriental religions.

Hindu fundamentalism

Reference is frequently made to Hindu fundamentalism. Yet one could ask whether Hindu fundamentalism, as advocated by the *Vishwa Hindu Panishad* and the Bharatiya Janata Party, is at all religious. It is much more in the nature of a nationalism appealing to religious sentiment. It can be seen as a reaction to Nehruvian secularism. This was not opposed to religion, but it included an agnostic streak: all religions should be allowed to exist side by side. Hinduism, the religion of the majority, was not thus favoured, and there developed a minority complex of the majority, a feeling of national inferiority. Further back is the historical memory of dominance by Muslims. Hence the emotive element in the broad appeal to Hinduism as the real cultural cement in India, the call for *hindutva*, devotion to Hinduism.

What can be noticed here is the instrumentalization of religious motivation. Nor should one neglect the economic factor, the widening gap between rich and poor as India's industrial power develops. Political leaders are using religion to fight for a greater share of the wealth. The poor are being used as pawns, but the benefits go to the powerful.

Sikh fundamentalism

Whereas religious minorities in India, in order to keep their identity, appeal to the secular character of the constitution according to which the state should not favour one religion over another, Hindu nationalism would imply that the minorities would have to secularize, i.e. lose their religious identities. This conflict in outlook has helped to consolidate Sikh fundamentalism as a reactive phenomenon, a defence mechanism.[10]

Sikh identity has both a doctrinal and a political dimension. Developing as an independent religion under the first guru, Guru Nanak (1469–1539), it established its own holy book, the Granth Sahib. For some Sikhs, after the death of the tenth guru the Granth remains the sole authority. Others recognize a living authority besides the holy book. Sikhs were able to establish their own state in the Punjab under Rajit Singh (1780–1839), but following the loss of power to the British many Sikhs became Hinduized. There are still Hindus today who do not wish to recognize that Sikhs belong to something other than Hinduism. This provokes a reaction that for some has taken on a political dimension, namely the call for a *khalistan*, or homeland, a 'land of the pure', where Sikhs will be able to live out their corporate identity.

The Sikh religion is intrinsically pluralistic in outlook. It allows the validity of all revelations since it holds that the Divine cannot be exhausted in any single revelation. Yet Sikh fundamentalism tends to exclude this broad outlook.

Sikhs give much importance to the veneration of the Granth Sahib, and to its chant, but the fundamentalist trend appeals less to the Scripture than to the traditions of the Gurus and the Martyrs. Sikhs have had to suffer much – one has only to see the gory pictures on the walls of some gurdwaras – and have had to fight for survival. It is this tradition that grounds the actions of the political activists. It must be emphasized that not all Sikhs approve of the violent methods of the nationalist fundamentalists.

Buddhist fundamentalism

According to Yukako Matsuoka, 'if the term fundamentalism can be used at all in Buddhism, it might apply only to parts of Theravada Buddhism',[11] that is to the Buddhism of the Ancients found in Sri Lanka, Myanmar, Thailand, Cambodia and Laos. The reason for this is that Theravada Buddhism has a body of ancient texts, *sutras* and *vinayas* (precepts) to which to refer, whereas for Mahayana Buddhism, the Buddhism of the Greater Vehicle spread from China to Japan in particular, the early texts are not so important and have been supplemented by later compositions. There are, nevertheless, some groups that insist on the importance of certain *sutras*, for instance the Lotus Sutra. A further reason why the Zen form of

Mahayana Buddhism should not be fundamentalist is its attitude towards truth. There can be no fundamental position to refer to, since truth is to be realized, not grasped.

Turning then to Theravada Buddhism, an example of fundamentalism can be found in modern Sri Lanka.[12] Several features already noticed in other forms of fundamentalism can be observed. There is the influence of a charismatic leader, David Hevavitarana (1864–1933). Taking the name of Anagarika Dharmapala (The Homeless Guardian of the Dharma), he founded the Mahabodhi Society of Colombo in order to spread a knowledge of Buddhist texts. Anagarika Dharmapala was known in the West, since he took part in the first World Parliament of Religions, at Chicago, in 1893.

In the teachings of Dharmapala an ambivalent attitude to the West is noted. Its immorality is attacked while at the same time the morality of Christian missionaries is adopted. In fact the influence of Victorian missionary Protestantism is strongly evident. It can be said that this modern Theravada Buddhism, a Buddhism of revival and reformation, is based on historical roots but has been fashioned within the context of the Westernization of European colonialism.

What is developed is a religious ideology. Buddhism as it has been lived in Sri Lanka is demythologized, purified of its Hindu elements except for those that can serve a purpose. Thus Buddhist festivals and the pilgrimage to the Temple of the Tooth are maintained since they can help to reinforce the sense of Buddhist culture. Similarly the myth of Sri Lanka being the island of *Dhamma* is preserved since this can serve a nationalistic goal. Here is the clue. This ideology, constructed through a selective simplification of rules and rites, has as its aim the restoration of Sinhalese national pride. It therefore leads to a drawing of lines, between Buddhist and non-Buddhist Sinhalese, between Sinhalese and non-Sinhalese.

Islamic fundamentalism

Turning finally to Islamic fundamentalisms, a few general remarks can first be made. First, the appeal to a past ideal as a model for the present ordering of society is nothing new in Islam. Throughout Islamic history there have been numerous examples of Islamic fundamentalism of this kind. One could think of the Almohads, the Fulani *jihād*s in West Africa, the rise of Wahhabism, to mention only a few. What is new, I think, is what anthropologists would call 'enlargement of scale'. Whereas the movements mentioned were confined to particular areas and hardly impinged on the rest of the Islamic world, today we see an internationalization and globalization of fundamentalism. Networking is the order of the day.

Second, the selective aspect of fundamentalism is apparent. There is a call for society to be regulated according to the *sharī'a*, without perhaps taking into account the complicated nature of the *sharī'a* as a construct dating much later than the period set up as a model.

Third, there is an evident anti-Western trend. The West is accused of corruption. It is held responsible for economic and political failures. Islam is hailed as the solution.

Yet, fourth, modern Islamic fundamentalism is not primarily the accomplishment of those with little experience of the West. It has been shown that many activists within the *jamā'at islāmiyya* in Egypt are science graduates, a number of whom have studied in the West. The Muslim Brothers have always been willing to use modern technology to further their aims.

In the fifth place, and finally, Islamic fundamentalist movements are concerned with Muslims rather than with non-Muslims. This was true in the past. The wars of the Almohads, the Fulani *jihād*s, the puritanical drives of the Wahhabis, were all directed against Muslims considered not to be authentic Muslims. The same is true in modern times. To give just one example, the Society of Muslims, formed by the Egyptian Shukri Mustafa in the wake of the Muslim Brother Sayyid Qutb, applied the principle of *al-takfīr wa'l-hijra*. It asserted the right to declare other Muslims unbelievers (*kuffār*) and the need to withdraw (*hijra*) from Egyptian society considered as *jāhiliyya*, ignorance and barbarism.[13]

Rather than try to present a panorama of Islamic fundamentalist movements it may be interesting to compare and contrast two movements that arose in the twentieth century and are still active, *Tabligh* and *Jama'at-i-Islam*.[14]

Tabligh was founded in the mid-1920s by Maulana Muhammad Ilyas (1885–1944), a graduate of Deoband. Jama'at-i-Islam was founded in 1941, before the partition of India, by Abul Ala Maududi (1903–75), who was not a traditional religious scholar (*'ālim*) but who was well known as the editor of a monthly magazine dedicated to the exegesis of the Qur'an (*Tarjuman al-Qur'an*).

Both movements relied on a selective retrieval of the past, based on a literalist interpretation of the Qur'an and Hadith. They both displayed hostility towards Islamic liberalism. Yet there was a difference in their goal. Maududi was working for a totally Islamic system of life and this he felt could only be attained with the establishment of an Islamic state. Ilyas aimed at the moral and spiritual uplift of individual believers so that they could live an integral Islamic life whether an Islamic state existed or not.

The difference in goal is reflected also in the organization of the movements. Maududi's support came mainly from the educated middle classes. The Tabligh is much more of a grass-roots movement. The Jama'at-i-Islam has developed in Pakistan into a modern-type political party, highly structured and hierarchical. It has had links with similar groups in other Muslim countries, such as the Rifah Partesi in Turkey and with the Islamic National Front in Sudan. Tabligh has also international connections, indeed it is an international movement, but it is much more free-flowing and apolitical. It is a *da'wa* movement which aims to purify Islam.

The Jama'at-i-Islam makes a distinction between Westernization, which it opposes, and modernization, held to be acceptable. By Westernization is understood certain features of modern society in the West, the breakdown of the family, sexual laxity, but also the primacy of reason over revelation, and above all the marginalization of religion. In the Islamic state, as advocated, religion plays a dominant role, but at a price. As Mumtaz Ahmad remarks, 'one of the characteristics of "political religion" is that although it retains religion as the basis of legitimacy, its religious content tends to become increasingly instrumental'.[15]

What characterizes the Tabligh, and perhaps qualifies it to be considered as a fundamentalist movement, is that it represents a closed system. No encouragement is given to read any literature other than that of the movement itself, nor is there any openness to criticism from within. The original methods continue to be followed without change. Yet, because of its apolitical stance, it can be said to have favoured secularism, for it has drained off energies which might otherwise have been channelled into political action. It might be interesting to examine whether the activities of the Tabligh among Muslims in the West will favour advocacy of the *sharī'a* for Muslim communities or the acceptance of a pluralist society. In other words, will revived religious fervour create support for more militant fundamentalism?

Conclusion

This leads to a final quotation which can be taken as an open-ended conclusion since it contains an implicit question about the way to react to fundamentalism.

> The sheer physical power of the modern state to suppress opposition assures that it has the ability to affect the development of fundamentalism and, under certain conditions, to curtail its effectiveness. However, a policy of suppression without nuance is less effective and perhaps even counter-productive in areas in which a generalized popular return to religion has forged a broad sympathy for even the most militant of fundamentalists. In addition, in instances in which nonviolent expressions of fundamentalism have been allowed to become a visible and credible part of the political system, the appeal of the violent marginal groups has been reduced.[16]

15

Witnessing to Christ: Ecumenism and interreligious dialogue

The 'Our Father', an expression of real but imperfect unity

When Christians gather together to pray, they often find unity, despite their differences, in the common recitation of the Lord's Prayer. This prayer unites them in praise of the Father, as they ask that his name be hallowed. It binds them together as they pray that his will be done. It commits them to a common mission in the desire that God's kingdom may come.

It can be noted that the fruit of the prayer is not confined to Christians only, for holiness can be found in people who do not profess faith in Christ, just as the search for God's will and the desire to fulfil it are not restricted to Christians, and the values of God's kingdom can be found outside the visible boundaries of the Church.

The fact that the words and the sentiments can be shared with people who do not hold the same faith as us should make us aware that the unity we experience can coexist with serious differences in belief. It is therefore an imperfect unity. It was perhaps for that reason, the emphasis being put on the disunity rather than the unity, that, when I was a boy, Catholics would not normally join other Christians in prayer, even for the recitation of the 'Our Father'. This is still the case for some Christians today.

The fact that Christians are divided is indeed a grave scandal. It is something that people of other religions naturally note. Instead of saying 'See how they love one another', they are inclined to remark 'See how they squabble with one another.' If we examine the Qur'an we shall find that almost every time Christians are mentioned, so too are their divisions. In *Sūrat Maryam*, for instance, after having recounted the Annunciation to Mary and the birth of Jesus, the text concludes: 'Such is Jesus, the son of Mary. This is a statement of truth about which they dispute' (Q. 19.34), and a later verse adds: 'But the parties among them (i.e. the Christians) differ among themselves' (Q. 19.37).

Surely then there is a need to do everything we can to bring about the will of Jesus Christ as expressed in his prayer 'That they may all be one, as you, Father, are in me and I in you, that they also may be in us, that the world may believe that you sent me' (John 16.21).

Thus is highlighted the need for a common witness, for Christians to relate together, in so far as it is possible, to people of other religions. The *Directory for the Application of the Principles and Norms of Ecumenism*[1] takes notice of this fact. It states:

> There are increasing contacts in today's world between Christians and persons of other religions. These contacts differ radically from the contacts between the Church and ecclesial communities, which have for their object the restoration of the unity Christ willed among all his disciples, and are properly called ecumenical. But in practice they are deeply influenced by, and in turn influence ecumenical relationships. Through them, Christians can deepen the level of communion existing among themselves, and so they are to be considered an important part of ecumenical cooperation. (PNE 210)

It could rightly be said, then, that interreligious relations provide a stimulus for ecumenical endeavour.

Comparing ecumenism and interreligious dialogue

The quotation just given, while noting the connection between ecumenism and interreligious dialogue, stresses the difference between these two. Although the spirit that animates these two activities and the methods that are employed in them are similar, the end that they pursue is not the same. Let me start with the latter point.

Ecumenism has as its aim 'the restoration of the unity Christ willed among his disciples'. It is evident that what is intended is unity in diversity, for there can be no question of doing away with all the particular rites and practices to be found in the various expressions of Christianity. Yet there must be a unity in belief sufficient to allow the members of the different communities to recognize one another not only with respect but as being in communion. It is this communion in belief that is the foundation for communion in practice.

With regard to interreligious relations, however, this communion of belief is necessarily lacking. This does not mean that there are no commonalities between Christianity and other religions, particularly with those religions, such as Judaism and Islam, which believe in the One Creator God who is the Judge of humankind. Yet these religions do not accept Jesus as the Son of God, the one Lord and Saviour. If they did they would cease to be themselves and would become expressions of Christianity. The aim of interreligious dialogue cannot therefore be to try to bring about a unity of all religions (such has been the aim of some 'universalist' movements, but they have in fact resulted in the formation of new religions). Its purpose is, at one level, somewhat more modest, namely the pursuit of harmony and peace among the followers of different religions. Yet it does go further:

> Interreligious dialogue does not merely aim at mutual understanding and friendly relations. It reaches a much deeper level, that of the spirit, where exchange and sharing consist in a mutual witness to one's beliefs and a common exploration of one's respective religious convictions. In dialogue, Christians and others are invited to deepen their religious commitment, to respond with increasing sincerity to God's personal call and gracious self-gift.   (DP 40)

It is for this reason that interreligious dialogue can truly be called a 'dialogue of salvation'. The fact that, in the Christian understanding of salvation, God's personal call and gracious self-gift 'always passes through the mediation of Jesus Christ and the work of his Spirit' (DP 40), does not invalidate the profound scope of interreligious relations.

If ecumenical and interreligious relations have a radically different finality, do they have anything in common? Surely it can be said that they display a similarity of spirit and often use comparable methods. Without going into great detail, I would like to suggest respect, love and humility as being essential elements of the spirit of both ecumenism and interreligious relations.

Respect comes from the conviction that God is working not only in the heart of individuals, but also in the rites and traditions of their communities. We know that this respect has not always been shown. When the Vatican Council declared in *Nostra Aetate* that 'the Church has also a high regard for the Muslims' (NA 3), this was something of an eye-opener for many Catholics. Religious traditions command our respect because they bear witness to the effort to provide answers 'to those profound mysteries of the human condition' (NA 1) that have exercised human minds and hearts since the beginning of time. They are also to be treated with respect because of the spiritual and human values that they enshrine. In ecumenical terms we may think of the liturgical and spiritual traditions of the Oriental Churches, the attention accorded to the word of God by the various Protestant communities, the vitality of praise among Pentecostals, while with regard to other religions we remember the family focus in Shabbat celebrations, the rich Sufi tradition in Islam, and the spirit of service in Sikhism.

This respect has practical consequences. It means being careful in the way we speak about other people. The Vatican Council's Decree on Ecumenism states that every effort is to be made 'to avoid expressions, judgements and actions which do not represent the condition of our separated brethren with truth and fairness and so make mutual relations with them more difficult' (UR 6). This could surely be applied to our relations with people of other religions and, we would hope, to their relations with us. Perhaps one application is that we no longer speak about 'separated brethren', just as we try to avoid using the term 'non-Christians'.

Yet respect does not mean indifference or laissez-faire. When it is combined with love it sees other Christians, as well as the people of other religions, as brothers and sisters, as members of the one human family. John Paul II, in his encyclical on ecumenism *Ut Unum Sint*, noted some of the applications of this 'universal brotherhood'. He spoke of communities that were once rivals subsequently helping one another, with regard to places of worship or scholarships for further studies, in making approaches to civil authorities on behalf of those being persecuted, and in helping to restore the good name of those who had been slandered (cf. UUS 42). All this could be applied, *mutatis mutandis*, to interreligious relations. The document *Dialogue and Proclamation* stresses that the spirit of brotherhood leads to unselfish action:

> There is need to stand up for human rights, proclaim the demands of justice, and denounce injustice not only when their own members are victimized, but independently of the religious allegiance of the victims. There is a need also to join together in trying to solve the great problems facing society and the world, as well as in education for justice and peace. (DP 44)

This appeal is addressed immediately to Christians, to local churches, but has a wider application.

Finally, one could point to humility as an essential requisite for sound ecumenical and interreligious relations. However convinced we are that our religious traditions teach us the truth – and we, as Christians, confess Jesus Christ as the way, the truth and the life – we know that we, ourselves, have not fully grasped that truth. As long as we are on earth we are in a state of pilgrimage. We are conscious of our human limitations; we know that we are not perfect. This holds good for us as individuals and also for our communities, which are always in need of renewal and reform. Above all, we are conscious that it is God who rules the universe, and that our task is to follow the promptings of his Spirit. The conviction that the Spirit is leading us is a source of courage and perseverance. When faced with obstacles, with misunderstandings, we can take solace in the fact that we are under God. We can realize that we are 'invited by God to enter into the mystery of his patience, as human beings seek his light and truth', for 'only God knows the times and stages of the fulfilment of this long human quest' (DP 84).

With regard to the methods used in ecumenism, the *Ecumenical Directory* has a chapter entitled 'Communion in life and spiritual activity among the baptized', and a further chapter on 'Ecumenical cooperation, dialogue and common witness'. The documents on dialogue, for their part, distinguish four types: *dialogue of life, of action, of discourse* and *of religious experience.* To some extent these two divisions overlap, though there are major differences.

One might think that community of life and dialogue of life would be the same, but the operative word in the title of the chapter in the *Directory* is 'baptized'. The fact of sharing a common baptism puts Christians in a special situation. Common prayer becomes possible, whereas among the followers of different religions it remains problematic. For Christians, joint services can be prepared in which the participants recite or sing the same words. Joint services for interreligious gatherings raise many difficulties. It is usually safer to have a succession of prayers led by representatives of different religions in turn with the others listening respectfully. Again, among Christians, under certain conditions, sharing in sacramental life and especially in the Eucharist is permissible. For people of other religions to share in Christian worship or for Christians to share in the worship of another religion would be condemned as *communicatio in sacris* (sharing in those things which are reserved for the people of that religion). The most that could be done would be to assist reverently at such worship. Such a practice should not be despised, for it can form part of what is known as the dialogue of religious experience.

Ecumenical cooperation can take on a multitude of forms. The *Directory* mentions common Bible work, common liturgical texts, cooperation in catechesis, joint theological study and formation, joint study of social and ethical questions, work together in the field of development, humanitarian need and the protection of the environment, common endeavours in the medical field, and also with regard to social communications. While the first items on this list, closely dependent on a sharing of the Christian faith, would hardly be applicable to interreligious cooperation, the more one looks outward to the service of the world, so the possibility of cooperation can be envisaged. In a religiously pluralistic society, where religious education must necessarily embrace different religious traditions, collaboration among these traditions in preparing and implementing programmes becomes desirable. Similarly religious traditions can find themselves united in sustaining common values or in common action for the benefit of the needy. Indeed the possibilities for cooperation are vast. What is needed, of course, is the will to engage in joint action and this, in turn, requires a high degree of mutual confidence.

Dialogue can help to create the necessary climate for such cooperation. The *Ecumenical Directory* gives some indications regarding the nature of this dialogue, which are to some extent relevant also in interreligious relations.

> Dialogue involves both listening and replying, seeking both to understand and to be understood. It is a readiness to put questions and to be questioned. It is to be forthcoming about oneself and trustful of what others say about themselves. The parties in dialogue must be ready to clarify their ideas further, and modify their personal views and ways of living and acting, allowing themselves to be guided in this

by authentic love and truth. Reciprocity and mutual commitment are essential elements in dialogue, as is also a sense that the partners are together on an equal footing. (PNE 172)

There are of course fundamental differences, following the difference of finality between ecumenical and interreligious dialogue already mentioned. Whereas in ecumenical dialogue the aim will be to arrive at a common statement of faith, in interreligious dialogue the aim can only be to clarify ideas and achieve greater understanding by eliminating prejudices and over-simplified approximations of the truth.

Opportunities for an ecumenical approach to interreligious dialogue

After having compared briefly the aims and methods of ecumenism and interreligious dialogue, I would now like to illustrate some opportunities for an ecumenical approach to interreligious dialogue. I shall do this following the fourfold division of dialogue, and then give some practical examples.

The dialogue of life really takes place at a human level, where people are relating to one another primarily as fellow human beings. Nevertheless faith motivations can strengthen the desire to reach out to other people, even if they belong to different religious traditions.

This is not always easy. Because of differences, often cultural as well as religious, there may well be a tendency to cut oneself off from others, or to relate to them at a very superficial level. So initiatives will be required to create a climate where everyone is at ease. Celebrations can be organized to mark the feasts of the different communities. Newcomers to the area can be welcomed, or a farewell party be arranged for people when they are leaving the neighbourhood. The variations are almost limitless.

At this level it would seem that differences among Christians should not have any weight. If in a neighbourhood Christians of different denominations are living together with, say, Muslims and Buddhists, then it would be as Christians that they relate to these others rather than as Catholics, Episcopalians and Pentecostals. What is often required here is a degree of communication. If someone has an idea to improve the relations in a particular village or quarter of a town, then perhaps this idea should be shared and discussed with others before being implemented.

The *Ecumenical Directory* distinguishes several types of cooperation. These can easily be adapted to interreligious cooperation. There is first participation in programmes already set up by one particular religious tradition. Or cooperation may take the form of coordinating independent initiatives, making sure that there is no unnecessary overlapping. Finally there may be joint initiatives (cf. PNE 163).

The programme in question may be to take care of AIDS orphans. Is it the Catholics who are going to do this, perhaps engaging Muslim nurses and seeking financial support from a wealthy businessman from another Christian community? Will the Catholics take care of the home for orphans and leave education about AIDS to others? Or will an attempt be made to bring everyone on board to tackle the specific problem of AIDS orphans, since these belong to all religious communities?

Since most religious bodies have their own structures and their own funding agencies, it is much easier to go it alone. It takes a deliberate effort to bring in people of other traditions. It requires, one might say, an ecumenical instinct. But surely, if Christians are united when approaching others to cooperate with them, they probably stand a better chance of receiving a positive reply.

The different types of cooperation mentioned above are relevant also for the more academic or more formal kind of dialogue that may take place among people of different religious traditions. Here again, it may well be one Church body, or one academic institution, which organizes a symposium and invites members of other Christian traditions to take part on the Christian side. Very often, of course, the organizer may be an ecumenical body, a national or regional council of Churches, since these are paying ever more attention to interreligious relations. Fortunately, in many places the Catholic Church is a full member of such councils, and therefore will be involved from the start.

It must be said that such ecumenical cooperation in formal dialogue is easier when the topics being discussed are of a social nature. When the exchanges deal with matters of belief, there may be some embarrassment to find that the Christians are not agreeing among themselves. Yet these differences can arise also regarding ethical issues. Since, as has been mentioned above, theological dialogue of an interreligious nature is not designed to bring about full agreement anyway, the fact that there are differences of opinion among the partners on one side of the dialogue may not matter too much. In fact, the airing of differences may encourage a less monolithic approach on the other side.

It may be in the dialogue of religious experience that ecumenical cooperation will be the most difficult. Of course, if the sharing takes the form of an academic exchange on respective spiritual traditions, there is no reason why different Christian traditions should not be brought into the picture. If, however, the sharing takes the form of presence at worship, this will normally be the worship of one particular community. Even in this case, however, there would not be any real reason for not inviting Christians of other traditions to attend respectfully together with their partners of the other religion or religions. It may well be profitable for Buddhists to experience at one time a Catholic ceremony and at another a Protestant form of worship, just as Christians would find it interesting to be present in a Theravada temple on one occasion, at Zen meditation another time, and have a further opportunity to assist at a Tibetan ceremony. What is useful is to give the opportunity to discuss the experience afterwards.

Some examples of ecumenical cooperation

After this rather theoretical approach, let me give some concrete examples. These are taken from my own experience in the years that I have been working in the Pontifical Council for Interreligious Dialogue (PCID).

For almost 30 years now there has been much contact between the Vatican's office for interreligious dialogue and the corresponding office in the World Council of Churches. In the mid-1970s the Secretary and Under-Secretary of the then Secretariat for Non-Christians were invited to take part in the WCC meeting on 'Dialogue in Community' at Chiang Mai, Thailand. In 1979 the leading staff members of the Sub-Unit for Dialogue with Living Faiths and Ideologies were invited to participate in the first Plenary Assembly of the Secretariat. Since then, these reciprocal invitations have continued, and in more recent years there have been annual joint staff meetings.

A further step taken has been to engage in joint projects. The first of these concerned interreligious marriages. Questionnaires were sent out, the literature produced by different Christian bodies was studied, and then a joint document was written.[2] The document remains very general in tenor, partly because it was dealing with interreligious marriages in general, and partly because it could not propose the legislative position of any one particular Christian tradition. Yet it does usefully present the problems such marriages pose, as also the opportunities for interreligious relations that they may give rise to.

The second project concerned interreligious prayer. There were three stages. First a survey among different Churches on the practice of interreligious prayer, then a consultation of people experienced in this field, and finally a consultation of a more theological nature. The findings of the two consultations and some of the papers presented were jointly published in *Current Dialogue* and *Pro Dialogo* 98 (1998). Here again Christians will not find the position of their own particular tradition, but they certainly have available material that will help them if they wish to consider whether and how to engage in prayer with people of other religions.

The current project engaging the joint efforts of the PCID and the WCC's Office on Inter-Religious Relations and Dialogue is concerned with Africa. It is designed to highlight the richness of the spiritual traditions of Africa as a contribution to the spiritual heritage of the world.

The Conference of European Churches (KEK, which groups practically all the main Churches in Europe with the exception of the Catholic Church) and the Council of Episcopal Conferences of Europe (CCEE) formed the Islam in Europe Committee. The purpose of the committee is to help the various Churches face up to the challenge of the growing Muslim presence in Europe. One distinctive feature of the committee is that, even before the enlargement of the European Union, it had always included the countries of Central and Eastern Europe. On one occasion it held a joint meeting with the Middle East Council of Churches.

The committee has made proposals on how best Islam should be studied during the formation of priests and ministers. It has tackled the question of marriage between Christians and Muslims. It issued a rather controversial document on reciprocity. As with other ecumenical bodies, the committee has no authority apart from the value of its work. It can merely propose reflections to the Churches which then have the responsibility to act upon them if and as they think fit.

In more recent years the Islam in Europe Committee has actively engaged in dialogue with Muslims. So it was that at the time of the terrorist attacks of September 11, 2001 the members of the committee were engaged in a Christian–Muslim symposium in Sarajevo. Such meetings are occasions for Muslims to be exposed to a great variety of Christian traditions.

There is another ecumenical group in Europe that deals with Christian–Muslim relations. This is an informal meeting held annually since 1980. It convened first in Arras, at a time when the bishop of that city in Northern France was responsible for the Secrétariat pour les Relations avec l'Islam, the official office set up by the French hierarchy for this matter. Although the meeting may take place now in any part of Europe, Milan or Marseille, Stockholm or Selly Oak, Birmingham, the week's gathering is still known as the Journées d'Arras. Its purpose is essentially an exchange of information on the situation of Christian–Muslim relations in the different countries of Europe. Enquiries are made and papers presented, but the emphasis is on personal communication. The meeting enables people from different Church structures or from study centres to discuss issues of common concern and to share progress in research.

The Federation of Asian Bishops' Conferences (FABC) has for many years been running its own programme on interreligious dialogue. This is only natural in a continent where Christians, apart from in the Philippines, are a rather small minority. First there came the Bishops' Institutes for Inter-Religious Affairs (BIRA) series, institutes for bishops to make them aware of the issues involved in inter-religious relations. The aim was to have all Catholic bishops in Asia attend one of these institutes. There followed a series of BIRA II, which were actual exercises in dialogue, with Muslims, with Hindus, with Buddhists, and with the Confucian-Taoist traditions. Now FABC is engaged in the FIRA series, where the F stands for formation. These sessions are not for bishops only, but are also offered to priests, religious and laypeople.

Precisely because in Asia Christians in most countries form a very small minority, the ecumenical dimension of their relations with people of other religions is of extreme importance. This has led to cooperation with the Christian Conference of Asia (CCA). Already a joint meeting was held in Singapore, in 1987, with 55 participants from 14 countries. The concluding joint statement shared fundamental insights and a series of practical recommendations. It is interesting to note that ecumenism is presupposed in this statement rather than addressed specifically. Only in one recommendation, that dealing with the appropriate structures for dialogue, is it stated that 'as far as possible, these efforts should be carried out in an ecumenical spirit'.[3]

My final example comes from the Philippines. Mindanao has long been beset by the conflict between certain Islamic factions and the national army. In an attempt to overcome the conflict by encouraging negotiations, religious leaders have come together. At first it was the Catholic bishops who met with the leading religious authorities among the Muslims. Then the forum was opened to bishops of other Churches. This was surely on account of the realization that in the Philippines of today all religious forces have to be engaged if a lasting result is to be achieved.

The bishops and *'ulamā'* have been meeting regularly and cultivating good relations among themselves. Their wish is that these good relations should filter down to other levels, to that of the local parish priests and ministers and the local imams. Much of interreligious relations is an exercise in confidence building. Now the Philippines forum has taken the step to spread the initiative to other countries of Asia.

In the 1970s in the continent of Africa, the various Protestant Churches set up a structure to help Christian communities in their relations with Muslims. The Islam in Africa Project eventually took the title Project for Christian–Muslim Relations in Africa (PROCMURA). Faithful to its origins this body, based in Nairobi, remains a Protestant structure. Nevertheless cooperation with Catholics is actively sought. Catholics often participate in the programmes run by PROCMURA, and a Catholic Sister from The Gambia is a member of the advisory board for West Africa. When PROCMURA was evaluating its work some years ago, a Catholic missionary priest, with a long experience in the field of Christian–Muslim relations, was invited to be a member of the evaluation team and help draw up the final report. This shows a high degree of mutual confidence. Cooperation could probably be increased. It might mean, on the part of Catholics, that instead of setting up their own structures and meetings, they would call on the expertise and organizational capacity of PROC-MURA. Even if separate structures are created within the Catholic Church, they should be ready to work together with their Protestant brethren.

Interreligious relations as a path to Christian unity

Faced with the scandal of the divisions among Christians, some people are tempted to say that ecumenism should have the priority. Once Christian unity has been achieved, then it will be the time to develop relations with people of other religions.

Without wishing to deny the importance of ecumenism, it would seem to me that this position is untenable for two reasons. One is that the sound development of interreligious relations cannot wait. The world is becoming ever more religiously pluralistic. There is practically no part of the world where people of different religions do not meet. It is important that they should learn to know, understand and respect one another. There are, for example, many Filipino workers in Saudi Arabia, the heartland of the Muslim world. Many of them are Christians. They need the backing of good relations between Christian and Muslim leaders so that their rights as human beings, and in particular their right to religious freedom, may be respected. It is vital then that interreligious matters be addressed.

A second reason is that relating to people of other religions helps Christians to understand better and appreciate more their own faith. They come to see how tremendous is the central tenet of that faith, namely that God so loved the world that he gave his only Son to be our Brother, Lord and Saviour. The contact with other systems of belief, and with people who are influenced by these systems, helps us to discern what is essential in Christianity and what is of lesser importance. It is by going to the roots of their faith that Christians will find the path to unity in diversity. This is surely what Christ wants of us.

16

Dialogue and spirituality: The example of Buddhist–Catholic dialogue in the USA

JOHN BORELLI

Christian–Buddhist dialogue

Buddhists and Christians draw close to one another in so many ways these days. They easily grow to be friends, colleagues, collaborators and companions, and at times become guides and instructors for one another, students together or of one another, or even partners in marriage. Friendship allows them to share sentiments sincerely and candidly, from everyday hopes and concerns to their deepest spiritual insights. Whenever Buddhists and Christians engage in interreligious dialogue, regardless of what they discuss and share, they do so as persons for whom their Buddhist practice and Christian faith are manifest dimensions of undeniable importance in their lives.

These relationships sometimes overlap, especially for individuals strongly committed to Buddhist–Christian dialogue. Colleagues on a faculty might hold ongoing conversations about their fields of study, especially as these reflect or impinge on aspects of their faith and practice. As members of learned societies, Buddhists and Christians might hold regular sessions of dialogue on topics of mutual interest. Buddhist and Christian religious and community leaders form associations that bring them together regularly for conversation, interreligious services of prayer, programmes and common projects or in times of crisis. A Buddhist centre, a Christian community or a monastic house of either group might invite speakers to introduce religious topics or to offer insights on similarities and differences between the Christian and Buddhist traditions. Therefore, when a

Buddhist–Christian dialogue group takes shape, several participants might already be familiar friends from other dialogues. This has been especially true in the USA, and such friendships lead to a sequence of events that reach a number of remarkable, if not singular, achievements.

Some dialogues benefit from formal institutional support; others are far more informal by accident or choice. No single kind of dialogue meets all the needs of everyone or every group. Some dialogues are theological discussions while others have a more pastoral focus to alleviate suffering and misery, to meet the needs of the poor and disadvantaged, and to address social and political problems. The latter are not less theological, because social engagement is at the heart of the message of both traditions, but some dialogues are unquestionably academic in nature, aimed at improving scholarly insight. While many may benefit from listening to these often erudite exchanges, few feel themselves qualified to prepare and deliver lengthy papers. Unfortunately, many think of these learned exchanges when they hear the term interreligious dialogue.

In fact, some persons, because of their cultural setting or background or a unique set of personal circumstances, sense that they are living interior dialogues and feel they belong to both Christianity and Buddhism. 'Double belonging' is the term used for this phenomenon, but the word refers to several kinds of experiences and has both ecumenical and interreligious usages. Whatever double belonging may mean in the context of Buddhist–Christian relations, it is a phenomenon that involves interiority, and it is quite different from erudite exchanges between two or more persons. Some dialogues focus on interiority and are contemplative in character, involving mutual exploration of meditation and spiritual insight. For a gradually increasing number of individuals, both Buddhists and Christians, working together in various ways, dialogue is not only an objective for their life and work but also an aspect of their spiritual practice. For many involved in Buddhist–Christian dialogue, interreligious dialogue itself is a natural way of being Christian or Buddhist. Three extraordinary examples illustrate this.

After their third intensive conversation in five days, Thomas Merton wrote in his Asian journal in 1968 of this experience with the Dalai Lama:

and at the end I felt we had become very good friends and were some-
how quite close to one another. I feel a great respect and fondness for
him as a person and believe, too, that there is a real spiritual bond
between us.[1]

Merton never returned from that trip to his Trappist home at Our
Lady of Gethsemani Abbey in Kentucky. Having left on his first and
only trip to Asia to participate in a conference in Thailand sponsored
by an international Benedictine group, he met an accidental death
shortly after delivering an address to that gathering. He died about a
month after he made the entry in his journal about meeting the Dalai
Lama. Many years later, in 1996, at a gathering of Buddhist and
Catholic monastics at Gethsemani Abbey, the Dalai Lama, now well
beyond Merton's age at the time of their meeting, commented on
their relationship:

As for myself, I always consider myself as one of his Buddhist brothers. So, as a close friend – or as his brother – I always remember him,
and I always admire his activities and his lifestyle. Since my meeting
with him, and so often when I examine myself, I closely follow some
of his examples. Occasionally I really have a deep satisfaction knowing
that I have made some contribution regarding his wishes for the
world. And so for the rest of my life, the impact of meeting him will
remain until my last breath. I really want to state that I make this commitment, and this will remain until my last breath.[2]

Interreligious dialogue became a natural part of Thomas Merton's
life as a monk. Likewise, it found a place in the spiritual practice of
the Dalai Lama, continuing to unfold but inextricably linked to their
friendship established in dialogue.

Pope Paul VI, who effectively established dialogue as an element of
Catholic self-understanding, knew how this dynamic played out
through personal contact. After speaking to a group of representatives of various religions of Japan in July 1978, he spontaneously
added to his prepared remarks: 'We thank you again for your visit
and pray to the Lord that we may always be worthy to love you and
to serve you.'[3] As it turned out, this was the Pope's last formal interreligious meeting. He died a few days later.

The documents of the Second Vatican Council offered only a
few principles and urgings for interreligious dialogue. In the 16

documents of the Second Vatican Council, there is only one direct reference to Buddhism:

> The religions which are found in more advanced civilizations endeavor by way of well-defined concepts and exact language to answer these questions . . . Buddhism in its various forms testifies to the essential inadequacy of this changing world. It proposes a way of life by which men can, with confidence and trust, attain a state of perfect liberation and reach supreme illumination either through their own efforts or by the aid of divine help. *(Nostra Aetate 2)*

General references in all these documents to interreligious dialogue and to peoples of other religions apply, of course, to Buddhists. From a Catholic perspective, Buddhists have divine assistance, discern the truths of conscience through grace, and are consistent with the gospel when what they hold is true and what they do is good. The documents of the council also urge Catholics to assist Buddhists to preserve what is true, good and holy along with their way of life and cultural traditions.

In his first address to the Second Vatican Council, after his election as pope, Paul VI urged the assembled bishops not to place limits on the love of the Church when they regard other religions. This love of the Church is God's love 'who showers his favors upon everyone (cf. Mt 5:45), and who so loved the world that for it he gave his only Son (cf. John 3:16).'[4] Paul VI's language in that 1963 speech would reappear in conciliar documents. For example, he stated, 'the Catholic religion holds in just regard all that which in them is true, good and human.' Eight months later, in May 1964, Paul VI established the secretariat in Rome that would eventually bear the name, the Pontifical Council for Interreligious Dialogue. On that occasion, he rejoiced that 'no pilgrim, no matter how distant he may be religiously or geographically, no matter his country of origin, will any longer be a complete stranger in this Rome.'[5] His words reflect the gospel messages of hospitality, loving kindness, service to one another for peace and mutual understanding, and fellowship in spiritual pilgrimage. Later, in August 1964, in his encyclical on the Church, Paul VI would remind the Church that 'the dialogue of salvation sprang from the goodness and the love of God' and urged 'our inducement, therefore, to enter into this dialogue must be nothing other than a love which is ardent and sincere' (*Ecclesiam Suam* 73). Similarly, Thich Nhat Hanh has written of how Christian–Buddhist dialogue rests on spiritual practice, 'when we are still, looking deeply, and touching the source of our true wisdom, we touch the living Buddha and the living Christ in ourselves and in each person we meet.'[6]

The context of the USA

Christians, of course, were present from the beginning of the European exploration and settlement of the territory that would become the USA. The overwhelming character of the population of the new nation before the Civil War in 1861 was Protestant Christian. The beginnings of Buddhism are far more recent by comparison. Chinese immigrants arriving on the West Coast in the 1840s were the first sizeable group practising Buddhism.[7] One source suggests that, with the discovery of gold and later opportunities for work on the railroad and wherever there was a need for labourers, one-tenth of the population of California in 1860 was Chinese.[8] With the building of the railroad, Chinese immigrants and their children spread to other states. Soon Montana's population was nearly one-tenth Chinese.[9] Thus, at first, Buddhist practice in the USA blended with Confucian and Taoist customs and rituals in typically Chinese fashion.

Life in the USA was not easy for Chinese immigrants because sentiment against them spread throughout the population of the west, leading to the enactment of several laws prohibiting Chinese from ownership, from marrying white Americans and even from immigrating. The Japanese began arriving in increasing numbers at the beginning of the twentieth century and seemed to have a greater impact on American society. In 1889, the first Japanese Buddhist priest arrived in Hawaii from the Honpa Honganji temple in Kyoto.[10] In the opening decades of the twentieth century, various Buddhist teachers and priests travelled to the West Coast from Japan to establish Buddhist temples and centres both for the slowly expanding Japanese population and to guide increasing numbers of white American aspirants to Buddhist practice. When President Roosevelt issued Executive Order 9066 in 1942 ordering the forcible internment of people of Japanese ancestry in camps, 60 per cent of the 110,000 relocated to the camps identified themselves as Buddhists.[11] After

President Johnson signed the Immigration and Nationality Act of 1965, Buddhists from many other parts of Asia came to the USA to put down roots. Some began to arrive as refugees because of war in South-East Asia, and today there are sizeable communities of Vietnamese and Cambodian Buddhists. Thai and Sri Lankan communities have grown. Numerous others have taken up Buddhism, especially Tibetan practice. Although Buddhists are a thriving, though small, minority in the USA, the decades since 1960 represent a period of phenomenal growth.[12]

The rapid increase in the Catholic population in the USA is a nineteenth-century phenomenon. Although Catholics probably held the same range of attitudes towards Asians as their fellow Christians, they too were met with suspicion and concern, as were Asians. Catholics first arrived in any numbers with the establishment of the Maryland colony in 1632, but they were never above suspicion and soon authorities forbade them from holding public office, carrying firearms and serving on juries.[13] Catholics served in the Revolution and enjoyed the same religious and other freedoms as their fellow citizens thereafter, but anti-Catholicism increased with the waves of immigrants first from Ireland and then from other Catholic countries of Europe. During the first 60 years of the nineteenth century, immigration changed the face of the USA, the population of which grew from 5 million to 31 million.[14] By 1850, Catholics composed 'the largest single body of church-goers in the nation'.[15]

The election of John F. Kennedy to the Presidency and the extraordinary changes of the Second Vatican Council brought Catholics to a level of acceptance they had not enjoyed up to that time in the USA. Collectively, the conciliar *Decree on Ecumenism*, the *Constitution on the Church in the Modern World*, and the *Declaration on Religious Liberty* improved the bonds of friendship and cooperation between Catholics and Protestants. The council's declaration on interreligious dialogue in 1965 set in motion a series of developments that would bear fruit in Buddhist–Catholic relations in the USA. Thus, as Buddhists grew in numbers and diversity, both through immigration and appeal to white Americans, Catholics drew from the council's strong encouragement to 'enter with prudence and charity into discussion and collaboration with members of other religions' (NA 2). By 1970, Buddhists and Catholics in the USA were prepared to reach out and form partnerships.

First steps

The international Benedictine group that invited the Trappist Thomas Merton to speak in Bangkok in 1968 was *Aide a l'Implantation Monastique* (AIM). The papal representative to the meeting was the Abbot Primate of the Benedictines, Dom Rembert Weakland, former Abbot of St Vincent's Archabbey in Latrobe, Pennsylvania. Following another meeting of AIM in 1973, Cardinal Sergio Pignedoli, president of the office established by Pope Paul VI for interreligious dialogue in Rome, known then as the Secretariat for Non-Christians but nowadays as the Pontifical Council for Interreligious Dialogue, wrote to Abbot Primate Weakland. The Cardinal asked the Abbot to encourage Catholic monastics to consider how they could serve as a bridge between the religions of the east and the west by fostering dialogue. In 1977, two groups of Catholic monks and nuns met in the USA and in Belgium and formed two branches of the same interreligious enterprise. In the USA, they named their group the North American Board for East-West Dialogue, and today the US and European branches are known respectively as Monastic Interreligious Dialogue (MID) and Dialogue Interreligieux Monastique (DIM).

At about the same time Catholic leaders were encouraging monastics to think about interreligious dialogue, a group of practitioners in the Tibetan strains of Buddhism, followers of Chögyam Trungpa Rinpoche, founder of the Naropa Institute in Boulder, Colorado, agreed to their founder's urgings to initiate a programme of interreligious contemplative studies. These were all converts who thought they had left their Jewish and Christian pasts for good. It took them a few years to come around to the idea but, in 1980, they invited members of the Catholic monastic board for dialogue to assist them in the planning of a series of conferences. The Naropa conferences eventually occurred through much of the 1980s (1981–6 and 1988). In 2005, Naropa University, heir of the Naropa Institute, hosted a reunion of the dialogue partners bringing together those planners and speakers still alive who contributed to the success of the series.[16]

The Dalai Lama participated in the first Naropa Conference in 1981, and during a conversation at that conference, members of the Catholic monastic group asked him if he would be willing to send his monks on visitations to Catholic monasteries in the USA. Hence, with the support of the Dalai Lama and the willingness of US male and female Catholic monastics to respond to the encouragement of their leadership, and at an interreligious conference initiated by American converts to Buddhism, the first long-term Buddhist–Catholic structure for ongoing dialogue took shape.

Monastic Interreligious Dialogue, a voluntary association of Catholic monastic houses of men and women in the USA, managed to sponsor a series of seven exchanges between 1982 and 1995. Four of these were visits of Tibetan monastics to Catholic monasteries in the USA, and three were visits of Catholic monastics to Tibetan houses in India and Tibet. Interspersed throughout this period were special events that brought the Dalai Lama and other Buddhist leaders together with Catholic speakers on various subjects of inter-monastic interest.[17]

There were other initiatives at this time in the broader area of Christian–Buddhist relations. In 1981, the East–West Religions Project of the University of Hawaii launched the annual *Buddhist–Christian Studies.* John Cobb, at Claremont School of Theology and Claremont Graduate School in California, and Masao Abe, from Nara University in Japan but for a time holding a position at the Pacific School of Religion in California, organized a dialogue of Buddhist and Christian scholars. They held their first meeting in 1984, and the group expanded gradually to slightly more than 20 over the course of five meetings. In 1997, Donald Mitchell, Purdue University, procured a sizeable grant from the Lilly Foundation, and a second round involving some members of the Cobb–Abe group plus others lasted seven meetings until 2004. Over the course of both rounds, perhaps only a few more than 50 scholars from North America, Europe and Asia participated in this dialogue. Academic by nature, the major impact of this dialogue was through publication. Several papers and reports appeared in *Buddhist–Christian Studies,* and participants published books and articles in various journals of theology and religion.

In 1987, many of these scholars and others founded the Society for Buddhist–Christian Studies. It gathers in conjunction with the annual meeting of the American Academy of Religion, and their sessions can draw 50 to 100 scholars. The Society assumed direction of the International Buddhist–Christian Conferences, convening every three to five years since 1980. The seventh conference met in June 2005 at Loyola-Marymount University, Los Angeles, on 'Buddhism and Christianity in Dialogue towards Global Healing'.

Buddhist–Catholic dialogue

Catholic scholars participated in all the foregoing occasions of Buddhist–Christian dialogue. On a diocesan level, when circumstances were conducive for forming relationships, Catholics met with Buddhist leaders. In 1982, the National Association of Diocesan Ecumenical Officers (NADEO) authorized the formation of a standing committee to provide assistance to dioceses for interreligious relations and dialogue. Diocesan staff from Chicago, Honolulu, Los Angeles, San Francisco and other dioceses with ongoing Catholic–Buddhist relationships have participated in this collective effort. The Faiths in the World Committee continues to meet, develop programmes, and provide advice and support to diocesan staff and the staff of the bishops' conference.

In 1989, the Archdiocese of Los Angeles and the Buddhist Sangha Council of Southern California inaugurated the Los Angeles Buddhist–Catholic Dialogue. In 1991, they published a report. They described how, in their first discussions, they had much to share regarding experiences of religious prejudice, and these honest exchanges were their first steps towards mutual respect and understanding. In their sessions, they had covered the usual introductory topics, the Buddha and the Christ, founder and follower, and key terms such as nirvana and resurrection. Among their observations, they noted that 'sometimes even after spending a whole session on a word, we found that we could not understand it completely.' Even without a precise understanding of one another, they could 'continue to speak and to hear each other' and they shared 'the expectation that if we continue to talk with each other long enough' they would understand one another better.[18] Similar dialogues have met over the years in other dioceses, but this one in Los Angeles still meets today.

By 1995, the necessary pieces had fallen into place for Catholic–Buddhist dialogue in the USA, with formal structure and sponsorship of institutions with regional or national constituencies. The bishops' conference had hired a specialist in 1987 in interreligious relations to promote interreligious dialogue and relationships and had appointed a bishop to serve as Moderator for Interreligious Relations in 1988. The Moderator, Bishop Joseph Gerry, a Benedictine, soon became an advisor to the Benedictines and Cistercians involved in Monastic Interreligious Dialogue (MID). Archbishop Weakland, the

Abbot Primate who had conveyed Cardinal Pignedoli's request for monastic assistance with relations with eastern religions, had become Archbishop of Milwaukee, and from 1990 to 1993 served as Chairman of the Bishops' Committee for Ecumenical and Interreligious Affairs (BCEIA). I was the specialist, serving on the secretariat to the BCEIA, and had been a founding member of NADEO's Faiths in the World Committee. As a scholar of the religions of India, I was already attending or soon began attending meetings of the Society for Buddhist–Christian Studies, the Cobb–Abe scholars' dialogue, and the International Buddhist–Christian conferences, and I served as an advisor to MID with Bishop Gerry.

The watershed event for Catholic–Buddhist dialogue in the USA was the Gethsemani Encounter in July 1996. It was planned and sponsored by MID's board members and advisors, and Donald Mitchell played a major role in making connections with Buddhist leaders. There were nearly 50 participants, almost equally divided between Buddhists and Catholics, most of whom were monastic women and men, and 100 observers in attendance. Several lineages of three major kinds of Buddhist practice were represented, including Theravada, Tibetan and the Chinese, Korean and Japanese forms of the meditation school or Zen. During the week-long meeting, Catholics and Buddhists discussed elements of the spiritual life with emphasis on prayer and community life and lived in community in the monastery that was the home of Thomas Merton. Much care was given to its preparation. Years of good will preceded it. The planning team wisely drew from lessons learned from the other developments in Christian–Buddhist relations.

Among the participants at the first Gethsemani Encounter were the Dalai Lama, Bhante Havanpola Ratansara, who co-founded the Los Angeles Buddhist–Catholic Dialogue, Bishop Gerry, David Steindl-Rast, OSB, one of the planners of the first Naropa conference, Judith Simmer-Brown, who coordinated the Naropa conferences, Bernardo Olivera, Abbot General of the Trappists, Donald Mitchell and Jeffrey Hopkins, participants in the Cobb–Abe group, Pierre-François de Béthune, OSB, of the European branch of MID, and many others, including myself. A schedule that combined intellectual reflection on aspects of monastic life with spiritual practice contributed to the success of the event. Participants exchanged views, challenged each other's concepts and explanations and inquired about aspects of practice. They attended each other's services of prayer, sat together in silent meditation for an hour before breakfast, remembered Thomas Merton and marked the closing of each day and the conference solemnly.[19]

Bishop Gerry's report to the Pontifical Council for Interreligious Dialogue stated that 'so intense was the engagement that a number of participants referred to the Gethsemani Encounter as the deepest experience of the Holy Spirit at work in a new level of awareness.' He also concluded that 'the most significant lesson of the Gethsemani Encounter for our future dialogues in the USA is the realization that every interreligious dialogue should include a spiritual dimension and an occasion to experience hospitality.'[20]

The Gethsemani Encounter spawned a number of unexpected discussions and outcomes. There were planned discussions of prayer and meditation, the role of the spiritual guide, the gifts and graces of prayer meditation, and organization of the contemplative community, but there were several unplanned discussions. One Buddhist challenged Catholics on the meaning of the crucifix so prominently displayed in each of the monastery's rooms. He called it a 'gruesome image'. Several Catholics rose to speak on the meaning of the crucifixion in their lives and in their habits of prayer. There were tense discussions of monastic witness in a world of violence. One afternoon, Cistercians spoke of their brothers beheaded in Algeria just a few months earlier, giving rise to a number of serious reflections on the role of monastic life and the causes and effects of political strife. Later, when the Buddhists were at odds with one another on what to do about political situations such as Tibet and Cambodia, the discussion had taken on the character of an argument. Finally, someone asked a Cambodian monk to lead everyone in a walking meditation to the grave of Thomas Merton. This did not resolve the opposing arguments on how involved monastics truly are in the violent world around them, but the brief, prayerful walk in silence reminded them that they are on this spiritual journey together with all its hazards. There were many other surprises.

Buddhist participants expressed a desire to study the Rule of Saint Benedict and eventually four Buddhists offered their reflections in a volume entitled *Benedict's Dharma*.[21] While the ideal would have included reciprocally Catholic monastic reflections on the Buddhist monastic rule, the Buddhists wanted to move forward with the project as a gesture of gratitude. When the book was ready for distribution, the secretary for MID hosted a conference for Buddhists and Catholics at Our Lady of Grace Monastery in Beech Grove, Indiana (21–23 September 2001).[22] Some of those scheduled to come did not attend because of the difficulties of air travel in the USA in the weeks immediately after September 11, 2001. Violence remained on everyone's minds. Yi Fa, a participant in the Gethsemani Encounter and the Rule of Benedict and a nun of the Fo Guang Shan order, followed with a reflection on violence, *Safeguarding the Heart.*[23]

Another Buddhist participant in the Gethsemani Encounter was quite taken with the use of the Psalms during recitation of the hours by the monastics. During the dialogue, the monastery's routine continued as usual, and those who wished joined the community in prayer. Norman Fischer, a former Abbot of the San Francisco Zen Center and by upbringing a Jew, later wrote, 'It was at Gethsemani that I first paid attention to what these texts were saying.' The passages, he says, 'that caught my ear during those early-morning and evening hours in that Kentucky summer' were those that spoke of 'violence, passion, and bitterness'. Astonished, he asked the monks why they intoned such expressions in their prayers. He received several explanations, but he was not fully satisfied. He believed these Christian monks to be 'true treaders of the path, sincere practitioners, possessed of wisdom and knowledge'. In the end, he produced a volume of Zen-inspired translations of the Psalms.[24]

The week after the July 1996 Gethsemani Encounter, the Society for Buddhist–Christian Studies convened the fifth International Buddhist–Christian Conference at De Paul University, Chicago. Members of NADEO's Faiths in the World Committee, several of whom were present at the Gethsemani inter-monastic dialogue, convened a working group to assess the current state of Buddhist–Catholic dialogue and to recommend steps for the future. Fr John Shirieda, Under-Secretary of the Pontifical Council for Interreligious Dialogue, had sent me a lengthy report on the Vatican's involvement in Buddhist relations since the close of the Second Vatican Council. That report and others on relations abroad were given. Donald Mitchell gave his personal reflections on the first dialogue with Buddhists convened by the Vatican, which he had attended in Taiwan at Fo Guang Shan Monastery a year earlier in August 1995. Buddhists and Catholics fresh from the dialogue at Gethsemani and brimming with enthusiasm offered their initial reflections on the meeting while representatives from the Los Angeles dialogue also spoke of their continuing progress.[25]

Catholics responsible for promoting interreligious relations on the diocesan level were searching for a format to convene a dialogue with the gravity and power of the Gethsemani Encounter. Catholic scholars and monastics expressed their willingness to help. Such a dialogue needed to combine in some way learned conversation with spiritual practice. The Los Angeles Buddhist–Catholic Dialogue also wanted to share its experiences of dialogue with those who could make practical use of the learning. Venerable Ratanasara and Dr Michael Kerze, the co-chairs, invited the Faiths in the World Committee and the bishops' secretariat for interreligious dialogue to come to Los Angeles and experience the good will and sharing they experienced in their monthly meetings.

The result of all these conversations and efforts was the West Coast Buddhist–Catholic Retreat/Dialogue, 1–4 October 1998, held at Serra Retreat in Malibu.[26] It resembled the Gethsemani Encounter in several ways. There were a few more than 50 participants, evenly divided between Buddhists and Catholics. There were presentations on the Buddha's conception of morality and the Christian conception of God, Buddhist spirituality and Christian spirituality, and Buddhist practice and Christian practice. There were periods for group dialogue and for assigned Buddhist–Catholic pairs, 'dyads' as they were called at Gethsemani, to hold private conversations. The day began with silent meditation, and there were opportunities for shared celebration. Catholics celebrated the Eucharist daily, and Buddhist chanting ceremonies took place. There were meals in common and ample time for informal discussion. The dialogue moved at the pace of a retreat, alternating between conversation and prayer. It was different from the Gethsemani Encounter in that most participants were not monastic men and women. About one-third of the participants were from the Los Angeles area, and most of them had participated in the Los Angeles dialogue. Two-thirds were from other parts of the USA. The retreat/dialogue was intended for diocesan staff persons, who were invited to come with a Buddhist contact from their area.

Several did. It was the hope of the planners that those in attendance would gain confidence, skills, insights and inspiration for developing similar encounters in their own cities and dioceses.

As a learning experience, the West Coast Retreat/Dialogue was a success. Those from Los Angeles shared their experiences of dialogue; speakers and participants exchanged ideas; practical suggestions for dialogue were shared; and participants learned the value of inter-religious encounters that offered both content and spirituality. The retreat/dialogue was a 'post-Gethsemani' event, not attempting to replicate the inter-monastic exchange but to capture its spirit, build upon its success, and make such a powerful experience available to a wider public.

After Gethsemani

The 1996 Gethsemani Encounter set in motion a whole series of developments in Catholic–Buddhist relations. It was fortuitous that the monastic men and women, who had taken the invitation of Cardinal Pignedoli seriously and applied themselves to promoting interreligious dialogue with discipline, care, and reflection, took the first major step. Buddhists and Christians were already in dialogue in a number of settings, mostly academic in character but not entirely. A few dioceses and other Christian agencies had formed relationships with Buddhists for various commendable reasons. Some Buddhist organizations and centres had organized and hosted events and dialogues for Buddhists and Christians. The Gethsemani Encounter was something new in that it was intended to do something more than share ideas and aim at mutual understanding and friendly relations. Dialogue, in the words of *Dialogue and Proclamation*, a document released in 1991 by the Pontifical Council for Interreligious Dialogue, 'reaches a much deeper level, that of the spirit, where exchange and sharing consist in a mutual witness to one's beliefs and a common exploration of one's respective religious convictions' (DP 40). There were many signs of the Spirit at Gethsemani and in the enthusiasm that led to subsequent developments.

Monastic Interreligious Dialogue hosted a second Gethsemani Encounter in 2002 on the theme of suffering and its transformation. Again, there were about 50 participants, but this time only one came from abroad. The Dalai Lama could not attend because of illness.

Msgr Felix Machado attended from the Vatican's office for interreligious dialogue and described it as 'a model of interreligious dialogue in action'. Noting that participants had received papers in advance and that only a few minutes were allotted to speakers, he characterized the ensuing, lengthy periods of discussion in this way: 'honest, open and deep reflections were shared, frank questions were asked, and convincing answers were suggested in an atmosphere of great friendship and mutual respect.'[27] The resulting volume is a very practical instruction on how Buddhists and Christians address the fact of suffering.[28] Following this second encounter, the MID board redirected its energies from convening nuns and monks in separate dialogue groups to addressing some of the specific issues and questions that they face. The dialogue entitled 'Nuns in the West' has met twice, in 2003 and 2005. 'Monks in the West' has met once, in 2004. Reports are available on the Monastic Interreligious Dialogue website.[29]

During the summer of 2000, the monks of New Camaldoli Hermitage in Big Sur, California, hosted a conference entitled 'Purity of Heart and Contemplation'. Most of the speakers were monastics, and most participants were either Catholic or Buddhist. The conference was generally a monastic dialogue alternating major presentations from Buddhist, Hindu, Chinese and Christian traditions, each with two formal responses, with time for prayer and silence. The planner collected the papers into an excellent and substantive resource on the purification of the heart and mind in the Hindu, Buddhist, Chinese and Christian traditions.[30]

Towards the end of this conference, several participants, all but one living in the San Francisco Bay area, considered the suggestion to inaugurate a Buddhist–Catholic dialogue in their region but with national sponsorship. Up to this point, the Bishop Moderator for interreligious relations and the bishops' conference staff and consultants for Buddhist–Catholic relations had gladly participated in activities and programmes of other organizations and principally those of Monastic Interreligious Dialogue and NADEO's Faiths in the World Committee. Since the bishops' conference had experienced recent success in starting regional dialogues with Muslims, the thought was to attempt a similar format for dialogue with Buddhists.[31]

Representatives of the Dharma Realm Buddhist Association (DRBA), a Chinese lineage with headquarters in Northern California, the San Francisco Zen Center, the Archdiocese of San Francisco and the US Conference of Catholic Bishops met over a period of three years at planning meetings and by conference call. Eventually a formula for a round of four dialogues surfaced from the conversations. A group of approximately 30 Buddhists and Catholics would meet annually for four years, twice sponsored by the bishops' conference and once each by the DRBA and the San Francisco Zen Center. Meetings would include presentations as well as time for meditation and prayer. More than half of those nominated to participate were scholars.

The initial meeting of the Northern California Chan/Zen–Catholic Dialogue took place at the City of Ten Thousand Buddhas in Talmage, California in March 2003. The topic for the first dialogue was 'Walking the Bodhisattva Path/Walking the Christ Path'. Each of the 28 participants spoke for about 10 minutes on what it means to follow one of these paths and shared a short passage from usually a traditional text on following the path. Some spoke to the passage they shared; others did not. It was a rich set of passages and reflections condensed into the time allotted, and during the unfortunately shorter designated periods of discussion, participants offered challenging questions and comments. The main planner felt that it was important for everyone to have a chance to speak at the first meeting of the dialogue, knowing there would be more time at the second, third and fourth meetings, for discussion.

At this first ongoing Buddhist–Catholic dialogue co-sponsored by the bishops' conference, there were representatives of four Catholic dioceses and three religious orders. The Buddhist participants represented six Buddhist lineages, and only one was born in Asia. Subsequent meetings in 2004 and 2005 have focused on 'Transformation of Hearts and Minds: Chan/Zen–Catholic Approaches to Precepts' and 'Practice: Means towards Transformation'. The planner had found a way for two communities, eager for dialogue but organized quite differently, to co-sponsor a dialogue with both a regional and national character. This was the first time that a Catholic bishop convened a Buddhist–Catholic dialogue with representatives of Buddhist organizations as a project of the bishops' conference. Bishop Tod Brown, chairman of the recently formed Bishops' Subcommittee on Interreligious Dialogue, recommended Bishop John Wester, Auxiliary Bishop of San Francisco, to chair the dialogue with the Buddhists. The chairman of the Bishops' Committee on Ecumenical and Interreligious Affairs appointed Bishop Wester to the dialogue. In the past, bishops were present at the inter-monastic dialogues and the retreat/dialogues sponsored by diocesan officers, but this regional dialogue was an event primarily of the bishops' conference on the Catholic side.

The Faiths in the World Committee sponsored a second retreat/dialogue for diocesan staff, and this was in 2003 on the east coast. The final number of those in attendance included 45 Catholics and 35 Buddhists. The opportunity developed out of a three-year relationship between the Franciscan Friars of the Atonement at Graymoor in Garrison, New York, and the monks and nuns of Chuang Yen monastery nearby in Carmel, New York. Previously, Graymoor's Spiritual Life Center had hosted a weekend retreat, 'The Buddha as Teacher: What Christians can learn from the insights and practices of Buddhists'. On that occasion, participants had visited Chuang Yen, headquarters of the Buddhist Association in the USA. That retreat was just one part of a series of exchanges between the communities.

The Spiritual Life Center, working with the Faiths in the World Committee, proposed to Chuang Yen that the two monasteries plan and host a weekend retreat/dialogue. This two-monastery model represented a new step in Buddhist–Catholic relations in the USA. Lectures focused on suffering and its transformation, Christ and the Buddha, and spiritual practice. Again, as in other meetings, participants meditated together in silence and attended one another's religious services. While some diocesan interreligious officers attended, most participants were Catholics and Buddhists wanting to know something more about one another's beliefs and practices and interested in improving their spiritual life. Buddhists experienced interest in learning more about the eucharistic liturgy, and Catholics expressed interest in learning how Buddhist practices of chanting and meditation differ from Christian practices. No one expressed a desire to be a Buddhist–Christian; rather, most left renewed and more confident in their own faith. Combining spiritual practice with intellectual exchange adds a practical dimension to dialogue and increases zeal for dialogue.

Concluding observations

Looking at Buddhist–Catholic dialogue sequentially, as developed in this reflection, is only one among several options for investigating how these two communities have interacted in formal ways in the USA. This approach reveals that balancing theological exchange with spiritual practice is successful not only for individual meetings but also for encouraging others to develop new occasions for dialogue. This approach also demonstrates how the richness of the two traditions offers limitless possibilities for mutual understanding, theological insight and spiritual growth. Repeatedly, participants in Buddhist–Christian dialogue return to the same themes – the human condition in need of transformation, the experience of God and nirvana, the Buddha and the Christ, and spiritual practice and commitment in service to others. These were the themes of the first meetings of the Cobb–Abe dialogue in the 1980s and the four broad themes of the Vatican's first Catholic–Buddhist Colloquium.[32] These same themes were repeated in some variation at the retreat/dialogues for diocesan staff. To some extent, these themes were always in the background and, from time to time, brought front and centre at the monastic encounters. Every generation will review these topics for themselves. Rich topics emerging from the heart of one belief and practice cannot be exhausted of insights and implications for those who believe and practice.

Advocates of interreligious dialogue also seem to create new ways for dialogue to serve as a tool for understanding as well as for living the spiritual practices that emanate from the religious experiences nurtured in each tradition. Monastic life in the USA, Buddhist or Catholic, has felt the effects of dialogue. Principally, it seems, monastic life now includes a charism for interreligious dialogue. This can also affect the comparative study of theology. The profound truths of the faith when placed in dialogue in the lives of individuals who take those truths seriously give rise to powerful experiences. This does not take away from erudite interreligious discussion, which is always needed if theology is to escape the shortcomings of isolation; rather, the spiritual dimension seems to enhance theological dialogue, giving an almost tangible feel to the grappling of the mind with the dense truths at the heart of both traditions. Theological reflection is not simply an exercise of the mind, although clarity, logic, accuracy and consistency are important. Theological reflection arises from practice, which is as much a discipline as study.

Finally, it seems that one test of a dialogue's success is whether or not there were unexpected insights among the participants and surprising diversions in the schedule. If the participants are truly listening to one another, something unexpected will happen with that many minds focusing on a topic. These surprises and the discovery of differences and similarities make interreligious dialogue interesting and even compelling. These signs are truly evident in the brief history of formal dialogues between Buddhists and Catholics in the USA.

17

'Forgiveness is beautiful'

During the Jubilee year 2000 I was asked to speak on the subject 'Perdonare è bello', 'Forgiveness is beautiful', and this put me in mind in the first place of various slogans of recent years: 'Black is beautiful', and in Italy 'Donna è bello' written on a wall in Trastevere in the early days of feminism. I thought too of Roberto Benigni's film 'La vita è bella'. This for me is pure fable, not reflecting the true nature of the Shoah. In proclaiming that forgiveness is beautiful, do we not run the risk of underplaying the harsh reality of what is involved in forgiveness?

My task was to examine how forgiveness is seen in the other religions. Is it correct in this context to speak of pardon, of forgiveness, of reconciliation? In answering these questions, I am basing myself on a chapter on 'Conversion of the heart in Hinduism, Buddhism and Islam', which I and two of my colleagues produced for a volume prepared for the Jubilee year.[1]

Hinduism

Conversion, intended in the Christian sense of *metanoia*, is not foreign to Hinduism. In the more popular devotional (*bhakti*) type of Hinduism, people often speak of religious experience as conversion towards God, which implies a continual return to the right path, commanded by the Eternal Truth (*dharma*). In Hinduism, the human being is essentially in search of the Absolute. It is possible to say that this search is undertaken particularly with the purpose of attaining the ultimate liberation (*moksha*) of the human being. The way to liberation may be long, by way of various transmigrations, a 'process of integration through which the *Atman* (the divine particle which is in every person) may return to its natural state in which birth and death are completely impossible'. That is, the final goal is to attain to 'the fixed, immobile state of *Brahman* (the divine being)'.[2]

This process does not explicitly involve pardon, but in a certain way implies it. It is necessary to be freed from every obstacle; it is necessary to rein in the senses, to fight against wicked attitudes, such as the desire for revenge. A refusal to forgive could create a bond hindering liberation. It is also possible to point to the notion of *ahimsa*, non-violence, which held an important place in the thinking of Gandhi. This seems to imply, if not precisely forgiveness, at least the idea of not returning evil for evil. The *Bhagavad Gita*, which shows God as the personal supreme being, gives the following instruction: 'So from (those) bonds which works (of their very nature forge), whose fruits are fair and foul, you will be freed; (your)self (now) integrated by renunciation and spiritual exercise, set free, you will draw nigh to me . . . On Me, your mind, on Me your loving-service, for Me your sacrifice, to Me be your prostrations; now that you have integrated self, your striving bent on Me, to Me you will (surely) come.'[3]

Buddhism

In Buddhism, which originated as a form of Hinduism, something similar can be found. Buddhism however, since it does not speak of God, does not present conversion as a return to the Absolute, and even less to a personal God. Nevertheless, Buddhism is a moral path. It is an invitation to liberate oneself from attachment, which is the cause of suffering. By purifying oneself, freeing oneself from attachment, one will arrive at nirvana, at the extinction of the ego, and thus to a state of peace and blessedness. It is noteworthy that Buddhism teaches, after the four noble truths (the existence of suffering, its cause, the possibility of eliminating this cause, and the method for doing so), the way to reach liberation. It is an eightfold path; one cannot choose *among* these but must travel them all together.

These paths include right perception and right thinking. To perceive the truth implies understanding the causes of a situation, the interdependent causality to which every being is subject. Such a perception will stop one from attributing blame where it does not exist or at least help one to realize where it is diminished. Thus one can be led to think well of persons even if they present themselves as enemies. Other paths are right speaking, right action, and right living, putting into practice in daily life both right perception and right thinking. Recognizing that to do this is not easy, Buddhism insists on the need for meditation. Thus the final three paths are right effort, right attention and right meditation. By following these eight paths it is possible to reach nirvana.

There is little here explicitly on forgiveness, yet to my mind this concept is in some way included. The search for purity of heart is not for the sole benefit of the individual; in Buddhism, the search for perfection and social liberation are interdependent. The ideal is not to be calm and in peace at the expense of others. Rather, the person who is detached is free to relate to other beings in a disinterested and harmonious way. Purification comprises freedom from envy and hate, and gives rise to the four great values: affectionate kindness (*metta*), compassion (*karuna*), solidarity (*mudita*), equanimity (*upekkha*). Finally, to quote the Buddha: 'Travel forth, monks, for the benefit of the many, for the happiness of the many, out of compassion for the world, for the well-being, benefit, and happiness of gods and humans.'[4]

A Hebrew vision of pardon

So far we have dealt with conversion, a process of liberation, which includes the need for good relations with other beings in general, and with humanity in particular. For the Jews also the idea of conversion is very important, but it includes a more personal relationship with God. Conversion (*teshuvah*) is the return to God to which the prophets call: 'Return, Israel, to the Lord your God, for your iniquity has made you fall' (Hos. 14.2). In this text we see that *teshuvah* is a collective action of the whole nation, which the rabbis have also extended to the individual. The notion became so important that the Talmud held that *teshuvah* was created before the universe. To the objection that sin did not yet exist, therefore *teshuvah* was not necessary, the reply was given that the Holy One, Blessed be He, foresaw the remedy before the illness.[5] Since for the Jew God, and the relationship with him, are of central importance, pardon will be considered first of all in relation to God.

The Jewish calendar has reserved a special day for pardon, Yom Kippur, the holiest day in the year. I think it useful to emphasize the meaning of the word *kippur*, following here the explanation given by Philippe de Saint Cheron. The term is derived from the word *kappara* which means to cover. Therefore, as distinct from the English word pardon (or forgiveness, French *pardon,* Italian *perdono,* or German *Vergebung*), it has nothing to do with 'gift'. De Saint Cheron says: 'It is possible to receive a gift without effort, and even without asking anything, without expecting anything more, whereas it is not possible to be cleansed of one's own faults without having effectively made amends for them through some work, a personal spiritual effort, and one cannot obtain reparation without having made some reparation of one's own.'[6] We can understand then why Yom Kippur, day of the Great Pardon, day of expiation, is consecrated exclusively to reparation for sins, to their expiation through fasting. On this day the Jewish people, freed to some extent from everyday needs, which are obstacles to the true freedom of spirit and body, can become themselves prayer. The Jews turn to God with penitence (*teshuvah*), with prayer (*tefilah*) and charity (*tsedakah*), and God gives to his sons and daughters pardon for the faults committed against him.

There arises now the problem of faults committed against fellow humans. Sin against the neighbour will be expiated only if the latter grants pardon. If a man commits a sin against his brother and is forgiven, God will also forgive him. It is necessary to ask forgiveness at least three times, said Rabbi Yosse, after which there is no further obligation. But every Jew should forgive anyone who asks forgiveness sincerely. To forgive is of benefit to oneself, meaning that it puts an end to the condition of victim, allows one to accept to give up that rancour which holds the mind and heart prisoner. The Buddhist, as we have seen, would say that pardon is a way of liberation.

What happens when the one who is offended wishes to forgive but the guilty party does not ask forgiveness? Jesus on the cross said: 'Father, forgive them, for they do not know what they do' (Luke 23.24), but the Jew, or perhaps one should say the Jew who remains tied to the attitude of his religion, since Jesus too is Jewish, does not share this sentiment. De Saint Cheron says: 'There must always be two involved in pardoning; if one goes by default, there is no more possibility of pardon. No one can forgive if the mind of the guilty one is against this.'[7]

Another problem arises when the person offended is no longer there, because in this case there is no possibility of granting pardon. No one can forgive in the place of another.

De Saint Cheron relates an episode from the Jewish author and activist Simon Wiesenthal. Detained in a camp in Lwow, he was asked one day to go to a military hospital to meet a young Nazi soldier who was dying. This young man, wishing in some sense to 'confess' to a Jew before dying, told of all the terrible things he had done, or had been made to do, and which were tormenting him at the end of his life. When he finished he asked forgiveness. Wiesenthal relates: 'I got up, I looked in his direction, I saw his two joined hands (his face was completely covered in bandages). A ray of sunshine seemed to pass in between us. My decision was taken. Without a word I left the room.'[8] This is a terrible conclusion, but Wiesenthal did not refuse to forgive, he did not say no, but he did not accept to forgive on behalf of others. De Saint Cheron quotes with approval from J. Maritain: 'I can only forgive the evil which has been done to me. The terrible things which you have done to others, how could I forgive *in their name?* What you have done is in human terms unpardonable. But *in the name of your God*, yes, I forgive you!'[9]

If to forgive is 'beautiful', perhaps we can understand here that forgiveness is not easy; yes, perhaps easy to understand, but not easy to practise. 'In a world in which pardon is at any moment possible, de Saint Cheron asks, is there not a risk of undervaluing it?'[10]

Islam and forgiveness

The universe of Islam is permeated by an atmosphere of submission (which is the meaning of the Arabic word *islām*) to God and to his will. Such submission, interior through the act of faith, and exteriorized through observing the divine commands, leads to true peace (*salām*). It is a peace which, like the Hebrew *shalom,* embraces all aspects of life. The call to Muslim prayer includes the call to success (*falāh*), which can be material as much as spiritual.

The Islamic ideal is thus to come close to God by means of observing his commands, and also through carrying out supererogatory works. Thus a tradition from the Prophet (*hadīth*) on doing good (*ihsān*) declares: 'It is to adore (and serve) God as if you saw him, for even if you do not see him, he sees you.' Sin puts a distance between oneself and God. It is an act of disobedience to the will of God and leads man to stray from the right path mapped out by God. At the same time sin is in itself a disorder, a lack of respect for the law that God has placed within his creatures, so that sin is not so much an offence against God as a wrong done to oneself.

Humankind is prone to sin. The Arabs speak of *insān nāsī*, the human being is by nature forgetful. He forgets the law of God; he rebels against his Creator. Thus Adam and Eve did not obey God, and consequently found themselves outside the garden in which God had placed them: 'Depart, in enmity one to the other' (Q. 2.36). But the story of Adam does not end here. The Qur'an continues: 'Adam received words from the Lord, who forgave him, for he is the Forgiver, the Merciful' (2.37). It is best here to refer directly to the Arabic text, since the translation does not give the complete meaning. Adam received words (*kalimāt*). The text does not specify what these are, words of inspiration or of forgiveness? God indeed is the one who pardons, but the verb used is *tāba 'alayhi*, he turned towards him. God is *al-tawwāb*, the one who turns continually, habitually. God's turning towards the creature, even a sinner, is the basis of the creature's turning towards God, conversion.

Divine mercy is a frequent theme in the Qur'an. Every *sūra*, except the ninth, begins with the invocation 'In the Name of God, the merciful, the compassionate' (*bi-smi llāhi l-rahmāni l-rahīm*). We see that the two words translated into English as 'merciful' and 'compassionate' have the same Arabic root, *RHM*. It could be said that God is in himself mercy, and that he shows himself to be merciful through his actions. A verse of the Qur'an says: 'Call upon God (*Allāh*), or call upon *al-Rahmān*, however you call upon him, to him belong the most beautiful names' (Q. 17.110).

For Islam God is merciful, or better he is Mercy, just as for Christians God is Love. Mercy is in an absolute sense a divine obligation: 'He has prescribed for Himself mercy' (Q. 6.12). In what way is divine mercy at work? It must be reconciled with his justice. God is merciful with those who repent after sin, but he is unbending in his justice towards those who do not turn to him, those who do not believe, those who remain in their unbelief (*kufr* – ingratitude towards the Creator).

Only God can pardon. There is no concept in Islam of a sacrifice for sin, of vicarious sufferings to renew friendship with God. Such a mediation would constitute *shirk*, associating with God that which is not God. For *shirk* goes right against the first principle of Islam, the belief in one sole God, and this is the only sin that cannot be forgiven. In this case even the mercy of God is constrained. It is worth noting that in Islam each person is responsible for himself. 'No soul shall be burdened with the burden of another' is a principle repeated several times in the Qur'an (cf. Q. 6.164). Noah wished to intercede for his son who refused to enter the Ark, insisting that he could save himself from the Flood, but God forbade this prayer (cf. Q. 11.25–48, especially 45–6).

Since everyone has responsibility for himself or herself, how is the return to God to obtain his mercy carried out? In the first place the faithful Muslim can seek the forgiveness of God through observing the pillars of Islam. By means of the *shahāda*, the profession of faith, is expressed the wish to serve God alone. Ritual prayer (*salāt*) includes ablution, a symbolic means of expressing the need for purification. The payment of community tax (*zakāt*) signifies the wish to use material goods in line with God's will. The fast during the month of Ramadan, undertaken in obedience to God, and accompanied by the prescribed prayers, opens the soul and the heart to divine forgiveness. During the pilgrimage (*hajj*), the pilgrims are the guests of God. If they call upon him, he will reply; if they ask pardon, this will be granted. In particular the standing on mount Arafat, a silent prayer, is already equivalent to a request for pardon.

Each one asks pardon of God for his or her own faults. But sin also has a social dimension. It disrupts social relations. True repentance includes therefore the obligation to repair the evil done in order to restore the established order. In this respect Islam puts the emphasis on justice, proposing the law of requital. Islamic law develops in detail the obligations of compensation for damage suffered. Yet the Qur'an, while allowing the law to be carried out in full, encourages mercy: 'We laid down for them (in the Torah) life for life, eye for eye, nose for nose, ear for ear, tooth for tooth, and for wounds the law of requital. But whoever foregoes the requital by way of charity, that will be for him an expiation' (Q. 5.45).

In the book already mentioned, *Le pardon*, Nassib Mahfouz writes: 'Unilateral forgiveness is one of the goals of the battle against oneself. It is a question of turning an enemy into a friend.' He goes on to quote a phrase attributed to Saladin: 'To forgive is in some way to transform.'[11]

The well-known spiritual author of Bihar, Sharafuddin Yahya Maneri (d. 1381 CE) said: 'As far as possible, make your peace with anyone who has a legitimate grudge against you.' If this direct effort at reconciliation is impossible or fails, God must be asked to effect satisfaction and happiness in the heart of the person offended. 'Be confident that, when the Lord realises how sincere-hearted His servant is, He, out of the infinite treasure of His mercy, will make your adversary happy.'[12]

In the relationship between human beings and God, the emphasis is above all on mercy and forgiveness, while in relationships between humans it is justice that is stressed. Nevertheless the Qur'an, as we have seen, while putting forward the demands of justice, invites the one wronged to forgive. This, as Nassib Mahfouz observes, supposes in the human being a high moral character. To respond to evil with good requires considerable moral energy and strength of character beyond the ordinary.[13] Mahfouz seems to mean that it is normal to demand just retribution, even if pardon is the better way.

Finally I should like to give an example from the modern political world. Mr Abdelaziz Bouteflika, President of Algeria, in a speech given at the Meeting of Rimini on 23 August 1999, remarked 'The truly great people are those who know how to live pardon and reconciliation.' These words were taken as the headline by the Algerian newspaper *El Moudjahid*, which published the speech in full. Bouteflika explained that in order to recover civil concord, Parliament voted unanimously for a law on amnesty. This law expresses the will of the Algerian state to pardon anyone implicated in acts of terrorism. He explained the different dispositions foreseen for those implicated in violence causing material damage and for those whose violence was directed against human lives. He indicated that there was to be a probationary period, as a proof of repentance, before acquittal. The President wished to submit the law on amnesty to a popular referendum, which, in fact, gave him the desired result. The referendum was necessary as a demonstration of the will of the Algerian people to extricate themselves from the crisis. Bouteflika said: 'Since peace and civil concord are the most valuable of political rights, it is our duty today to work with all our strength and all the means at our disposal to bring this about.' Even if, unfortunately, violence did not immediately cease in Algeria, it is right and proper to acknowledge the courage of the President and his clear vision in recognizing that without pardon and reconciliation it is not possible to build true peace.

18

Christ in the religions

The Jubilee of the year 2000 naturally focused on Jesus Christ. In inviting people to prepare for this Jubilee, Pope John Paul II expressed the hope that the representatives of other religions could share in the joy of Christians who would be celebrating this very special anniversary.

On 2 January 2000 in the Jesuit Church of Farm Street, Mayfair, a multireligious celebration was held in honour of Jesus. The Jesuit Michael Barnes describing this event pointed out that the name of Jesus is often divisive, but on this occasion the aim was to bring people together to listen to words from different traditions inspired by the person and teaching of Jesus. With the Jubilee and this celebration in mind Brother Daniel Faivre, the former director of Westminster Interfaith, and some others produced a small booklet: *Celebrating Jesus: a multifaith appreciation*, a collection of short extracts from texts about Jesus.

We might well ask how Jesus is viewed by the other religions. This echoes a question he put to his disciples: 'What do people say of the Son of Man?' (Matt. 16.13). In trying to answer this question by examining a series of texts of the other religions, we might have the impression of entering a hall of mirrors. We shall see the image of Jesus, but it will be an image somewhat modified, maybe unusual. We can meditate on this diversity, recognizing that the unique person of Jesus Christ lies at the origin of all these different reflections.

Jesus the Jew

If we look in the mirror of Judaism we shall find, as is natural, a Hebrew Jesus, Yehoshua ben Yosef, a master in religion and ethics, with a great knowledge of the Torah. He will not have the appearance of a new lawmaker or of the founder of a new religion. Martin Buber emphasizes the importance, and the limitations, of Jesus for a Jew in three points: Jesus was a perfect man, a perfect Jew, but he does not embody the fulfilment of the Jewish religion; he was a man of faith, but not an object of faith; he was a messianic man, but he is not the Messiah whom the Jews still await.

In the writings of a Jewish author, David Kossof, in *The Book of Witnesses* (1971), we have an impressive presentation of the baptism of Jesus. His narrator sees Jesus arriving at sunset, asking to be baptized. John seems rather hesitant, perhaps thinking that this is not right, but Jesus insists and they descend to the river. The narrator follows them together with a group of disciples. On the banks of the river John stops, but Jesus looks into his eyes and smiles, and so they enter the water. John does not say very much, probably not finding the right words, which would be understandable. Jesus bows his head, and John also. When they straighten up, after the baptism, there is an unusual change in the light, which makes the narrator look up – as does everyone else. In the sky there is a great band of light like an opening in the heavens. Everything is very quiet, there is no wind, no birds singing, no noise, but then right on high there appears what looks like a tiny white luminous point. As it comes nearer it is seen to be a bird, then a dove. It comes down to rest on the still dripping head of Jesus. A voice is heard, calm and loving like that of a father, saying 'This is my beloved, my only son.' The narrator adds that this was so long ago he is not sure whether he heard the voice himself or whether only John heard it and told others about it. But he would like to think that he did really hear it.

This account seems to say that also for a Jew, Jesus is someone special. This is surely something worth noting.

Jesus for Islam

It is obvious that we shall find no mention of Jesus in the Hebrew Bible, whose writings were completed before his birth in Bethlehem. Quite different, however, is the situation in Islam, since Muhammad's preaching, gathered together in the Qur'an, is six centuries later than Jesus' mission. Jesus is specifically named 25 times, and the term Messiah occurs 11 times.

In the two *sūras* 3 and 19, the Qur'an narrates the annunciation to Mary, the virginal conception, the birth of Jesus. He received the Book (the *Injīl*), is strengthened by the gift of the Holy Spirit, he works miracles. He has as supporters (*ansār*), the apostles. He meets with opposition from the Jews who wish to kill him. But God raised him to himself (cf. Q. 4.157–9).

Christians will be able to recognize in this portrait of Jesus many elements of their own tradition, but must also accept that the context is completely different and that it gives another meaning to the mission of Jesus. He is the son of Mary, a title that includes both a positive significance, the miracle of the virgin birth, and a negative, since it wishes to emphasize that he is not son of God. In the Qur'an Jesus in fact rejects the attribution to himself of divinity. He presents himself as the servant of God (*'abd Allāh:* servant-worshipper) (Q. 3.30).

While with Mary his mother he forms a sign for the universe (Q. 21.91 – see Chapter 12), this indicates that the virgin birth demonstrates the power of God who will be able to give back life even to the dead. The Qur'an says: 'Jesus is like Adam: He created him from the earth, said to him 'Be' and he was' (Q. 3.59). Jesus has the privilege of being one of the prophets, and Islam takes pride in recognizing all the prophets without exception, including of course Muhammad. Jesus himself had foretold the coming of a prophet by name Ahmad (a name which has the same root letters as Muhammad) (Q. 61.6). If in the Qur'an there is a hint of the passion of Jesus, this does not end with his death on the cross, and is not followed by the resurrection. Thus any salvific value of Jesus' life is denied. In Islam, God has no need of a mediator.

The Qur'an several times names the *Injīl* preached by Jesus but does not give details of his preaching. In the *hadīth* (words and actions attributed to Muhammad) some gospel sayings are reported. For example, Jesus said: 'Consider the birds: they do not sow nor reap, and make no provision, and God takes care of their existence day by day.' In a *hadīth qudsī*, a tradition in which Muhammad speaks in the name of God, we find this text: 'O son of Adam, I was ill and you did not come to visit me!' 'How could I have visited you, O master of the universe?' 'Did you not know that this servant of mine was sick, and you did not visit him? Did you not know that if you had visited him, you would have found me at his side? O son of Adam, I asked you for food and you did not give me any.' 'How could I have given you something to eat, O master of the universe?' 'Did you not know that this servant of mine was hungry, and you did not give him food? Did you not know that if you had given him something to eat, you would have found me at his side? O son of Adam, I asked you to give me to drink, and you did not relieve my thirst.' 'How could I have relieved your thirst, O master of the universe?' 'That servant of mine asked you for something to drink, you did not relieve his thirst. If you had done so you would have found me at his side.'

Abdallah ben Umar, reporting what the Messenger of God had said, relates a description of Jesus: 'One night when I was near the Ka'ba, I saw a dark-skinned man, one of the most beautiful dark-skinned persons that you have ever seen. He had hair more beautiful than you have ever seen. It was wavy and dripping with water. He was supported by two men and going around the shrine. When I asked who this person might be the answer was given "The Messiah the son of Mary".'

Even if Jesus is reduced in stature by Islam, he remains nonetheless a mysterious figure. A Muslim scholar, Ali Merad, has pointed out that the Qur'an presents Christ as a person beyond the ordinary condition of humanity. This is not only the fact of being born of a virgin. Of him, and only of him, it is said that he is a word (*kalima*) coming from God, and he is a spirit of God. To him are attributed actions usually reserved to God: he 'creates' birds from clay and 'breathes' life into them (Q. 3.49); he heals and, even more, raises the dead. He is proclaimed illustrious (Q. 3.45) in this world as in the next, and for him is reserved a place among those who are brought close to God (*muqarrabūn*), a term which can recall the cherubim; in fact the presentation of Jesus in the Qur'an appears closer to the Judaeo-Christian trend which included Jesus in the category of the angels.

Jesus is thus exalted above the other prophets to occupy a unique rank in the story of the human race. It is God himself who has raised Jesus, just as he has rescued him from death as a free act of his power. The raising of Jesus to the presence of God, and his final triumph, constitute at the same time the fulfilment of the divine mercy and a promise for all of humankind. One of the greatest of Muslim mystic writers, Ibn 'Arabi, did not hesitate to attribute to Jesus the title 'seal of holiness' (compared with Muhammad, who is called the 'seal of prophecy').

Jesus as seen by the Hindus

The majority of Hindus are fascinated by the mystery of Jesus Christ, and many have a very great devotion to him. For a good number of Hindus Jesus provides inspiration for a new attention to those in need. Apart from the south of India, where there exist ancient communities of Christians, the so-called 'St Thomas Christians', for the majority of Hindus knowledge of Jesus and his gospel came through Christian missionaries who arrived in India with the colonial powers. Three different attitudes can be distinguished. The most widespread is that of admiration for the message of Jesus without any commitment; this is often accompanied by a rejection of the Church seen as an obstacle rather than as a way to know Jesus. A second category comprises those who respond to the message of Jesus with a certain commitment, but they live out this commitment within Hinduism. Finally, others accept Jesus as Lord and ask for baptism, though they may still retain a critical attitude towards the Church.

The judgement of Mahatma Gandhi is well known. He admired Jesus but not the Christians. In common with many Hindus, Gandhi had no difficulty in recognizing the divinity of Jesus, but as one of the incarnations of God and not as someone unique. He said: 'I consider Jesus Christ as one of the great masters of humanity but not as the only Son of God.' He was struck by the teaching of the gospel, and in particular that of the Beatitudes. For him Jesus became a model of ethical behaviour, but of a symbolic nature. He wrote: 'I can say that the historical Jesus is of no interest to me. Nothing would change for me if someone demonstrated that Jesus never lived and that the gospel account of him was simply fiction. The message of the Sermon on the Mount would always remain true for me.'

To consider Jesus as a symbol is an approach common to other Hindu thinkers. Radhakrishnan, at one time President of India and an exponent of Neo-Vedanta, held that every event in the life of Christ, because he was born of the Spirit, is to be taken as a symbolic stage in the spiritual life with universal validity. Christhood is a state of illumination. Salvation consists in freeing oneself from the chain of illusory values that dominate us. This can be achieved by contemplating the divine mystery which is within. In this context Jesus Christ is one who has a better understanding of this process because he strongly believes in the interior light, excluding any sort of ritualism and showing complete indifference to a legalistic piety. The mystery of the cross is equivalent to abandoning one's ego and identifying oneself with a more intense life with a higher consciousness.

Ramakrishna, the founder of the Ramakrishna Order, an organization for the spread of Hinduism modelled on the Protestant missions, had a mystical experience of identification with Christ. In this way he experienced the truth of Christianity as a way towards God-consciousness. So he believed in Christ as an incarnation of God, not unique but one among others, Buddha, Krishna, etc.

The realization of God is central to Hinduism and is the foundation of the teaching of A. C. Bhaktivedanta Swami Prabhupada, founder of the International Society for Krishna Consciousness (ISKCON). He travelled widely to spread ISKCON and its doctrines. Once in Melbourne, when some Christians asked him what he thought of Christ, he replied: 'He is our guru. He teaches the realisation of God, and thus he is our spiritual master.' He went on to explain that the knowledge which comes from Jesus Christ is perfect, because the source is perfect. We ought to receive knowledge from the perfect source rather than trying to achieve it ourselves from below, which will bring with it the experience of failure. Moreover, this takes too much time. One should draw near to the one who is perfect, receiving knowledge from him, and thus become perfect oneself.

We can end with a very recent example, a letter written by a Hindu leader for Good Friday and taken by his disciples to the Christian community. It reads thus:

> Today is a very important day. It is a day to recall the Great Powerful One who sacrificed his life for humanity . . . We, gathered here today, have perhaps sinned. But the greatest sin is to forget God. In this our day, when humanity is straying from the path of morality, it is right to recall those who sacrificed their lives to uphold the two great virtues of the human being: faith in God, and faithfulness to God. To repent, to confess one's sins, brings about a new birth. The Hindu religion calls this *dvija*. There is nothing wrong in confessing one's sins to God because he is the one who will pardon. To the one who, during his lifetime, made no discrimination between rich and poor, developed or backward, who taught mutual love, who proposed to humanity the great principle of self-denial and of submission to the Lord, to this venerable person Jesus Christ, let there be eternal obedience! (Private communication)

Buddhist teaching

Buddhism, at least in the majority of its different forms, does not include any explicit faith in God. It does not speak of God, because it is not intent on seeking to understand the origin of things but rather freedom from attachment. Christ, the Son of God incarnate, is of no interest to Buddhists, but the Master and liberator is.

Buddhadasa, an exponent of Theravada Buddhism, wrote a book on Christianity for his fellow Buddhists, in which he presents Christ as the Redeemer. Jesus, sacrificing himself, wished to free the people from ignorance and blindness. He offered his own life to save humanity. The cross becomes the symbol of his sacrifice. Nailed to the cross, Jesus affirms the interior truth of every person. He does not impose his life on others but offers it, and it has to be accepted freely. Choosing Christ becomes the way of liberation. Buddhadasa speaks of the compassion of Christ which makes it possible for every person to become reconciled with their self. He speaks of love as the central element of Christ's message, a love that takes its origin not from the person of Christ but from God (he actually uses this term). At the end of his book Buddhadasa urges his disciples: 'love one another, sacrifice yourselves for others; everything you give, including the gift of yourself, is the surest way to salvation.'

An exponent of the Mahayana school, Masao Abe, centres his reflection on the *kenosis* of Christ. He says that the hymn in the letter to the Philippians (Phil. 2.5–11) does not describe an action, but indicates the true nature of Christ. Self-emptying, self-denial, is essential to the very being of the Son of God. In his paradoxical way of writing, Masao Abe says: 'The Son of God is *not* the Son of God; and just because he is not the Son of God, he is indeed the Son of God.' Denying himself, denying his 'ego', Christ truly becomes God. This is what all should do. Each one of us should deny their own ego, recognize their own sin, and renounce it. 'Every day the old person in us is dying and the new person in Christ is rising.'

The approach of the Dalai Lama is much less philosophical. Rather than academic discussions he prefers the exchange of religious experience. After going to Lourdes and standing in silence before the grotto of the apparitions, he said that the happiness that one experiences in visiting such a place cannot really be explained. For him, such a visit is not just a sign of solidarity with Christians. It is also an experience to be enjoyed, a face-to-face encounter with Jesus Christ, with his cross, with Mary carrying her child. These things, he said, cannot be learnt from books. To understand them properly it is necessary to practise the religion.

The Dalai Lama does not speak of God. He does not recognize Jesus as the Son of God, but he does accept that the life of Jesus influences millions of persons and brings about their liberation. In fact he says that for him as a Buddhist, he recognizes that Jesus Christ is a completely illuminated being . . . a *bodhisattva* of the highest spiritual quality.

Conclusion

We could continue our walk through the hall of mirrors by looking at other reflections of the image of Jesus Christ. The book *Celebrating Jesus* contains contributions of Sikhs, of Ahmadiyya Muslims, of Baha'i. But perhaps those we have looked at already are sufficient to give us an impression of how others consider Jesus. How do we, as Christians, respond to the various presentations of Jesus as master, guru, bodhisattva?

In the gospel Jesus puts a question to his disciples: 'Who do people say that I am?' As we know, the replies were varied: John the Baptist, Elijah, Jeremiah or one of the prophets. Jesus did not seem very worried about this. He did not say: 'Oh, that's terrible, I must take care of my image, we'll have to improve our communications!' He was not concerned with correcting the mistakes. Rather, he turned to his disciples and asked them: 'But you, who do you say that I am?' We know the reply. Peter in the name of all made his wonderful profession of faith: 'You are the Christ, the Son of the living God' (Matt. 16.13–16).

Should this not perhaps be our way of reacting to the images of Jesus that do not correspond to our faith? Rather than oppose them or say that they are false, should we not try to discern the inner motivation that leads to presenting Jesus in a particular way?

We can admire the guru who leads to a deeper spirituality and the bodhisattva who sacrifices himself so that all people can obtain liberation. We can also show respect for a sense of divine transcendence which is so strong that it denies the possibility of incarnation.

All this, however, is not enough. As Christians, as people who believe in Jesus Christ, we are invited, called even, to be his witnesses, to confess: You are the Christ, the Son of the living God. We are called to proclaim this central truth of our faith, not only in words, but also by our life. It may happen that, like Peter, we do not always have the courage to confess Christ and the fact that we belong to him. We must however, again like Peter, realize that we are loved by Jesus with a love that takes away all fear.

The fact that there is a positive appreciation of Jesus found among people of other religions can motivate us to try to help them to come to a deeper understanding of him. Respectful dialogue, accompanied by a spirit of prayer and a sincere search for truth, can lead us to mutual enrichment. It can encourage us to be open to each other, to appreciate the values held in common, to work together for our own benefit and that of the whole of humanity.

19

Prophets of dialogue

In his letter to the Ephesians, Paul speaks of Christ: 'He who has descended is the same who has ascended above the heavens, to fill the universe. And it is he who through grace has appointed some apostles, others prophets, other evangelists, others pastors and teachers' (Eph. 4.10–11). This text reminds us that prophecy did not end with the coming of Jesus. The Church, as this and other passages testify, recognizes prophets and seems to attribute to them a specific role. If in the Creed we acknowledge that the Holy Spirit 'has spoken through the prophets', perhaps we should also put the verb into the present, and say that he 'speaks' through the prophets.

We must then make a distinction between the prophets before Christ and those after him. The former can contribute to the formation of the revelation, while the latter interpret such revelation, bearing their personal witness to God and to Christ in the power of the Spirit. Keeping this in mind, it is certainly justifiable to speak of prophets of dialogue; that is, of persons who through their own experience, studies and teaching have contributed to making people understand that dialogue between the religions is a requirement of our time and indeed a demand of faith.

If, as Paul VI mentioned after his pastoral visit to India in 1965, quoting St Augustine, 'Also the Gentiles have their prophets', it would have been possible to choose persons from the various religions – for instance Mahatma Gandhi, whom Paul VI admired. I have, however, chosen to limit myself to three Christians, in fact three Catholics, and consider their contributions to dialogue with Muslims, Hindus and Buddhists.

Louis Massignon (1883–1962) and Islam

Louis Massignon, a well-known French Orientalist, was professor at the Collège de France from 1926 to 1954. Maybe more than any other individual, he prepared the way for the new attitude of the Catholic Church towards Islam expressed in the conciliar declaration *Nostra Aetate*.

Massignon was brought up as a Christian. Baptized despite his father's opposition, he had made his first Communion, but already at school abandoned his practice of religion. His spiritual journey began with a cultural and linguistic conversion. While travelling in North Africa to prepare for a diploma he was betrayed by an interpreter who did not translate his words faithfully. Massignon thereupon decided to study Arabic, and dedicated himself to this with all the strength of his 21 years. He went to Cairo to deepen his knowledge of the language, and there came across a verse of the Muslim mystic al-Hallāj which made a great impression on him:

> Two *rak'as* (of prayer) are sufficient for love
> but first the ablutions made in blood.

He was to choose Hallāj as the subject for his doctoral thesis, hoping in this way to come to understand Islam from within.

In late 1907 he left for an archaeological mission in Mesopotamia. During a journey on the Tigris, the only European on a Turkish boat, he felt himself threatened on suspicion of being a spy. He tried to flee but was captured. He felt that he would be condemned to death, and tried to commit suicide. Ill with a high fever, he prayed to all who might protect him. He felt a presence – God who is Love, who wishes to be loved for himself alone, and for ever. Massignon declared: 'The Stranger visited me.' Taken to Baghdad, at the hospital he was cared for by a Muslim family, the Alusi, and this experience of hospitality was to be fundamental for his spiritual development. On his way back to France, in Aleppo he had a strong sense of the presence of God the Father. At Baalbek he made his reconciliation with the Church, and on arriving in Paris he dedicated his life to God.

Massignon's conversion was not from one religion to another, but it was the rediscovery of his Christian faith, a rediscovery made in a Muslim milieu, 'en terre d'Islam', which was to determine the direction of his life.

Louis Massignon was a friend of Charles de Foucauld, who saw in him a possible successor as a Christian presence in the Sahara desert. Guy Harpigny, who wrote his thesis on Massignon, says: 'Massignon always considered that he had received a mandate from de Foucauld to continue his work. However, while he followed de Foucauld as regards his spiritual aspirations, the sanctification of Islam through continual intercession before God, in silence and prayer, he took another path for his presence among Muslims. Massignon was to choose the transformation of a mindset' (cf. Harpigny 1981, p. 77).

Praying for Islam, helping marginalized Muslims, in the spirit of substitution, this was the spirituality of Massignon which he developed as a result of his studies on Hallāj. To illustrate this I have chosen, from Massignon's vast corpus of writings, a fairly short text which came out in 1949: *Les trois prières d'Abraham*. Massignon meditates here upon the text of Genesis, but using his knowledge of Islam.

The first prayer, made at Mamre, is for Sodom. Abraham, having left his own country, has in accordance with God's will received hospitality in the country of Canaan. As a result of his alliance with the inhabitants of Canaan, he fights on behalf of Sodom (Gen. 14.8–24). Then, still under obligation for the hospitality received, he intercedes for Sodom (Gen. 18.16–33). One could say that, not being able to liberate Sodom by means of armed force, he tries to find within the city those righteous persons who could make it worthy of salvation. God's promise to Abraham remains in force, but God in prayer must be reminded of this promise. Applied to Islam, this means that one must remind God of the presence in this religion of righteous people such as Hallāj.

The second prayer of Abraham, made at Beersheba, is for Ishmael, when he is forced to make a migration (*hijra*), with his mother Hagar (Massignon notes the linguistic similarity). He will find water in the desert, but he will not find hospitality. He will be compelled to live as an exile. But Ishmael too had received from God a blessing of fruitfulness. Massignon saw in the expansion of Islam after Muhammad's *hijra* the realization of God's plan for Ishmael. In other words, he saw Islam as a mysterious answer to Abraham's prayer. He attributed to Islam a critical role in the plan of God. It is a living criticism of Israel, which claims to enjoy a special privilege, and also of the Christians who do not live out in full the message of Christ. Massignon called Islam 'the sword of divine transcendence'. The role of Islam, a community (*umma*) centred upon Mecca (hence the importance of the *qibla* – the direction of prayer – and of the *hajj* – the pilgrimage), a community forming an authentic and homogeneous spiritual bloc held together by the faith in God which comes from Abraham, will receive its fulfilment when the excluded Hagarenes will again be welcomed. This moment of reconciliation is to be prepared by people living out, in the lands of Islam, the holiness of Christ, living as strangers and welcomed as guests.

The third prayer is the offering of Isaac on Mount Moriah. Abraham is totally faithful to his covenant with God. He abandons everything, even the moral justification of his action: he is ready to sacrifice his son. But this son is restored to him. However, the interrupted sacrifice has to be completed by his descendance. Thus the third prayer of Abraham has a priestly character.

The sacrifice is made in Jerusalem. Massignon declared in a lecture given in Paris:

> It is there that one must go to hear, beneath a downpour of profanation announcing the final judgement, the invitation from the Father whom we have in common, who calls all the hearts which hunger and thirst for justice, to make pilgrimage to the Holy City: an invitation repeated here, after returning from a third visit, made not without a great desire, as yet ungranted, to die there. (Massignon 1963, p. 816)

His wish was not to be granted. He died in Paris in 1962, on the eve of the Second Vatican Council. The council was to agree with Massignon in its recognition that the Muslims with us adore the same God, in the importance given to Abraham as a model of faith, in the respect owed to Muslims. It did not however accept his emphasis on Ishmael. St Paul states that our prophecy is imperfect, something which could well be applied to Massignon. He was a complex man, a man of prayer and also of action, a thinker and an activist (as exemplified by his interventions on behalf of the North Africans living in France), an ordained priest yet exercising his orders in secret, a man of great intuitions which were not always well understood and not easily systematized. Yet Christian studies of Islam are greatly indebted to him.

Jules Monchanin (1895–1957) and Hinduism

On his way to India in 1939, on board ship in the Red Sea, Jules Monchanin reread Massignon's work on Hallāj. Ordained a priest in Lyon in 1922, he was a man of considerable culture, although due to delicate health he did not pursue his studies; he nevertheless dedicated himself to an intellectual apostolate. He collaborated in ecumenical activity with Abbé Couturier, the initiator of the Week of Prayer for Christian Unity. In Paris he led a Jewish–Christian group, and was in contact with Jacques Maritain and the Jew Walter Rieze and Madame Belenson. In the 'Thomas More Circle' he entered into dialogue with Marxists. Above all, however, he was attracted by India, an intellectual attraction in the first place, which did not immediately take the form of a specific vocation. He gave himself to the study of Sanskrit and Indology. Gradually, through his own reading and his contact with Indian students, and the advice he was called to give to those wishing to be missionaries, the idea grew of dedicating himself to the Church in India. He received permission from his bishop, and was then accepted by an Indian bishop. For ten years he was curate and parish priest in various villages in the diocese of Tiruchirapalli. Then in 1950, with another Frenchman, Dom Henri Le Saux (Abhishiktananda), he was able to realize his dream by founding at Kulitalai (Shantivanam) the ashram of Saccidananda (the Most Holy Trinity). He remained there for seven years until he was compelled by illness to return to Paris in 1957.

Monchanin held lofty ideals in going to India.

> With my Indian brother priests, always in the most humble place among them, my aspiration is to share in the same conditions of life. I wish, as much as possible, to become Indian, to feel and suffer as they do, to think in the traditional categories of their civilization, to pray with them and work to help the Church take root in India.
>
> (Monchanin 1965, p. 15)

In short, he gave himself to a work of reparation. He wished, in his own person, to make amends for the faults of the white people who had undervalued the Indians and had wished to impose their way of thinking on them. 'I must be hidden in this Indian land' (somewhat like Father de Foucauld in the land of the Sahara) 'to become holy and to make this earth bear fruit' (Monchanin 1965, p. 25). For him, 'It is Hinduism that must be converted, by taking upon oneself, by way of a mystical substitution (a sea of suffering!) whatever has been introduced there by the spirit of evil and men's rejection' (Monchanin 1965, p. 30).

We are here close to the spiritual vision of Massignon. Monchanin's ideal also contains a theological dimension. Before leaving for India he went to see a priest friend, who confirmed his way of thinking. Monchanin writes: 'He believes that it is in coming up against India that I shall be able to renew theology, rather than by trying to deepen theological problems in themselves' (Monchanin 1965, p. 22). He dreamt of an institute of study and research, which would provide a profound knowledge of the languages, the philosophy and the religions of India. In his opinion India needed to be thought of anew in the light of Christianity, and Christianity in the light of India (cf. Monchanin 1965, p. 98).

There is also a strong spiritual and contemplative dimension to his thinking. He wrote: 'To receive the Christian message, India will need a costly incarnation, or at least an extreme spiritualization requiring, here more than anywhere else, a great asceticism – and more than anywhere else contemplation of that which is essentially spiritual – the Trinity' (Monchanin 1965, p. 42). He expressed a desire: 'that from my life, from my very death, should come to birth a trinitarian contemplative life, which will be able to subsume, purify and transfigure the ancient thought, art, and experience of India' (Monchanin 1965, p. 29).

A Church without a contemplative basis is incomplete. That is true everywhere, but especially in India where there is such a great spiritual thirst. According to Monchanin, the Logos and the Holy Spirit are at work in the depth of the Indian soul. But he saw the Indian way to salvation as being damaged by errors and needing to meet with Christianity in order to purify itself.

Monchanin was thus open to Indian values. Thinking of his future ashram he said: 'I shall seek to have around me Indian things, to create an Indian atmosphere.' Moreover he wished to learn from the *sannyasi*: 'I wish to spend some days with Hindu spiritual men, being there as a Christian but also to be instructed in whatever in this spirituality can be separated from Hinduism' (Monchanin 1965, p. 31). He recognized that his openness towards Hinduism, although moderate, would be misunderstood: 'It has been too often said to Indian Catholics that Hinduism is an invention of Satan. Thus an attitude of understanding and sympathy causes astonishment.'

With the permission of the bishop he was finally able to found his ashram. However, cooperation with Dom Le Saux was never going to be easy. There was too great a diversity of character, and also too great a difference in their attitudes towards Hinduism. Le Saux (while remaining a Christian monk) became almost a Christian *sannyasi* of *advaita* (non-duality), while Monchanin could not accept such a compromise. Le Saux gave priority to experience, to what lies beyond all thought, while for Monchanin *advaita* was incompatible with faith in a trinitarian God. Despite all this, the ashram of Shantivanam has continued, even after the death of Monchanin, first under Le Saux, then under the direction of Dom Bede Griffiths, and now with Camaldolese monks.

Can we consider Jules Monchanin a prophet of dialogue? His life in India did not contain much actual dialogue. In the villages he did not find anyone ready for dialogue. In the ashram he was ready to welcome Hindu spiritual men, but few came. But in his reflection there was a continual dialogue between Hinduism and Christianity. He did not condemn Hinduism, he was open to its values, and can be considered a pioneer in opening the Church to the spiritual contribution of India. Thus he helped prepare the way for the Second Vatican Council, which briefly but precisely described Hinduism:

> Thus, in Hinduism men explore the divine mystery and express it both in the limitless riches of myth and the accurately defined insights of philosophy. They seek the release from the trials of the present life by ascetical practices, profound meditation and recourse to God in confidence and love. (NA 2)

Thomas Merton (1915–68) and Buddhism

The third of our prophets, Thomas Merton, after eventful early years spent in the USA and in Europe, converted to Catholicism and became a Trappist monk. Enclosed in the monastery of Gethsemani, Kentucky, he became paradoxically well known through his writings, in the first place his autobiography *Seven Storey Mountain* (published in England as *Elected Silence*), and then his essays on spirituality.

A contemplative, he was not withdrawn from the world. Thus in the last years of his life, moved by a 'passion for peace' he was involved in activity against war and in particular against the possibility of nuclear war. This was an unexpected but almost natural progression. Finding in solitude the God who is Love, the hidden foundation of all that exists, he opened his heart to the troubles of the world. He wrote: 'A certain openness to the world and a genuine participation in its sufferings helps to preserve the sincerity of the duty of contemplation' (Merton 1961, p. 175). As the editor of his writings on peace has observed, his was a compassion born in solitude, like the *karuna* of the Buddha born from illumination (cf. Shannon 1995, p. 3).

The reference to Buddha is not a casual one. Merton saw a real possibility of contact at a profound level between the contemplative and monastic traditions of the west and the various contemplative traditions of the east. He studied Buddhism, and in particular Zen. He was in contact with experts in Zen, for instance D. T. Suzuki. He travelled to Asia to deepen his knowledge, and died in Bangkok, where he had gone to take part in a monastic meeting on interreligious dialogue.

Merton's interest in Buddhism preceded the Second Vatican Council, and was strengthened by it. He worked in the spirit of the council and wished to contribute to spreading this spirit more widely. He says of his own efforts that he has attempted to present religious traditions in an objective way but, going beyond this, he has tried to share, at least to some extent, in the values and the experiences that they enshrine.

Merton characterizes as a 'protestant' reaction diffidence and repugnance towards the mysticism of other religions. He also criticizes Catholic 'activists' who disregard the contemplative dimension. He writes, with some exaggeration, 'all the types of mysticism except those which are contained within the ambit of the Roman Church are frequently attributed by Catholics to the direct or indirect intervention of Satan' (Merton 1961, p. 177). He rebelled against such positions. If we recognize, as we should, that God is not limited with regard to his gifts, we should admit the possibility of supernatural mystical grace being given to believers of other religious traditions.

Recognizing the great value of the monastic life in Buddhism, he was the prime mover of a dialogue that was not limited to a discussion of concepts. He explains his thinking in this way:

> While at the level of philosophical and doctrinal formulations serious obstacles can be encountered, it is often possible to arrive at a truly clear, simple and satisfying understanding through comparing accounts of contemplative life, its various disciplines, its exaggerations, its rewards. (Merton 1961, p. 180)

For him communication should become communion, a sharing in an authentic experience at pre-verbal and post-verbal levels. The pre-verbal level consists in a free and open attitude that is favourable to the encounter. The assimilation of one's own tradition from within provides the ability to meet a person from another religious tradition and to find common ground. The post-verbal level coincides with the meeting in silence after the spoken exchange, which will have prepared the way for a new common experience.

Merton attributed a special value to dialogue on the 'ultimate ground' of faith. He considered such a communication not only possible and to be desired, but as having great importance for human destiny. But he set out two conditions. First, to undertake dialogue 'in an Asian way', that is, without rushing, with great patience, without looking for immediate results. Second, faithfulness to one's own tradition, avoiding any syncretism that might deprive dialogue of its true contents. For the Christian, Merton wrote in strong terms:

> Christian contemplation is based not on a vague interior appreciation of the mystery of man's spiritual being, but on the Cross of Christ which is the mystery of Kenosis, the emptying, the self-denial of the Son of God . . . In this mystery we find the full Christian expression of the dialectic between fulness and vacuity, *todo y nada*, emptiness and infinity, which appears at the centre of all the major traditional forms of contemplative wisdom. (Merton 1961, p. 182)

Faithfulness and openness, silence and word, individual contemplation and community discipline, are some of the apparent opposites that Merton tried to keep united. He has made a very valuable contribution, given an impetus, perhaps a decisive one, to monastic interreligious dialogue which has developed and become structured over the last 20 or more years.

Conclusion

Massignon, Monchanin and Merton: three men with different experiences, but holding a similar position. All three were inspired by a desire for a greater openness of the Church towards other religions. They advocated this not for ambiguous humanistic reasons, but out of faithfulness to the true nature of the Church, 'a sacrament or as a sign and instrument ... of communion with God and of the unity of the whole human race' (LG 1). The Second Vatican Council and the post-conciliar documents have shown them to be right. Pioneers then certainly, but prophets of dialogue? I would say that what William Shannon wrote about Thomas Merton is also valid for Louis Massignon and Jules Monchanin:

> Merton believed that he was called to be a prophet, despite his lack of preparation for such a role. He had a clear perception of the limits of the prophetic vocation. The prophet is not necessarily one who has the correct response to everything; he is one who knows, at a precise moment in history, the true problems which humanity has to face, the goals to be sought, the real questions to be put. (Shannon 1995, p. 3)

Appendix
The PCID: A Vatican structure for dialogue

The Secretariat for Non-Christians

In 1964, while the Second Vatican Council was still in progress, Pope Paul VI set up what was then known as the Secretariat for Non-Christians, to form a structure within the Church with special responsibility for interreligious relations. As with the other offices of the Roman Curia, the Secretariat was made up of a certain number of members, who are in fact bishops residing in different parts of the world, and a group of consultors or advisors, also representing different regions and a variety of expertise. Running the office in the Vatican is a permanent staff, whose numbers have gradually increased. The office is headed by a president assisted by a secretary and an under secretary.

The concern of the first president, Cardinal Paul Marella (1964–73), was to establish a sound basis for fruitful dialogue. The teaching of the Second Vatican Council, particularly with regard to the new attitude towards people of other religions, had to be conveyed to the Church at large. Experts were called upon, and with their help a whole series of *Guidelines* was produced for dialogue with Buddhists, Hindus, Muslims and for the encounter with African traditional religions. This went hand in hand with theological and pastoral reflection, which was made available to the public through a journal founded for this specific purpose: *Bulletin. Secretariatus pro Non Christianis* (later, under Cardinal Arinze, to be renamed *Pro Dialogo*).

The presidency of Cardinal Sergio Pignedoli (1973–80) saw a great increase in the number of contacts with religious leaders in different parts of the world. Cardinal Pignedoli travelled to meet them, and he also encouraged them to visit Rome. Formal meetings were organized, both of Catholic authorities in order to encourage them in the way of dialogue – the first Plenary Assembly of the Secretariat took place in 1979 – and also with representatives of other religions.

The brief mandate of Archbishop Jean Jadot (1980–84) was a time of reflection and consolidation. During this period, the Secretariat prepared its first document, *The Attitude of the Church towards the Followers of Other Religions. Reflections and Orientations on Dialogue and Mission*

(DM), finally published in 1984. This document summarized the teaching of the Second Vatican Council on interreligious relations. At the same time, the Secretariat encouraged local churches to establish adequate structures for dialogue.

The Pontifical Council for Interreligious Dialogue

In 1984 Pope John Paul II appointed Archbishop Francis Arinze, at that time Archbishop of Onitsha, Nigeria, to be Pro-President of the Secretariat for Non-Christians. The following year came his creation as Cardinal and appointment as President of the Secretariat. In 1988 the Constitution *Pastor Bonus*, the most recent reform of the Roman Curia, stipulated that from now on this office was to be known as the Pontifical Council for Interreligious Dialogue. This document gave the aims of the council as follows:

> Art. 159 – The council promotes and regulates relations with the members and groups of those religions that are not included under the name of Christian and also with those who in any way are endowed with a sense of religion.

> Art. 160 – The Council works so that the dialogue with followers of other religions takes place in a suitable manner, and it promotes various forms of relationships between them; it promotes opportune studies and conventions so that these may produce reciprocal knowledge and esteem and so that, through common work, the dignity of man and his spiritual and moral values are favoured; it also provides for the formation of those who devote themselves to this kind of dialogue.

Four elements in the mission entrusted to the council can thus be distinguished:

- *to give advice* on the way dialogue is to be practised;
- *to establish relations* with persons belonging to other religions;
- *to engage in studies*, above all with a view to human promotion;
- *to ensure the formation* of persons engaged in dialogue.

The document Dialogue and Proclamation

Since the concept of dialogue could be seen as in conflict with the Lord's command to proclaim the gospel, the decision was taken to prepare a new document which would study the relationship between dialogue and proclamation, and a first draft was presented to the Plenary Assembly of 1987. It became evident that the matter under discussion concerned also the Congregation for the Evangelization of Peoples, and so further work on the document was undertaken by a joint commission.

During the same period the missionary encyclical of Pope John Paul II, *Redemptoris Missio,* was also in preparation. The decision was taken not to alter DP, but to delay its publication and include in it a statement that it should be read in the light of the encyclical. DP was eventually published at Pentecost, 19 May 1991.

The Commission for Religious Relations with Muslims

On 22 October 1974 Pope Paul VI set up two new commissions: one for Religious Relations with Jews, within the Secretariat for Christian Unity, and the other for Religious Relations with Muslims as part of the structure of the Secretariat for Non-Christians (now the PCID). The President and Vice President of the Commission are respectively the President and the Secretary of the PCID, while its Secretary is the head of the Office for Islam. The rest of the Commission is formed by a group of eight consultors. Since dialogue with Muslims already represents a large part of the work of the PCID, the Commission has been transformed into a special advisory body engaging in studies and preparing papers for publication. Topics addressed so far are the following:

- Contemporary trends and movements in Islam
- Religion and violence
- Praying with Muslims
- The reception of *Nostra Aetate*
- Religion and politics
- Religious freedom

Nostra Aetate Foundation

This Foundation was established by the PCID in 1993. Its main purpose is to provide scholarships for students belonging to other religions who wish to improve their knowledge of Christianity by studying in one of the Pontifical academies or universities in Rome. Almost 50 students have taken advantage of this possibility. A monthly meeting brings together the current scholarship holders and some local people who are interested in dialogue. The Foundation also occasionally gives small grants to support dialogue activities in different parts of the world.

Notes and references

Forty years ago: Vatican II, dialogue and lay leadership

1 Giuseppe Alberigo (ed.), *History of Vatican II*, Vol. 3 (Maryknoll, NY, Orbis, 2000), p. 379.

2 See The Constitution on the Sacred Liturgy (*Sacrosanctum Concilium*) 14: 'In the restoration and promotion of the sacred liturgy the full and active participation by all the people is the aim to be considered before all else, for it is the primary and indispensable source from which the faithful are to derive the true Christian spirit.' Austin Flannery, OP (ed.), *Vatican Council II. The Conciliar and Post Conciliar Documents*, new revised edition (Northport, Costello Publishing Company, 1996), p. 8.

3 *History of Vatican II*, Vol. 3, pp. 220–1.

4 R. W. Southern, *Western Views of Islam in the Middle Ages* (Cambridge, Harvard University Press, 1962), p. 72.

5 See 'The Attitude of the Church toward Followers of Other Religions', a document of the Secretariat for Non-Christians (10 May 1984), 26, published in Francesco Gioia (ed.), *Interreligious Dialogue. The Official Teaching of the Catholic Church (1963–1995)* (Boston, Pauline Books & Media, 1997), p. 574.

6 Paul Lakeland, *The Liberation of the Laity. In Search of an Accountable Church* (New York, Continuum, 2003), p. 109.

7 *Documents of the Thirty-Fourth General Congregation of the Society of Jesus*, Decree 5, 'Our Mission and Interreligious Dialogue', 3 (Saint Louis, Institute of Jesuit Sources, 1996).

3 Religious pluralism in the USA today: A Catholic perspective

1 National Opinion Research Center (NORC), University of Chicago, 20 July 2004.

2 *Faith Communities Today* is available on the Hartford Seminary website: <http://fact.hartsem.edu/>.

3 See Diana L. Eck, *A New Religious Pluralism* (New York, Harper & Collins, 2001), pp. 6–11, 61–79.

4 This is how 'religious pluralism' was discussed in the project 'Confessing Christian Faith in a Pluralistic Society' (Institute for Ecumenical and Cultural Research, Collegeville, MN 56321–6188, 1995). One sentence in particular demonstrates this purpose: 'We can no longer think and act without attention to our neighbors from other traditions' (p. 11).

5 Originally published by Anchor Books in 1960, it is now available with an introduction by Martin E. Marty, The University of Chicago Press, 1983.

6 Eck, p. 61.

7 The most prominent defender of this metaphysical usage of religious pluralism as a hypothesis for a theology of religions is John Hick, *A Christian Theology of Religions* (Louisville, John Knox, 1995), pp. 11–30.

8 See James B. Wiggins, *In Praise of Religious Diversity* (New York, Routledge, 1996), pp. 55–71.

9 James L. Fredericks, *Faith Among Faiths. Christian Theology and Non-Christian Religions* (New York, Paulist Press, 1999), p. 116.

10 See, for example, Jacques Dupuis, *Toward a Christian Theology of Religious Pluralism* (Maryknoll, NY, Orbis, 1997), pp. 330–56.

11 See, James Fredericks, 'The Catholic Church and Other Religious Paths: Rejecting Nothing That is True and Holy', *Theological Studies* 64, 2 (June 2003): 225–54.

12 Published in Francesco Gioia (ed.), *Interreligious Dialogue. The Official Teaching of the Catholic Church (1963–1995)* (Boston, Pauline Books & Media, 1997), p. 38.

13 For an account of history of the Catholic response to religious pluralism around the question of salvation outside of the Church, see Francis A. Sullivan, SJ, *Salvation Outside the Church?* (New York, Paulist Press, 1992). A useful historical review of Catholic reflections on religious pluralism can be found in Jacques Dupuis, *Toward a Christian Theology of Religious Pluralism*, chapters 1–5.

14 *Interreligious Dialogue*, p. 102.

15 The occasion was the release of the letter *Dominus Iesus*, by the Vatican's Congregation for the Doctrine of the Faith in September 2000 and the strong reaction by Catholics, other Christians, Jews, and many others. See Fredericks, 'The Catholic Church and Other Religious Paths' and my own 'Interreligious Dialogue and Mission: Continuing Questions', in Thomas P. Rausch, SJ (ed.), *Evangelizing America* (New York, Paulist Press, 2004), pp. 172–98.

16 Published in *Pro Dialogo*, the bulletin of the Pontifical Council for Interreligious Dialogue 106 (2001/1): 20–1.

17 *Apostolic Letter 'Novo Millennio Ineunte'*, published in *Origins*, CNS Documentary Service, 30/31 (18 January 2001): 506.

4 Pluralism and the parish

1 'Dialogue' would be a better translation of the Latin text.

2 Jean-Marie Gaudeul, *Called from Islam to Christ. Why Muslims become Christians* (London, Monarch Books, 1999).

3 Gaudeul, p. 283.

4 Andrew Wingate, *Encounter in the Spirit. Muslim–Christian Meetings in Birmingham* (Geneva, WCC Publications, 1988).
5 *The Tablet*, 17 July 2004, p. 16.

6 Christian–Muslim dialogue: Developments, difficulties and directions

1 Ali Merad, 'Dialogue islamo-chrétien: pour la recherche d'un langage commun', *Islamochristiana* 1 (1975), p. 4.

7 Recent Muslim–Catholic dialogue in the USA

1 Published in Francesco Gioia (ed.), *Interreligious Dialogue. The Official Teaching of the Catholic Church* (Boston: Pauline Books & Media, 1997), p. 117.
2 This is how the term 'religious pluralism' was used in the project 'Confessing Christian Faith in a Pluralistic Society' (Institute for Ecumenical and Cultural Research, Collegeville, MN 56321–6188, 1995). The project was sponsored and facilitated by the interreligious offices of the National Conference of Catholic Bishops and the National Council of Churches along with the staff of the Institute at Collegeville.
3 *Apostolic Letter 'Novo Millennio Ineunte'*, 55, published in *Origins*, CNS Documentary Service, 30/31 (18 January 2001): 506.
4 Sayyid Qutb, quoted in Yvonne Y. Haddad, 'Sayyid Qutb, Ideologue of Islamic Revival', in John Esposito (ed.), *Voices of Resurgent Islam* (New York, Oxford, 1983), p. 70.
5 Haddad, p. 67.
6 Shahrough Akhavi, 'Sayyid Qutb', in John L. Esposito (ed.), *The Oxford Encyclopedia of Modern Islam* (New York, Oxford, 1995), p. 404.
7 Paul Berman, 'The Philosopher of Islamic Terror,' *The New York Times Magazine* (23 March 2002): 29.
8 These points appear in a news release on the USCCB website, dated 10 March 2003: <http://www.usccb.org/comm/archives/2003/03-056.htm>.
9 The report, dated December 2003, appears on the USCCB website under official dialogues of the Ecumenical and Interreligious Affairs department: <http://www.usccb.org/seia/friends.htm>.

8 From heresy to religion: Vatican II and Islam

1 Jean-Marie Gaudeul, *Encounters and Clashes* (Rome, Pontificio Istituto di Studi Arabi e d'Islamistica, 1984), Vol. 2, p. 78; cf. Vol. 1, pp. 106–12.
2 Gaudeul, *Encounters and Clashes*, Vol. 2, p. 19; cf. Vol. 1, pp. 67–8.
3 Gaudeul, *Encounters and Clashes*, Vol. 1, p. 67.
4 Gaudeul, *Encounters and Clashes*, Vol. 2, p. 9; cf. Vol. 1, pp. 28–30.

5 Saint Thomas Aquinas, *Reasons for the Faith against Muslim Objections*, translated by Joseph Kenny, OP, *Islamochristiana* 22 (1996), p. 33.

6 Cf. Joseph Farrugia, *The Church and the Muslims* (Gozo, Media Centre, 1988), p. 39.

7 Cf. R. Caspar, 'Les Versions arabes du Dialogue entre le catholicos Timothée I et le Caliphe Al-Mahdī', *Islamochristiana* 3 (1977), pp. 107–75; Gaudeul, *Encounters and Clashes*, Vol. 1, pp. 34–7, Vol. 2, pp. 234–45.

8 Gaudeul, *Encounters and Clashes*, Vol. 2, p. 242.

9 Robert Caspar, 'Islam according to Vatican II', in Michael L. Fitzgerald and Robert Caspar, *Signs of Dialogue. Christian Encounter with Muslims* (Zamboanga City, Philippines, Silsilah Publications, 1992), p. 240.

10 See for instance Ataullah Siddiqui, *Christian–Muslim Dialogue in the Twentieth Century* (London, Macmillan, 1997), p. 35.

11 On this whole question see GRIC (Muslim–Christian Research Group), *The Challenge of the Scriptures. The Bible and the Qur'an* (Maryknoll, NY, Orbis, 1989) (original French edition 1987).

12 On Abraham, see PISAI Forum – 26 January 1996, 'Abraham-Ibrahīm in the Monotheistic Traditions', in *Encounter: Documents for Christian–Muslim Understanding*, 1996, nos 222–3.

13 R. Caspar, 'La religion musulmane', in *Vatican II. Les relations de l'Eglise avec les religions non chrétiennes* (Paris, Cerf, 1966), p. 215.

14 Joseph Farrugia, *The Church and the Muslims*, p. 74.

15 For a more detailed study see Michael L. Fitzgerald, 'Other Religions in the Catechism of the Catholic Church', *Islamochristiana* 19 (1993), pp. 29–41; also Mohammed Arkoun, 'Réflexions d'un Musulman sur le "Nouveau Catéchisme"', *Islamochristiana* 19 (1993), pp. 43–54.

16 Cf. Francesco Gioia (ed.), *Interreligious Dialogue. The Official Teaching of the Catholic Church* (Boston, Pauline Books & Media, 1997), no. 339.

17 Cf. Gioia, no. 474.

18 Cf. Gioia, no. 263.

19 Cf. Gioia, no. 360.

20 Cf. Gioia, no. 363, emphasis in the original.

9 Muslims in Europe: A religious and cultural challenge to the Church

Angelescu, Nadia, 'La minorité musulmane en Roumanie', *Islamochristiana* 25 (1999): 125–37.

Bishops' Conference of England and Wales, *Catholic Schools and Other Faiths* (London, 1995).

Fitzgerald, Michael L., 'Muslims in Europe. Managing as Minorities', in *Religion et politique: un thème pour le dialogue islamo-chrétien*, Dossiers de la Commission pour les Relations Religieuses avec les Musulmans (Vatican City, 1999), pp. 63–78.

Fitzgerald, Michael L., 'Christians and Muslims in Europe: perspectives for dialogue', *Encounter. Documents for Muslim–Christian Understanding* (Pontifical Institute of Arabic and Islamic Studies) no. 247 (July–August 1998).

Galindo, Emilio & Alonso, Emilia, 'Les relations entre Musulmans et Chrétiens en Espagne', *Islamochristiana* 22 (1996): 161–91.

Goncalves, T., 'Le Synode pour l'Europe et la dimension interreligieuse', *Bulletin. Pontificium Consilium pro Dialogo inter Religiones* no. 79 (1992), pp. 27–36.

Hristova, Milka Andonova, 'Musulmans et Chrétiens en Bulgarie du XIVème siècle à nos jours', *Islamochristiana* 28 (2002): 125–47.

Nielsen, Jorgen, 'Christian–Muslim Relations in Western Europe', *Islamochristiana* 21 (1995): 121–31.

Nielsen, Jorgen, *Muslims in Western Europe* (Edinburgh, Edinburgh University Press, 1992).

Sakowicz, Eugeniusz, 'Islam and Christian–Muslim Relations in Poland', *Islamochristiana* 23 (1997): 139–46.

Schacht, Joseph & Bosworth, C. E. (eds), *The Legacy of Islam*, 2nd edition (Oxford, Clarendon Press, 1974).

Schmidt De Friebourg, Ottavia & Borrmans, Maurice, 'Musulmans et Chrétiens en Italie', *Islamochristiana* 19 (1993): 153–98.

Troll, Christian, 'Germany's Islamic Charter with a commentary by Christian Troll SJ', *Encounter* no. 290 (December 2002).

10 Dialogue and proclamation in the perspective of Christian–Muslim relations

1 Cf. Ataullah Siddiqui, *Christian–Muslim Dialogue in the Twentieth Century* (London, Macmillan, 1997), especially pp. 50–6.

2 R. Caspar, 'Islam according to Vatican II', in Michael L. Fitzgerald and Robert Caspar, *Signs of Dialogue. Christian Encounter with Muslims* (Zamboanga City, Philippines, Silsilah Publications, 1992), pp. 233–45.

3 Cf. Khurshid Ahmad and David Kerr (eds), 'Mission and Da'wah', a special issue of *International Review of Mission* vol. 65 no. 260 (October 1976); and also J.-M. Gaudeul and M. L. Fitzgerald, 'A Difficult Dialogue: Chambésy 1976', *Encounter. Documents for Muslim–Christian Understanding*, 36 (June–July 1977), Pontifical Institute of Arabic and Islamic Studies, Rome.

4 Francesco Gioia (ed.), *Interreligious Dialogue. The Official Teaching of the Catholic Church (1963–1995)* (Boston, Pauline Books & Media, 1997), no. 263.

5 Cf. *Insegnamenti di Giovanni Paolo II*, Libreria Editrice Vaticana Vol. 21, no. 2, 1998, p. 250; English translation in Pontifical Council for Inter-religious Dialogue, *Journeying together. The Catholic Church in dialogue*

with the Religious Traditions of the world (Vatican City, Libreria Editrice Vaticana, 1999), p. 13.

6 See the various articles on this topic by Mahmoud Ayoub and Sami A. Aldeeb Abu-Sahlieh in *Islamochristiana* 20 (1994).

7 On the elimination of these prejudices, see Maurice Borrmans, *Guidelines for Dialogue between Christians and Muslims* (New York/ Mahwah, NJ, Paulist Press, 1990), pp. 70–7.

8 Cf. Maurice Borrmans, *Jésus et les musulmans d'aujourd'hui* (Paris, Desclée, 1996).

9 Borrmans, *Jésus et les musulmans d'aujourd'hui*, p. 237 (my own translation).

11 Christians and Muslims together: Creating a culture of peace

1 Cf. Pontifical Council for Interreligious Dialogue, *Peace: a Single Goal and a Shared Intention* (Vatican City, 2002), p. 91.

2 PCID, *Peace*, p. 91.

12 Mary as a sign for the world according to Islam

1 The translation I am using is that of Yusuf Ali, a Sunni Muslim: *The Holy Qur'an. Text, Translation and Commentary* (Beirut, Dar al Arabia, 1968). Where his explanatory notes are used, they will be referred to by the initials YA. I have also made use of the translation and commentary by a Shi'ite Muslim, Mir Ahmed Ali: *The Holy Qur'an. With English Translation of the Arabic Text and Commentary according to the Version of the Holy Ahlul-Bait* (Karachi, Muhammad Khaleel Shirazi, 1964). Quotations from his work will be signalled by the use of the letters MAA.

13 The witness of monotheistic religions

1 Pontifical Council for Interreligious Dialogue, *Towards a Culture of Dialogue* (Vatican City, 2000), p. 79.

2 PCID, *Towards a Culture of Dialogue*, pp. 79–80.

14 Modern religious fundamentalisms

1 Martin E. Marty & R. Scott Appleby (eds), *Fundamentalisms Observed* (Chicago and London, University of Chicago Press, 1991).

2 Cf. Marty & Appleby (eds), *Fundamentalisms Observed*, pp. ix–x.

3 Ashis Nandy, 'Fundamentalism', in John S. Augustine (ed.), *Religious Fundamentalism. An Asian Perspective* (Bangalore, South Asia Theological Research Institute, 1993), pp. 1–10.

4 Quoted by Nancy T. Ammerman, 'North American Protestant Fundamentalism', in Marty & Appleby (eds), *Fundamentalisms Observed*, p. 2.

5 Cf. Ammerman, 'North American Protestant Fundamentalism', pp. 4–8.

6 Cf. Françoise Smyth-Florentin, 'A Christian Understanding of Fundamentalism', in Augustine (ed.), *Religious Fundamentalism. An Asian Perspective*, p. 57.

7 cf. Ammerman, 'North American Protestant Fundamentalism', pp. 38–49.

8 R. Scott Appleby, 'The new Christian "Fundamentalists"', in *Proceedings of the Asian Journey – 95* (Cagayan de Oro), pp. 14–31.

9 Samuel C. Heilman and Menachem Friedman, 'Religious Fundamentalism and Religious Jews: The Case of the Haredim', in Marty & Appleby (eds), *Fundamentalisms Observed*, pp. 197–264; Gideon Aran, 'Jewish Zionist Fundamentalism: The Bloc of the Faithful in Israel (Gush Emunim)', in Marty & Appleby (eds), *Fundamentalisms Observed*, pp. 265–344.

10 The following paragraphs are based on T. N. Madan, 'The Double-Edged Sword: Fundamentalism and the Sikh Religious Tradition', in Marty & Appleby (eds), *Fundamentalisms Observed*, pp. 594–627, and J. S. Ahluwalia, 'A perspective on Sikh Fundamentalism', in Augustine (ed.), *Religious Fundamentalism. An Asian Perspective*, pp. 11–19.

11 Yukako Matsuoka, 'Zen Buddhism and Fundamentalism', in Augustine (ed.), *Religious Fundamentalism. An Asian Perspective*, p. 48.

12 For what follows see Donald K. Swearer, 'Fundamentalist Movements in Theravada Buddhism', in Marty & Appleby (eds), *Fundamentalisms Observed*, pp. 628–51.

13 Cf. John O. Voll, 'Fundamentalism in the Sunni Arab World', in Marty & Appleby (eds), *Fundamentalisms Observed*, pp. 380–2.

14 Cf. Mumtaz Ahmad, 'Islamic Fundamentalism in South Asia: The Jamaat-i-Islami and the Tablighi Jamaat of South Asia', in Marty & Appleby (eds), *Fundamentalisms Observed*, pp. 457–530.

15 Ahmad, 'Islamic Fundamentalism in South Asia', p. 485.

16 Voll, 'Fundamentalism in the Sunni Arab World', p. 395.

15 Witnessing to Christ: Ecumenism and interreligious dialogue

1 Pontifical Council for Promoting Christian Unity, *Directory for the Application of the Principles and Norms of Ecumenism*, Pontificium Consilium ad Christianorum Clnitatem Fovendam, *Directory for the Application of Principles and Norms on Ecumenism*, Vatican City, as March 1993, No. 210, p. 95. Available Online at <http://www.Vatican.Va/Roman_Curia/Pontifical_Councils/Chrstuni/Documents/Rc_Pc_Chrstuni_Doc_25031993_Principles-and-Norms-on-Ecumenism_En.Html>.

2 Cf. *Pro Dialogo* 96 (1997), pp. 324–39.

3 Cf. *Bulletin Secretariatus Pro Non Christianis* 66 (1987), p. 246.

16 Dialogue and Spirituality: The example of Buddhist–Catholic Dialogue in the USA

1 *The Asian Journal of Thomas Merton*, edited by Naomi Burton, Brother Patrick Hart and James Laughlin (New York, New Directions, 1975), p. 125.

2 *Spiritual Advice for Buddhists and Christians*, edited by Donald W. Mitchell (New York, Continuum, 1998), pp. 23–4.

3 Published in Francesco Gioia (ed.), *Interreligious Dialogue. The Official Teaching of the Catholic Church* (Boston: Pauline Books & Media, 1997), p. 207.

4 Gioia, *Interreligious Dialogue*, p. 117.

5 Gioia, *Interreligious Dialogue*, p. 121.

6 Thich Nhat Hanh, *Living Buddha, Living Christ* (New York, Riverhead, 1995), p. 12.

7 Charles S. Prebish and Kenneth K. Tanaka (eds), *The Faces of Buddhism in America* (Berkeley, University of California Press, 1998), p. 3.

8 Rick Fields, *How the Swans Came to the Lake. A Narrative History of Buddhism in America*, 3rd edition (Boston, Shambala, 1992), pp. 70–1.

9 Diana L. Eck, *A New Religious America* (San Francisco, Harper, 2001), p. 165.

10 Louise Hunter, *Buddhism in Hawaii* (Honolulu, University of Hawaii Press, 1971), p. 32.

11 Eck, *A New Religious America*, p. 178.

12 For an engaging overview of this history, see the first chapter, 'American Buddhism, a Brief History', in Charles S. Prebish, *Luminous Passage* (Berkeley, University of California Press, 1999), pp. 1–50.

13 Mark S. Massa, SJ, *Anti-Catholicism in America* (New York, Crossroad, 2003), p. 19.

14 James Hennesey, SJ, *American Catholics* (New York, Oxford University Press, 1981), p. 117.

15 John T. McGreevy, *Catholicism and American Freedom* (New York, W. W. Norton, 2003), p. 91. See also Hennesey, *American Catholics*, pp. 126, 185.

16 The first four of the Naropa conferences were reported in Susan Walker (ed.), *Speaking of Silence* (New York, Paulist Press, 1987). The book will be reissued in 2005 by Vajradhatu Press, edited by Susan Szpakowski.

17 For an excellent review of this history, see Pascaline Coff, OSB, 'How We Reached This Point: Communication Becoming Communion', in Donald W. Mitchell and James Wiseman, OSB (eds), *The Gethsemani Encounter* (New York, Continuum, 1997), pp. 4–9.

18 'An Early Journey,' published in *Origins, Catholic News Service Documentary Service*, vol. 20, no. 44 (11 April 1991): 713, 715–19.

19 Mitchell and Wiseman, *The Gethsemani Encounter*.

20 'Interreligious Dialogue in Europe and America', report of the 1998 Plenary summarized by Felix A. Machado, *Pro Dialogo* 101 (1999/2): 261. Bishop Gerry's complete report first appeared in *Pro Dialogo* 95 (1997/2): 216–19.

21 Patrick Henry (ed.), *Benedict's Dharma* (New York, Riverhead, 2001).

22 A report on the Monastic Interreligious Dialogue, which provides much information on interreligious dialogue, is available online at <monasticdialogue.org>.

23 Yi Fa, *Safeguarding the Heart. A Buddhist Response to Suffering and September 11* (New York, Lantern, 2002).

24 Norman Fischer, *Opening to You* (New York, Viking Compass, 2001).

25 For a report of this working group see: Leo D. Lefebure, 'Buddhists and Catholics in Dialogue: Report of the Working Group on Catholic–Buddhist Dialogue', *Pro Dialogo* 95 (1997/2): 220–7.

26 A report was published in *Buddhist–Christian Studies* 19 (1999): 191–2.

27 Msgr Machado's reflections appear in *Pro Dialogo* 110 (2002/2): 231–2.

28 Donald W. Mitchell and James Wiseman, OSB (eds), *Transforming Suffering* (New York, Doubleday, 2003).

29 <www.monasticdialogue.org>.

30 Bruno Barnhart and Joseph Wong (eds), *Purity of Heart and Contemplation* (New York, Continuum, 2001).

31 My most recent published reflection on regional Catholic–Muslim dialogues was in 'An Overview: Christian–Muslim Relations in a Post-9/11 World', *Origins* 32, 37 (27 February 2003): 615–24.

32 The meeting was reported in *Pro Dialogo* 90 (1995/3). The final statement was also published in *Origins* 25, 14 (21 September 1995): 222–4 and in *Buddhist–Christian Studies* 16 (1996): 203–8. In the last reference, Donald Mitchell writes an excellent explanation of how the colloquium came to be.

17 'Forgiveness is beautiful'

1 These reflections are mainly based on a contribution to a book prepared for the Jubilee 2000, Francesco Marinelli (ed.), *Il Giubileo del 2000* (Roma, Editrice Rogate, 1997), in particular the chapter written together with Giovanni Bosco Shirieda and Felix Machado on 'Conversion of the heart in Hinduism, Buddhism and Islam', pp. 438–51.

2 Shirieda & Machado, 'Conversion of the heart'.

3 R. C. Zaehner, *The Baghavad Gita* with a commentary based on the original sources (Oxford, Clarendon Press, 1969), pp. 284, 286.

4 Kevin Trainor (ed.), *Buddhism. The Illustrated Guide* (London, Duncan Baird Publishers, 2001), p. 38.
5 Cf. Mark L. Solomon, 'Teshuvah. A Jewish Perspective', in *SIDIC*, 29/1, 1996.
6 Philippe de Saint Cheron, 'Le pardon et l'impardonnable', in Philippe de Saint Cheron, Xavier de Chalendar and Nassib Mahfouz, *Le Pardon* (Paris, Centurion, 1992), p. 30.
7 De Saint Cheron, 'Le pardon et l'impardonnable', p. 62.
8 De Saint Cheron, 'Le pardon et l'impardonnable', p. 57.
9 De Saint Cheron, 'Le pardon et l'impardonnable', p. 58.
10 De Saint Cheron, 'Le pardon et l'impardonnable', p. 49.
11 Nassib Mahfouz in *Le pardon*, p. 148.
12 Cf. *Hundred Letters of Spiritual Guidance*, no. 2, quoted by C. Troll, 'Islam and Reconciliation' in *Encounter*, no. 104, April 1984, p. 5.
13 Cf. Nassib Mahfouz in *Le Pardon*, p. 153.

18 Christ in the religions

Faivre, Daniel (ed.), *Celebrating Jesus. A Multifaith Approach* (Daniel Faivre, 2000).
Kossof, David, *The Book of Witnesses* (London, Fount, 1971).

19 Prophets of dialogue

Harpigny, G., *Islam et Christianisme selon Louis Massignon* (Louvain-la-Neuve, Coll. Homo Religiosus no. 6, 1981).
Massignon, L., 'Les Trois Prières d'Abraham', *Opera Minora*, Vol. 3 (Beyrouth, Dar Al-Maaref, 1963), pp. 804–16.
Massignon, D., 'Le voyage en Mésopotamie et la conversion de Louis Massignon en 1908', *Islamochristiana* 14 (1988): 127–99.
Merton, T., 'Monastic Experience and the East-West Dialogue', *Bulletin Secretariatus pro non-Cristianis* 10 (1969): 39–45.
Merton, T., *Mystics and Zen Masters* (Gethsemani, 1961).
Monchanin, J., *Écrits Spirituels* (Paris, Centurion, 1965).
Monchanin, J. & Le Saux, H., *Ermites de Saccidānanda* (Tournai, Casternau, 1956).
Rodhe, S., 'Christianity and Hinduism. A comparison of the views held by Jules Monchanin and Bede Griffiths', *Vidyajyoti* 59 (1995): 663–77.
Shannon, William H., 'Introduction', in Thomas Merton, *Passion for Peace*, ed. William H. Shannon (New York, Crossroad, 1995).

Appendix: The PCID – A Vatican structure for dialogue

Arinze, Francis, 'Dialogue and Proclamation. Two aspects of the evangelizing mission', *Bulletin. Pontificium Consilium pro Dialogo Inter Religiones* 77 (1991): 201–3.

Burrows, W. R. (ed.), *Redemption and Dialogue* (Maryknoll, NY, Orbis, 1993).

Dupuis, Jacques, 'The Church, the Reign of God and the "Others"', *Pro Dialogo* 85–6 (1994): 107–30.

Dupuis, Jacques, *Toward a Christian Theology of Religious Pluralism* (Maryknoll, NY, Orbis, 1997), especially pp. 360–77.

Fitzgerald, Michael, 'Dialogue and Proclamation', *Bulletin. Pontificium Consilium pro Dialogo Inter Religiones* 82 (1993): 23–33, with further bibliography.

Fitzgerald, Michael, 'PCID/CEP: Dialogue and Proclamation. Introducing a document on the Evangelizing Mission of the Church', in Chidi Denis Isizoh (ed.), *Milestones in Interreligious Dialogue* (Rome/Lagos, Ceedee Publications, 2002), pp. 209–17.

Mbuka, Cyprian, 'Annonce et Dialogue inter-religieux: une compréhension inclusive', *Pro Dialogo* 88 (1995): 54–68.

Thottakara, A. (ed.), *Dialogical Dynamics of Religions* (Rome, CIIS, 1993).

Tomko, J., 'Dialogue and Proclamation. Its Relation to *Redemptoris Missio*', *Bulletin. Pontificium Consilium pro Dialogo Inter Religiones* 77 (1991): 204–9.

Sources of original articles and talks

1 The Catholic Church and interreligious dialogue
Based on 'Developing Dialogue,' *SEDOS Bulletin* 30 (June–July 1998).

2 Theological considerations on pluralism
Based on 'Religious Pluralism – a Theological Consideration', *Bulletin Dei Verbum* 62–3 (1–2/2002).

3 Religious pluralism in the USA today: A Catholic perspective
Based on lectures for the Georgetown University Summer Institute for Undergraduate Student Leaders, sponsored by the US State Department, Bureau of Educational and Cultural Affairs and the Middle Eastern Partnership Initiative (MEPI), administered by the US Department of Government and the Center for Intercultural Education and Development (CIED), Georgetown University, July 2004.

4 Pluralism and the parish
Based on talks given to the National Conference of Priests of England and Wales, in London, September 2004.

5 The role of the laity in interreligious dialogue
Based partly on a contribution to Michael Fuss (ed.), *Tenrikyo–Christian Dialogue* (Nara, Tenri University Press, 1999): a symposium co-sponsored by Tenri University and the Pontifical Gregorian University.

6 Christian–Muslim dialogue: Developments, difficulties and directions
Based on a talk given in Sarajevo, November 1999.

7 Recent Muslim–Catholic dialogue in the USA
Based partly on 'An Overview: Christian–Muslim Relations in a Post-9/11 World', published in *Origins* 32, 35 (27 February 2003), partly on 'Christian–Muslim Relations in the United States: Reflections for the Future After Two Decades of Experience', published in *The Muslim World* 94, 3 (July 2004), and partly on addresses at Duquesne University,

2 April 2003, and Theological College, The Catholic University of America, 16 February 2004.

8 From Heresy to religion: Vatican II and Islam

Based on a contribution to M. S. Elsheikh (ed.), *Europe and Islam: Evaluations and Perspectives at the Dawn of the Third Millennium. Proceedings of an International Conference* (Pontifical Gregorian University – Rome 6–8 May 2000) (Florence, Florence University Press, 2002), pp. 53–71.

9 Muslims in Europe: A religious and cultural challenge to the Church

Based on a talk given in Graz, May 2003, published in French in Bernard Ardura & Jean-Dominique Durand (eds), *Culture, incroyance et foi: Nouveau dialogue* (Rome, Edizioni Studium, 2004).

10 Dialogue and Proclamation in the perspective of Christian–Muslim relations

Based on a contribution to D. Kendall and G. O'Collins (eds), *In Many and Diverse Ways. In Honor of Jacques Dupuis* (Maryknoll, NY, Orbis, 2003).

11 Christians and Muslims together: Creating a culture of peace

Partly based on a talk given in Washington DC, and published in *Origins*, Washington DC 33/1 (15 May 2003).

12 Mary as a sign for the world according to Islam

Based on a talk given to the International Conference of the Ecumenical Society of the Blessed Virgin Mary, in Bath, UK in August 2004.

13 The witness of monotheistic religions

Partly published in *Salaam (ISA)* 25/2 (April 2004).

14 Modern religious fundamentalisms

Based on a talk given to a group of Franciscans in Rome, August 1995.

15 Witnessing to Christ: Ecumenism and interreligious dialogue

Based on a talk given at the Istituto San Bernardo, Venice, in November 2003 and published in *Studi Ecumenici* 21 (2003), pp. 397–412.

16 Dialogue and spirituality: The example of Buddhist–Catholic dialogue in the USA

Written entirely for this volume with notes from presentations at the 7th International Buddhist–Christian Studies Conference, Loyola-Marymount University, 7 June 2005, and at 'Suffering to Liberation', a Buddhist–Christian Retreat/Dialogue, Graymoor, Garrison, New York, sponsored by the Faiths in the World Committee of the National Association of Diocesan Ecumenical Officers; the Buddhist Association of the United States – Chuang Yen Monastery, Carmel, NY; the Buddhist Council of New York; and the Franciscan Friars of the Atonement.

17 'Forgiveness is beautiful'

Adapted from 'Perdonare è bello', *San Benedetto,* Parma, 4 (2000).

18 Christ in the religions

Adapted from 'L'immagine di Gesù Cristo nelle Religioni', a talk given in Vercelli, February 2000.

19 Prophets of dialogue

Adapted from 'I Profeti del Dialogo', a talk given to the Alleanza Ebraica-Cristiana in Rome, May 1996.

Appendix: The PCID – A Vatican structure for dialogue

Based on a contribution to *Milestones in Interreligious Dialogue. Essays in Honour of Cardinal Arinze* (Rome/Lagos, Ceedee Publications, 2002).